GREAT MEALS
ON A
Tight Budget

Other Books by Family Circle

Recipes America Loves Best
Family Circle *Hints Book*
Delicious Desserts

GREAT MEALS

ON A
Tight Budget

More Than 250 Recipes and
Dozens of Tips to Save You Money

•

THE EDITORS OF

FamilyCircle

Times
BOOKS

SPECIAL PROJECT STAFF

PROJECT EDITOR • *Linda Speer*
FAMILY CIRCLE FOOD EDITOR • *Jean Hewitt*
FAMILY CIRCLE ASSOCIATE FOOD EDITOR • *David Ricketts*
FAMILY CIRCLE GREAT IDEAS EDITOR • *Marie Walsh*
TYPE SUPERVISOR • *Wendy Hylfelt*
TYPESETTING • *Vickie Almquist*
SPECIAL ASSISTANTS • *Helen Russell*
Denise Johnson · Michael Giaquinto
Margaret Chan Yip

PROJECT MANAGER • *Annabelle Arenz*

Published by TIMES BOOKS,
The New York Times Book Co., Inc.
130 Fifth Avenue, New York, N.Y. 10011

Published simultaneously in Canada by
Fitzhenry & Whiteside, Ltd., Toronto

Copyright © 1984 by The Family Circle, Inc.

All rights reserved. No part of this book may be reproduced
in any form or by any electronic or mechanical means,
including information storage and retrieval systems,
without permission in writing from the publisher,
except by a reviewer who may quote brief passages
in a review.

Library of Congress Cataloging in Publication Data

Main entry under title:

Great meals on a tight budget.

    Includes index.
    1. Low budget cookery.   I. Family Circle.
TX652.G726   1984   641.5'52   84-40098
ISBN 0-8129-6340-7

Designed by Giorgetta Bell McRee/Early Birds

Manufactured in the United States of America

84 85 86 87 88 5 4 3 2 1

Dedicated to the millions of **Family Circle** *readers,*
who know you can serve a meal fit for a king
without spending a king's ransom for it.

CONTENTS

FOREWORD

Family Circle magazine is published seventeen times a year, and each issue has an average of four food stories. That's a lot of recipes and a lot of planning. In creating these recipes throughout the year, we try to anticipate your needs and address your grocery-shopping and meal-planning problems. We also keep you up-to-date on new food trends and food products appearing on supermarket shelves. We know you are busy people—fifty percent of you work either full- or part-time and fix family dinners at least five times a week. We know, too, that your food budgets will not stretch to allow frequent use of convenience foods, so you are always looking for quick-to-make, inexpensive recipes to make "from scratch."

In response to your needs, we try to come up with tasty, "do-able" recipes for all occasions. We look for new ideas and new twists on old favorites for fast-to-fix, easy, economical, and nutritious meals. We always keep in mind that fresh produce, such as asparagus, nectarines, and cranberries, at the peak of their season are not only more nutritious but are also more economical. Once in a while real families who prepare balanced, good-looking, delicious meals, and snacks on restricted food budgets send us their menu plans, recipes, and shopping lists, and we share them with you. And occasionally we run stories on inexpensive American regional, ethnic, and international favorites that have been adapted in *Family Circle* test kitchens.

For this book, Special Editor Linda Speer has chosen the very best budget recipes from all categories of food in our bulging files, all of which have been triple-tested in our kitchens. She has also put together an introduction that explains how to save money at the supermarket and how to plan exciting and tasty meals that will not upset your tight food budget, even when you entertain. More specific money-saving tips and hints are also scattered throughout the book. Whether you are looking for a recipe for a family-style casserole, a sophisticated appetizer for a Saturday night buffet, or a vegetarian main dish to satisfy a hungry teenager, they are all here. And they're all easy on your pocketbook.

Happy Cooking!

Jean D. Hewitt
Family Circle Food Editor

GREAT
MEALS
ON A
Tight Budget

INTRODUCTION

How We Feel
About Saving Money

When you're on a tight budget, it's so easy to fall into the trap of humdrum family meals and lackluster entertaining. But there's no reason to let that happen to you. Instead, take on the challenge of cooking inexpensive, imaginative, and nutritious meals every day. This book will provide you with the tools to breeze through family meals or parties with the greatest ease. There are hundreds of money-saving tips, techniques, and mouth-watering recipes to make your meals so delicious that no one but you will ever be aware of how little they cost.

All of the recipes have been triple-tested in the kitchens of *Family Circle*, and all are easy on your pocketbook. Main-course dishes cost less than $1.00 per serving; side dishes less than 50 cents. And to make menu planning a snap, main-course dishes are followed by serving suggestions. The serving suggestions that are based on recipes from this book are indicated by the symbol ■.

You'll find every kind of recipe you need to create appealing meals throughout the year. There are homey and luscious ones, such as

Apple Griddle Cakes and Corn Frittata, as well as sophisticated ones for entertaining—Miniature Sausage-Crêpe Quiches and Frozen Grand Marnier Mousse. International and regional specialties include Cuban Chicken Tacos, Genoa Salami and Black Olive Crostata, Florida Citrus Burgers, and Cuban Chicken Tacos. Dozens of exciting meatless main-course dishes (based on kasha, pasta, rice, legumes, eggs, and cheese) will delight everyone. And there are plenty of recipes that stretch a little meat or poultry a long way.

BUDGET SAVVY

In order to develop budget savvy, you must first become a knowledgeable consumer. This means being aware of current economic conditions as well as marketing strategies used by manufacturers and retailers. You can become enlightened through experience, and you can learn from books, magazine and newspaper articles, media programs, and educational courses. When armed with specific consumer know-how, you'll be able to judge if a product is really for you. Here are some basics:

• Read the label. Many labels provide nutritional information that may steer you from an unwise purchase. For instance, a canned fruit product may be inexpensive, but if the label reveals a very high sugar and water content, it's probably not a good buy.

• While many coupons do provide excellent savings, you must evaluate them carefully. If you are persuaded to buy an item you really don't need, then you don't have a bargain. If a coupon influenced you to buy a nationally advertised brand that is higher in price (even with a coupon) than a store- or private-label brand, you don't save money.

• Set up a filing system to make using your coupons more convenient. Then, as you make up your shopping list, simply pull as many coupons as fit your needs. Keep coupon expiration dates in mind and trade those you can't use with a friend.

• Enjoy the benefits of refund offers in the form of cash, premiums, or coupons for a free or reduced-price product. These are the reward from a manufacturer who wishes to entice a consumer to try a new product.

• Pursue a premium if you can really use it. This is usually an inexpensive product that relates to another product from a manufacturer. For instance, a tea manufacturer may offer inexpensive mugs or a cheese company may entice you with a slicing device.

• Beware of loss-leaders. If you've been lured to a store by a low price on a featured item but find yourself surrounded by higher prices on everything else, watch out.

• Understand what is meant by the terms "fortified" and "enriched." A fortified food has had a substantial amount of nutrients added that were not there originally. For instance, a cereal may be fortified with vitamin C. An enriched food has regained the nutrients lost during processing. An example is enriched flour that regains vitamin B.

• Today there is an imitation for just about everything, including food. The Federal Drug Administration (FDA) defines an imitation food as one that is not as nutritious as the food it imitates; its label must state "imitation." Examples are imitation cheese or maple syrup. If, however, a product mimics another and is just as nutritious, it is not labeled imitation. It stands on its own merits and has its own name.

MENU PLANNING

Plan your menus a week in advance, taking into account your budget, the principles of good nutrition, family preferences, current store specials, coupons on hand, seasonal food, and what's already in your pantry. If you're a full-time employed homemaker, you'll probably rely more heavily on convenience foods than a stay-at-home homemaker. Here are some other menu considerations to keep in mind:

• Base your menus on a *variety* of nutritious foods. Resolve to spend most of your food dollars on the Basic Four Food Groups—not *empty-calorie* foods. Include the following in each day's menus:

Proteins—2 servings of meat, poultry, fish, peanut butter, peas, or dried beans.
Dairy Products—2 servings for adults (4 servings for children) of milk, cottage cheese, yogurt, or hard cheese.
Grains—2 servings of cereals, breads, rice, or pasta.

Fruits and Vegetables—4 servings, including 1 fruit high in vitamin C, and 1 dark green leafy or deep yellow vegetable.

● Emphasize meatless sources of protein and serve more vegetarian meals. Get familiar with brown rice, soybeans, kasha, couscous, and many other alternative-protein foods. (This book presents exciting vegetarian dishes such as Mexican Cheese Enchiladas with Beans, Bulgur Chick-pea Salad, and Nutted Zucchini-Rice Loaf with Cheddar Cheese Sauce.)

● Plan your menus so that different types of incomplete proteins are in one meal. The complementary incomplete proteins enable the body to assemble a complete protein, but all of the needed protein building blocks (amino acids) must be available at one time. Any of the following combinations work fine:

   legumes (dried beans and peas) and grains
   legumes and rice
   legumes and corn
   legumes or grains with small amounts of eggs or cheese

● Stretch expensive protein foods. When you do cook meat, poultry, or fish, don't serve a larger portion than is needed to fulfill nutritional needs. Allow 2½ to 3½ ounces per person and round out the dish with pasta, rice, etc.

● Plan to use foods already on hand in your pantry. Many a dollar has gone down the drain because food spoiled. So check your cupboards, refrigerator, and freezer on a regular basis and incorporate your finds in next week's menu.

SMART SHOPPING

Budget savvy and menu planning get you ready for smart shopping. You're now aware of exactly how to get the best value for your food dollar and what your needs are. Armed with your shopping list and coupons, you'll head toward the store in your area that gives the best value. Here are some things to keep in mind:

- Choose the best time to shop. Early morning is usually not the best time to shop; a better time may be mid-morning, when store shelves are stocked with items on "special." The best shopping day varies by market. Pinpoint the day when produce, etc., are freshest and most plentiful in your market.

- Use the price-per-serving, not the price per pound, to determine the actual price of food. For instance, inexpensive but fatty cuts of meat, or meat cut with a great deal of bone will yield only 1 to 2 servings per pound, but more expensive boneless cuts will give 4 to 5 servings per pound. So, the latter may be the better buy.

- Switch the form of a product if another one is cheaper. If the fresh grapefruit crop has been damaged by frost, for example, buy canned grapefruit juice instead.

- Although some health food store vegetables are not sprayed with insecticides, the carrots and honey from your supermarket are just as nutritious and wholesome and much cheaper than their much touted "health" food counterparts.

- Buy generic items, rather than national or store brands, if appearance is not critical. The nutritional value is likely to be just as good. For instance, the generic applesauce is just perfect for your applesauce cake, and canned carrots are fine in your stew. Although consumers were reluctant to try generic products at first, they do seem to be here to stay. Give them a try!

- Buy produce when in season to avoid paying top prices. Although certain produce is available all year (carrots, potatoes, or bananas), most have a definite season.

- Buy in bulk when it makes sense to do so. A 25-pound bag of rice can be stashed away in a dry place for a long time. Occasionally you may wish to buy a case of canned goods and split it with a neighbor.

- Don't spend more money than you have to by buying a higher food grade than you need. In the case of canned fruits and vegetables, if you need them uniformly shaped and evenly colored, buy US Grade A or Fancy. If slightly less uniformly shaped and colored foods will do, buy US Grade B or Choice. If appearance is not important, buy US

Grade C or Standard. As for meats, if your budget dictates less expensive meats, seek out USDA Good, a grade found in large meat markets. (Supermarkets usually offer just USDA Choice grade meats, which are more expensive.) If you're buying a wholesale cut, be sure it shows the stamped logo—US INSP'D & P'S'D (US Inspected and Passed).

- Steer clear of impulse items that defeat your budget.

CLEVER COOKING

Clever cooking is the efficient management of resources—ingredients, time, effort, and energy—to create pleasing family meals within your budget. We're going to cover many points that will allow you to cook clever meals that are inexpensive, beautiful, delicious, and nutritious.

- Storing food. Proper food storage avoids waste. The process starts the moment you get home from smart shopping, when you'll need to prepare all perishables for the refrigerator or freezer as quickly as possible.

- If necessary, first subdivide foods for the freezer and wrap with the appropriate freezer wrap.

- Place cheeses, meats, and other highly perishable foods in the coldest part of your refrigerator.

- Store ripe fruit unwashed, in your crisper; keep unripe fruits in a brown paper bag and allow them to ripen at room temperature.

- Put a date on packaged or canned goods before you put them in your cupboard. This will help you later when you need to decide which can of lima beans to use first.

- Read package labels for specific storage instructions.

- Transfer foods, such as flours and grains, to an airtight container to preserve the quality and flavor and to prevent insect infestation.

• Check your cupboard periodically and discard any canned goods that show signs of leaking or any bulging.

Freezer Know-How. The fuller your freezer is, the more efficiently it runs, and the more foods you have at your fingertips. Think of your freezer as a food bank that allows you to stock up on supermarket specials, preserve your leftovers, and stash away your garden's bounty. It also enables you to make the most efficient use of your time by preparing double and triple quantities of a recipe and freezing the extras for future meals.

• Keep a list of the foods in your freezer handy so that you can keep track. Use the list when preparing each week's menus.

Be a Star Cook. When you understand basic cooking principles and know how to combine ingredients, you'll have very few cooking failures and very little food waste.

• Buy good-quality ingredients and store them properly. Remember, a dish is only as good as the ingredients that go into it.

• Enhance dishes with herbs and spices. This is definitely one of the least expensive ways to add an exotic touch.

• Pay attention to aesthetics. A menu should have a variety of colors and textures. Garnish foods attractively. Set a pretty table, complete with an inexpensive centerpiece. Use candles and your best dishes.

• Make creative use of your leftovers. Most leftovers can be used for TV dinners and snacks as well as in soups, salads, and casseroles.

• Plan nutritious snacks. Don't let your family fall into the trap of high-priced, empty-calorie foods. Instead, offer fruits, popcorn, raw vegetables with a cheese dip, peanut butter sandwiches, or cookies made with oatmeal.

Be Energy-Efficient

Harness your kitchen watts and get the greatest mileage from them. Since most of the energy is used by your major appliances, let's concentrate on them.

● Use your oven to its fullest capacity by cooking several foods at once. If two recipes have slightly different temperatures, you can usually compromise; for instance, if your casserole calls for 350° and your roast for 400°, bake them both at 375°. Simply adjust the baking times accordingly. (Even if you're not serving an entire oven-cooked meal, you can prepare for future meals.)

● Follow the same principle for broiler meals. Toast the bread and broil the vegetables along with the poultry.

● Don't preheat an oven unnecessarily. Except for baked goods, foods baked over an hour do not require preheating. When you do preheat, make it no longer than 10 minutes. (If you want to be super efficient, use this time to make melba toast.)

● When you've just turned off the oven, take advantage of the residual heat and use it to freshen baked goods or to warm the dinner plates.

● Cook with minimal amounts of water or oil. Not only will you save energy by shortening your cooking time, but your food also will be more nutritious.

● Choose energy-efficient cookware for range-top cooking. Skillets and saucepans should be the approximate size of your burners to avoid wasting energy. They should have flat bottoms, straight sides, and tight-fitting lids. Choose materials that conduct heat efficiently— aluminum, aluminum alloys, or stainless steel, cast iron, and copper.

● Open your freezer and refrigerator as little as possible. Keep the freezer full with stacked foods. But don't stack foods in your refrigerator, or you'll inhibit air circulation.

● Run the dishwasher only once a day and eliminate the heating cycle. Air-dry dishes once they've been rinsed.

1

Breads

Bread baking is more popular than ever these days because it's fun. And what's more pleasing than the aroma of freshly baked bread? This chapter contains recipes of every type: quick breads, such as Cinnamon Muffins and hearty Sausage and Zucchini Cornbread, and glorious yeast breads, such as Autumn Barley Loaf and Nut and Raisin Bread.

These breads not only taste delicious, they're also inexpensive to make and a great way to round out a meal. Many of them contain especially nutritious ingredients: alfalfa sprouts, wheat germ—even carrots. Bread also freezes well, and can be defrosted and warmed in a twinkling.

WHITE HONEY BREAD

Bake at 375° for 45 minutes.
Makes 2 loaves.

2	envelopes active dry yeast	6	tablespoons vegetable oil
⅓	cup nonfat dry milk powder	1	cup very warm buttermilk
⅓	cup honey	1	cup very warm water
1	teaspoon salt	3¾	cups unbleached all-purpose
¼	cup wheat germ		flour

1. Combine yeast, dry milk, honey, salt, wheat germ, and oil in a large bowl. Stir in the very warm buttermilk and water. Beat mixture until well blended, about 30 seconds.

2. Stir 2 cups of the flour into the yeast mixture. Beat with an electric mixer on medium speed for 2 minutes. Stir in another cup of flour; beat 1 minute. Beat in remaining flour by hand until a heavy, sticky dough forms, about 2 minutes. If dough seems too stiff, beat in 2 extra tablespoons of vegetable oil while adding the last of the flour.

3. Grease well two 7⅜ x 3⅝ x 2¼-inch loaf pans. Divide dough evenly between prepared loaf pans. Cover with clean cloths, and let rise in a warm place, away from drafts, about 20 minutes. Preheat oven to 375°.

4. Bake in a preheated moderate oven (375°) for 45 minutes or until loaves sound hollow when lightly tapped on the bottom of the loaf. Remove from pans to wire racks. Cool completely.

ACTIVATING DRY YEAST

The liquid must be at proper temperature when you are ready to activate dry yeast. If the liquid is too hot, it will kill the yeast; if it's too cool, it will inhibit the yeast and the dough will not rise. It's best to check the temperature with a thermometer, but if you don't have one, use the following methods:

• If yeast is to be dissolved in water (conventional method), have the water just lukewarm (105° to 115°). Learn to test the temperature of the water yourself: If it feels warm on your wrist, it's probably the correct temperature for the yeast.

• If the yeast is first mixed with dry ingredients (rapid-mix method), then the temperature of the added liquid should be higher (120° to 130°). The liquid should feel quite warm but comfortable—not hot. Note: The rapid-mix method does not work with Canadian yeast.

HONEY AND CREAM CHEESE
WHOLE WHEAT BREAD

An excellent bread to slice in ¾-inch slices, wrap in aluminum foil, and freeze. The individual slices can then be removed and warmed or toasted for breakfast and slathered with peanut butter, jam, or cream cheese. And it's great with soup.

Bake at 325° for 45 minutes.
Makes 2 loaves.

2 envelopes active dry yeast	3 cups whole wheat flour
½ cup warm water	½ wheat germ
½ cup honey	1½ teaspoons salt
1 can (5.33 ouncs) evaporated milk (⅔ cup)	2½ to 3 cups all-purpose flour
Water	1 tablespoon water
4 ounces cream cheese, softened (from an 8-ounce package)	½ teaspoon honey
	2 teaspoons sesame seeds

1. Sprinkle yeast over warm water in a 1-cup measure; stir in 1 teaspoon of the honey (from the ½ cup). Stir to dissolve yeast; let stand until bubbly, about 10 minutes.

2. Pour evaporated milk into a 2-cup measure; add water to make 1½ cups liquid. Pour into a medium-size saucepan; add remaining honey and the cream cheese. Heat slowly until cheese starts to melt; beat slightly with a wire whisk until mixture is blended. Pour into a large bowl; cool to lukewarm. Stir in yeast mixture.

3. Stir in whole wheat flour, wheat germ, and salt until smooth; beat in enough all-purpose flour to make a soft dough.

4. Turn out onto a lightly floured surface; knead until smooth and elastic, about 10 minutes, using only as much flour as needed to keep the dough from sticking.

5. Place dough in a large buttered bowl; turn to coat. Cover with a damp towel. Let rise in a warm place, away from drafts, about 1 hour or until doubled in volume.

6. Punch dough down and turn out onto lightly floured surface. Knead a few times; invert bowl over dough and let rest about 10 minutes. Butter two 8 x 4 x 2-inch loaf pans.

7. Divide dough in half and knead each half a few times; shape into 2 loaves. Place loaves in prepared loaf pans; cover with a towel.

8. Let rise again in a warm place, away from drafts, 45 minutes or until doubled in volume.

9. Combine water with the remaining honey in a small cup; brush over loaves after second rising; sprinkle with sesame seeds.
10. Place rack in lowest position in the oven. Preheat oven to 325°.
11. Bake in a preheated slow oven (325°) for 45 minutes or until browned, and loaves sound hollow when tapped on the bottom of the loaf. Cover loaves loosely with a piece of aluminum foil after 30 minutes if loaves are browning too fast. Remove from pans to wire racks; cool completely.

CRACKED WHEAT, CORN, AND SESAME LOAF

The flavor of these loaves improves after standing 24 hours.

Bake at 400° for 20 minutes, then at 350° for 15 minutes.
Makes 4 loaves.

2 cups water	¼ cup vegetable oil
1 cup cracked wheat (bulgur)	1 tablespoon salt
1½ cups warm water	1½ cups whole wheat flour
3 tablespoons honey or brown sugar	4½ to 5 cups all-purpose flour
2 envelopes active dry yeast	1 egg white
½ cup yellow cornmeal	2 tablespoons water
⅓ cup sesame seeds	Sesame seeds for topping

1. Bring 2 cups water to a boil in saucepan. Stir in cracked wheat. Lower heat; simmer, uncovered, 7 minutes, stirring once or twice. Cool.
2. Combine ½ cup of the warm water and the honey in a large bowl. Sprinkle yeast over top; stir to dissolve yeast. Let stand until bubbly, about 10 minutes.
3. Add cornmeal, ⅓ cup sesame seeds, oil, salt, cooled bulgur mixture, and the remaining 1 cup warm water; beat until smooth. Beat in whole wheat flour. Beat in all-purpose flour, 1 cup at a time. When dough is too stiff to stir, turn out onto a floured surface. Knead in as much of the remaining all-purpose flour as needed to make dough that is elastic but not sticky. Form into a ball; place in large oiled bowl; turn to coat. Cover; let rise in a warm place, away from drafts, about 1 hour or until doubled in volume.

4. Punch dough down; turn over; cover; let rise again until doubled, about 45 minutes.

5. Divide dough into fourths; push out any large air bubbles in dough. Flatten into ovals 1 inch thick. Cover; let rest 10 minutes.

6. Sprinkle 2 cookie sheets with cornmeal.

7. To shape loaves, flatten each piece on lightly floured surface into an oval about 12 inches long. Roll each up from long side; pinch dough together along seam; pinch ends closed. Place 2 loaves, seam side down, on each cookie sheet. Cover; let rise about 45 minutes or until doubled in volume.

8. Preheat oven to 400°.

9. Beat egg white with the 2 tablespoons water. Brush over loaves; sprinkle with sesame seeds. Make 3 shallow diagonal slashes along top of each loaf.

10. Bake in a preheated hot oven (400°) for 20 minutes. Switch pan positions in oven. Lower oven temperature to moderate (350°). Bake 15 minutes longer or until loaves sound hollow when tapped on the bottom of the loaf. Remove loaves to wire racks; cool completely.

11. Wrap in plastic wrap and store at room temperature. Flavor improves after 24 hours. The loaves can be frozen.

FREEZE NOW, ENJOY LATER

• Make efficient use of your time by baking an extra large batch of bread or rolls; store the extras in your freezer to enjoy in the future. In general, it's best to freeze baked goods, rather than dough, because most yeast doughs lose volume during the freezing and thawing process.

• Wrap the cooled baked goods in aluminum foil or freezer wrap, using the drugstore wrap method on page 227. Seal tightly, label, and date. For best quality, use breads within 3 months; longer storage may result in a loss of flavor or moisture.

• Thaw baked goods in their wrappings and unwrap just before serving. Bread will thaw at room temperature in about 2 hours. Foil-wrapped bread may be quickly thawed and warmed by placing it in a preheated moderate (350°) oven for about 20 minutes.

AUTUMN BARLEY LOAF

An extremely soft bread that holds up well in sandwiches.

Bake at 325° for 1 hour, 15 minutes.
Makes 2 loaves.

⅓ cup barley	2 tablespoons margarine
4 cups water	1 teaspoon salt
2 envelopes active dry yeast	3 cups whole wheat flour
⅓ cup firmly packed light brown sugar	1½ cups raisins, finely chopped with 1 tablespoon flour
¼ cup warm water	5 to 6 cups all-purpose flour

1. Rinse barley in a coarse strainer under cold water; turn into a large saucepan; cover with the 4 cups water. Cover saucepan with a lid or plastic wrap. Let stand overnight at room temperature.

2. Next day, bring barley and soaking liquid to a boil; lower heat; simmer 45 minutes or until barley is tender. Reserve 2 cups of the barley water; drain and discard remaining water.

3. Place barley in the container of an electric blender; cover. Whirl until smooth; reserve.

4. Sprinkle yeast and 1 teaspoon of the brown sugar over the ¼ cup warm water in a 1-cup measure. Stir to dissolve yeast. Let stand until bubbly, about 10 minutes.

5. Heat reserved barley water, margarine, remaining brown sugar and salt in a medium-size saucepan until margarine melts. Pour into a large bowl and add reserved pureed barley. Cool to lukewarm. Stir in yeast mixture.

6. Stir in whole wheat flour and raisins until smooth; beat in enough of the all-purpose flour to make a soft dough.

7. Turn out onto a lightly floured surface. Knead until smooth and elastic, about 10 minutes, using only as much flour as needed to prevent dough from sticking.

8. Place in a large buttered bowl; turn to coat. Cover with a damp towel. Let rise in a warm place, away from drafts, about 1 hour or until doubled in volume.

9. Punch dough down and turn out onto lightly floured surface. Knead a few times; invert a bowl over dough and let rest 10 minutes. Grease two 9 x 5 x 3-inch loaf pans.

10. Divide dough in half and knead each half a few times. Shape into 2 loaves. Place loaves in the prepared pans. Cover with a damp towel.

11. Let rise again in a warm place, away from drafts, about 45 minutes or until doubled in volume. Preheat oven to 325°.

12. Place rack in lowest position in the oven.

13. Bake in a preheated slow oven (325°) for 1 hour and 15 minutes or until golden brown and loaves sound hollow when tapped on the bottom of the loaf. Cover loaves loosely with aluminum foil after 30 minutes to prevent over-browning. Remove from pans to wire racks; cool completely.

SAVORY BREADS

- Cut buttered rye slices into triangles for a casserole topper.
- Sprinkle refrigerated rolls with basil and bake in a cake pan.
- Slice Italian bread and spread with garlic butter; heat in aluminum foil.
- Cut a round loaf, as shown, and stuff with sharp cheese.

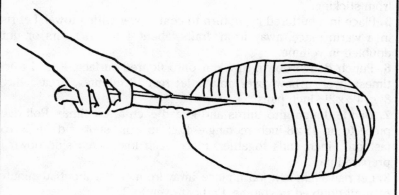

- Top unrolled refrigerated rolls with cubed cheese; roll and bake.
- Score club rolls with a sharp knife; brush with parsley butter, then heat.
- Toss 1-inch bread cubes in butter and arrange, checkerboard-style, on top of a casserole; then brown in oven.

WHEAT GERM BREAD

The potato flakes help to keep this moist, soft loaf fresh longer. This bread is especially good as delicate, tender breakfast toast.

Bake at 375° for 45 minutes.
Makes 3 loaves.

2	envelopes active dry yeast	1	tablespoon salt
1	cup warm water	½	cup instant potato flakes
2	cups buttermilk	½	teaspoon baking soda
½	cup (1 stick) butter or	1	cup plain wheat germ
	margarine	7	to 8 cups *sifted* all-purpose
¼	cup honey		flour

1. Sprinkle yeast over warm water in a large bowl. Stir to dissolve yeast.

2. Heat buttermilk with butter, honey, and salt in a small saucepan until butter is melted; stir in potato flakes. Add to yeast mixture in large bowl.

3. Stir in baking soda, wheat germ, and 3 cups of the flour until smooth; beat in enough additional flour to make a soft dough.

4. Turn out onto a lightly floured surface. Knead until smooth and elastic, about 10 minutes, using enough flour to prevent the dough from sticking.

5. Place in a buttered bowl; turn to coat. Cover with a towel. Let rise in a warm place, away from drafts, about 1 to 1½ hours or until doubled in volume.

6. Punch dough down; turn out onto floured surface. Knead a few times; invert a bowl over dough; let rest 10 minutes. Grease three 8½ x 4½ x 2½-inch pans.

7. Divide dough into thirds and knead each a few times. Roll each piece to an 18 x 8-inch rectangle. Roll up from short side, jelly roll fashion. Pinch ends together. Place each loaf, seam side down in prepared pan.

8. Let rise again in a warm place, away from drafts, about 30 minutes or until doubled in volume. Preheat oven to 375°.

9. Bake in a preheated moderate oven (375°) for 45 minutes or until golden brown and loaves sound hollow when tapped on the bottom of the loaf. Loosely cover tops with aluminum foil if tops are browning too fast. Remove the loaves from pans to racks; cool completely.

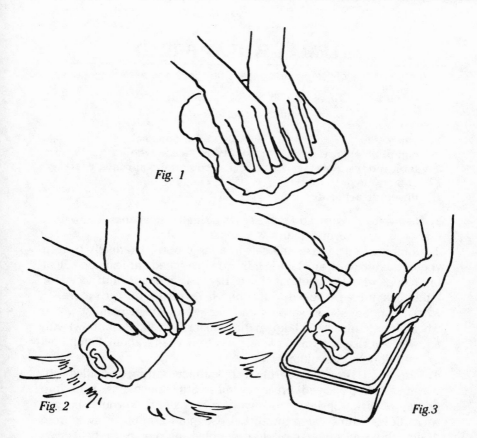

Fig. 1

Fig. 2

Fig. 3

SHAPING A LOAF OF BREAD

Shaping a loaf of bread is easy (Fig. 1). Simply roll or pat out dough to a rectangle, no wider than the length of the baking pan (Fig 2.). Bring short side of dough toward you (Fig. 3). Press ends of dough gently with thumbs or heel of hand (Fig. 4). Place shaped loaf, seam side down, in the greased baking pan.

"SOCK" A ROLLING PIN

A stockinette helps to prevent dough from sticking to your rolling pin. If you don't have one, improvise one. Simply cut a full-sized, clean, white, fine-woven cotton sock just above the heel. Slip it over the surface of a rolling pin and secure the ends with rubber bands. Dust with flour and you're ready to roll.

ALFALFA-WHEAT BREAD

A nutty, moist casserole bread that's nutritious and easy to prepare.

Bake at 375° for 30 to 35 minutes.
Makes 1 round loaf.

1	cup water	2	teaspoons salt
½	cup plain yogurt	1½	to 2 cups whole wheat flour
2	tablespoons molasses	1	cup alfalfa sprouts, coarsely
1	cup all-purpose flour		chopped
1	envelope active dry yeast		

1. Heat water, yogurt, and molasses in a small saucepan over low heat just until very warm. Mixture will appear curdled.

2. Combine flour, yeast, and salt in a large bowl. Gradually beat in yogurt mixture with an electric mixer on low speed until blended. Beat in 1½ cups whole wheat flour slowly. Beat batter on medium speed for 2 minutes; increase speed to medium-high; beat 2 minutes more.

3. With spoon, stir in sprouts and enough of the remaining whole wheat flour to make a soft dough that will form a ball. Cover bowl with a towel. Let rise in a warm place, away from drafts, about 45 minutes or until doubled in volume.

4. Grease a 1½-quart casserole dish; sprinkle bottom and sides with cornmeal or packaged bread crumbs. Stir dough and turn into prepared dish. Sprinkle top with more alfalfa sprouts if, you wish. Cover with a damp towel. Let rise in a warm place, away from drafts, about 45 minutes or until doubled in volume. Preheat oven to 375°.

5. Bake in a preheated moderate oven (375°) for 30 minutes or until golden brown and bread sounds hollow when tapped on the bottom of the loaf.

6. Loosen bread around edge with a metal spatula; remove to a wire rack; cool completely. Wrap in aluminum foil or plastic wrap; store in refrigerator.

IS THE BREAD DONE?

Don't rely just on a rich brown color to judge when your yeast bread is done. Check also by the sound. If the bread is done, it will sound hollow when lightly tapped on the bottom of the loaf.

WHOLE WHEAT-RAISIN BREAD

An old-fashioned quick bread.

Bake at 325° for 1 hour.
Makes 1 loaf.

1 cup *sifted* all-purpose flour	¼ cup (½ stick) butter or
¼ teaspoon salt	margarine, softened
2 teaspoons baking powder	¾ cup sugar
1½ cups whole wheat flour	1 egg
1 cup raisins	1 cup milk

1. Sift all-purpose flour, salt, and baking powder onto a large sheet of wax paper; blend in whole wheat flour. Toss raisins with flour mixture. Grease a 9 x 5 x 3-inch loaf pan. Preheat oven to 325°.

2. Combine butter, sugar, and egg in a large bowl. Beat with an electric mixer until well blended.

3. Add flour mixture alternately with the milk to butter mixture, beginning and ending with flour mixture. Turn batter into prepared loaf pan, smoothing top.

4. Bake in a preheated slow oven (325°) for 1 hour or until center springs back when lightly pressed with fingertip. Cool 10 minutes in pan on a wire rack. Remove from pan; cool completely. Store in a tightly covered container or wrap in aluminum foil or plastic wrap.

PANS DO MATTER

Although light-colored, thick aluminum baking pans give the most uniform baking results, other pans can be used successfully. However, you may have to adjust the baking time or temperature. For instance, if you are using glass pans, you should reduce the baking temperature by 25 degrees. Pans with a nonstick coating or dark colored exterior tend to absorb more heat and will produce a harder crust than an uncoated aluminum pan. Check for doneness before the recommended baking period when using these pans. Very shiny metal pans, such as tin, reflect the heat away from the bread and deter browning; in this case, it will be necessary to bake the bread slightly longer.

NUT AND RAISIN BREAD

Bake at 375° for 50 minutes.
Makes 1 loaf.

2	envelopes active dry yeast	2	cups very warm milk
⅓	cup nonfat dry milk powder	1½	cups whole wheat flour
2	tablespoons honey	1½	cups unbleached all-purpose
2	tablespoons molasses		flour
1	teaspoon salt	½	cup raisins
¼	cup vegetable oil	½	cup chopped walnuts

1. Combine yeast, dry milk, honey, molasses, salt, and oil in a large bowl. Stir in the very warm milk. Beat mixture until well blended, about 30 seconds.

2. Blend the whole wheat and all-purpose flours in a medium-size bowl. Stir 1½ cups of the flour mixture into the yeast mixture. Beat with an electric mixer on medium speed for 2 minutes. Stir in another ½ cup of flour; beat 1 minute. Beat in the raisins, walnuts, and remaining flour by hand until a heavy, sticky dough forms. If dough seems too stiff, beat in 2 extra tablespoons of vegetable oil while adding the remaining flour. Grease a 9 x 5 x 3-inch pan.

3. Turn dough into prepared loaf pan. Cover with a clean cloth, and let rise in a warm place, away from drafts, about 20 minutes or until doubled in volume. Preheat oven to 375°.

4. Bake in a preheated moderate oven (375°) for 50 minutes or until loaf sounds hollow when lightly tapped on the bottom of the loaf. Remove from pan to a wire rack; cool completely.

BUBBLY AND FRESH

Always use yeast before the date stamped on the package. but if you doubt its freshness, observe the yeast mixture carefully. When fresh yeast is dissolved in warm water (105° to 115°) with a little bit of sugar, it will bubble within 10 minutes. This is known as proofing the yeast. If it doesn't, don't waste your time and ingredients. Run out to buy some fresh yeast.

KNEADING THE DOUGH

Kneading the dough can be fun, even therapeutic, as you watch the dough change from an uneven, sticky mass into a smooth, nonsticky, elastic dough. It takes about 8 to 10 minutes for this transformation. To knead, fold the dough toward you and then push it away with the heel of your hand in a rocking motion. Rotate the dough a quarter turn and repeat the kneading procedure until the dough is smooth.

READY TO RISE

Kneaded dough should be formed into a ball and placed in a greased bowl. Turn the dough greased side up. The greased top allows the dough to stay soft and to stretch easily as it rises. Cover the dough and keep in a warm, draft-free place. If the kitchen is cool, place the bowl of dough in a turned-off oven and cover with a towel.

DOUGH KNOW-HOW

• All ingredients should be room temperature before starting.
• Be sure your dough has plenty of room to rise. The bowl should hold about 3 times the volume of dough put into it.
• Use as little flour as possible during the kneading process to ensure tender breads and rolls.
• A new, clean paint scraper or putty knife works well for cutting dough into smaller portions or for scraping the board or counter top when kneading.
• If you use only a small amount of bread at a time, you will find it convenient to slice baked loaves of bread before freezing. When needed, the frozen slices will pull apart easily and thaw in a flash.

CARROT CORNBREAD

Bake at 425° for 20 minutes.
Makes 12 servings.

1	cup *sifted* all-purpose flour	1	egg
1	cup cornmeal	1	cup buttermilk
¼	cup sugar	2	medium-size carrots,
3	teaspoons baking powder		shredded (1½ cups)
1	teaspoon salt		
¼	cup (½ stick) butter or margarine, softened		

1. Grease a 9 x 9 x 2-inch baking pan. Preheat oven to 425°.
2. Combine flour, cornmeal, sugar, baking powder, and salt in a large bowl. Cut in butter with a pastry blender until mixture is crumbly.
3. Beat egg until frothy. Stir in buttermilk and carrots. Pour into dry ingredients; stir until blended. Pour into prepared pan.
4. Bake in a preheated hot oven (425°) for 20 minutes or until center springs back when lightly pressed with fingertip. Cool in pan on a wire rack. Cut into 12 rectanglar pieces. Leftovers are delicious toasted.

SAUSAGE AND ZUCCHINI CORNBREAD

A quick cornbread batter, mixed with shredded zucchini and grated Parmesan cheese is layered with sausage links to make this hearty bread. Reheat leftovers for a snack.

Bake at 400° for 30 minutes, then at 350° for 30 minutes.
Makes 6 servings.

½	cup (1 stick) unsalted butter or margarine	1	cup cornmeal
1	clove garlic, minced	3	tablespoons all-purpose flour
2	cups packed shredded zucchini (about ¾ pound)	1	tablespoon baking powder
		1	cup grated Parmesan cheese (¼ pound)
2	teaspoons salt	1	cup dairy sour cream
8	pork sausage links (½ pound)	2	eggs, lightly beaten
½	cup water	¼	cup thinly sliced green onions

1. Melt butter with garlic in a small saucepan over low heat. Cool to room temperature.

2. Toss zucchini with salt in a colander. Let drain 20 minutes. Rinse the zucchini with cold water; squeeze dry; blot with paper towels. Set aside.

3. Meanwhile, place sausages and the ½ cup water in a medium-size skillet. Bring to a boil; boil gently until water evaporates, about 7 minutes. Continue cooking sausages in their fat, turning frequently, until browned, about 3 minutes. Drain sausages on paper towels.

4. Preheat oven to 400°. Coat bottom and sides of an 8½ x 4½ x 2½-inch loaf pan with 2 teaspoons of reserved garlic butter.

5. Combine cornmeal, flour, baking powder, and Parmesan cheese in a large bowl; stir to mix well. Stir in sour cream, eggs, green onions, remaining garlic butter, and zucchini just until dry ingredients are moistened.

6. Spread one third of the batter evenly over the bottom of prepared pan. Arrange 4 of the sausages in 2 lengthwise rows over batter. Repeat layers with another third of the batter and the remaining sausages; cover with the remaining batter; smooth top.

7. Bake in a preheated hot oven (400°) for 30 minutes. Lower oven temperature to moderate (350°); bake 30 minutes longer or until wooden pick inserted in center comes out clean. Cool pan on a wire rack 15 minutes. Turn bread onto rack; cool another 15 minutes. Cut into ½-inch slices; serve warm. To reheat leftovers, heat slices in ungreased skillet over low heat, about 2 minutes on each side.

SERVING SUGGESTIONS: Tossed green salad and Apricot-Yogurt Whip ■.

COOLING AND SLICING

Unless the recipe tells you otherwise, remove bread from the pan immediately after baking and cool on a wire rack to prevent the bottom crust from becoming moist and soggy. If the bread is to be served warm, you'll find it's much easier to slice the bread with a bread knife, common serrated knife, or even an electric knife.

A SOUPÇON OF GARLIC

- Rub a halved garlic clove on slices of toast; cube and add to salad.
- Sprinkle garlic salt on rolls before baking.
- Mash garlic clove into butter; spread on bread.

MEXICAN CORN STICKS

Bake at 400° for 7 minutes.
Makes 21 corn sticks.

2 eggs	½ cup vegetable oil
1 cup yellow cornmeal	½ cup buttermilk
1 can (8¾ ounces) cream-style corn	1 teaspoon baking soda
	½ teaspoon salt
4 ounces sharp Cheddar cheese, shredded (1 cup)	3 canned jalapeño peppers, chopped

1. Preheat oven to 400°. Grease 3 corn stick pans with vegetable shortening; put in oven to warm while oven is preheating. (If you have only 1 pan, bake, regrease, and refill until all batter has been used.)
2. Beat eggs slightly in a large bowl. Add cornmeal, corn, cheese, oil, buttermilk, baking soda, and salt; beat until blended. Stir in peppers. Spoon into prepared pans* until almost full.
3. Bake in a preheated hot oven (400°) about 7 minutes or until firm and golden brown. Remove pans from oven; invert over a wire rack; tap sharply. Sticks should drop out; otherwise gently loosen with a table knife.

---

*Batter may be baked in a greased 8 x 8 x 2-inch pan for 20 minutes. Cut into squares to serve.

POST-DATED BREADS

Breads are one of the few foods where freshness is not always critical. You can buy bread that is a few days old, at a substantial discount, and use it in dozens of tasty ways. Store the extra bread in your freezer and use when needed for bread crumbs, croutons, puddings, etc.

BUTTER STRETCHER

Save money and calories by "stretching" your butter with this simple technique: Whip a pound of softened butter with a pound of softened margarine and a cup of water in a large bowl until light and fluffy. Serve butter spread with your favorite breads, rolls, waffles, pancakes, etc.

PARATHAS

It takes practice to make these tasty unleavened breads truly round in shape, but triangular ones taste just as good.

Makes 12 parathas.

10 tablespoons (1¼ sticks)   ½   teaspoon salt
    butter or margarine   ¾   cup hot water
2   cups all-purpose flour

1. Melt butter in a small saucepan; pour into a measuring cup; let stand a few minutes for milk solids to settle to the bottom. Pour off the clear liquid (clarified butter) into another container; discard solids at bottom of measuring cup.

2. Stir flour with salt in a medium-size bowl. Slowly stir in water until dough pulls from side of bowl and forms a ball.

3. Knead on a lightly floured surface until smooth. Divide dough into 12 pieces. Roll 1 piece at a time into a 5-inch circle; brush with a little of the clarified butter; fold over and roll out again. Repeat procedure 3 more times to make a total of 5 times. Stack uncooked parathas with a piece of wax paper between them.

4. Brush a small skillet with a little of the butter; heat. Cook parathas until lightly browned on both sides, about 3 to 3½ minutes for each side. Brush skillet with butter for each paratha.

STALE BUT VERSATILE

Don't discard stale bread; it can be used in dozens of tasty ways.
• To prepare bread crumbs, crush slices of stale bread in a tightly closed plastic bag with a rolling pin or whirl in your food processor or electric blender. Combine the bread crumbs with grated cheese and herbs for a flavorful casserole topping.
• Make croutons easily by brushing stale bread slices with vegetable oil or melted butter; sprinkle with seasonings, if desired. Cut into small cubes. Toast in a moderate oven until lightly browned. Use the croutons to perk up salads and soups.
• Large bread cubes can star in a poultry stuffing or fruited bread pudding.
• Slices of leftover French bread can provide the basis of a wonderful soup such as À l'Oignon Gratinée on page 38.

GIANT WHOLE WHEAT TWISTS

Spread with butter or cream cheese.

Bake at 425° for 10 to 12 minutes.
Makes 1 dozen 5-inch twists.

2	envelopes active dry yeast	½	cup unprocessed bran*
	Pinch sugar	3½	cups bread flour
2¼	cups warm water	2	quarts water
2	tablespoons vegetable oil	6	tablespoons baking soda
1½	cups whole wheat flour		Kosher salt for topping
1	teaspoon salt		

1. Sprinkle yeast and sugar over ½ cup warm water in a large bowl. Stir to dissolve yeast. Let stand until bubbly, about 10 minutes.

2. Add remaining 1¾ cups water, oil, whole wheat flour, and salt to yeast mixture; beat until smooth. Add bran; beat well. Mix in 2½ cups of the bread flour.

3. Spread remaining 1 cup bread flour on a work surface. Turn out dough. Knead until smooth and elastic, incorporating bread flour. Form into a ball; place in ungreased bowl. Cover; let rise in warm place away from drafts, about 45 minutes or until doubled in volume.

4. Turn dough out onto lighly floured surface; divide in half. Wrap half; refrigerate. Cut other half in 12 equal pieces. For each pretzel, roll 2 pieces into 2 smooth 12-inch ropes. Cover dough with a towel and set aside while making pretzel. Moisten 1 tip of each; join, to make 1 long rope, rolling seam to smooth. Form the 24-inch rope into large "pretzel"; place on a lightly floured baking sheet to rise. Form remaining pieces into twists. Repeat with remaining half of dough. Cover; let rise in a warm place until almost doubled in volume.

5. Lightly grease a cookie sheet. Preheat oven to 425°.

6. Combine the 2 quarts of water and baking soda in a large skillet; bring to a simmer. Cook twists, one at a time, in simmering water for 20 seconds; turn; cook 20 seconds more. Drain briefly on cloth towel. Place right side up on prepared cookie sheet. Sprinkle with a little kosher salt. Repeat, placing twists well apart on cookie sheet.

7. Bake in a preheated hot oven (425°) for 10 to 12 minutes or until

---

*You may substitute whole wheat flour or white flour for the unprocessed bran.

well browned. Cool slightly on wire racks. Serve warm. Store in an airtight container.

8. To reheat twists, place in a preheated slow oven (325°) for about 10 minutes. These twists may also be frozen.

PUNCHING DOUGH

When yeast dough has doubled (or risen as directed by the recipe), it's ready to be punched down and shaped. Punch center of dough with your fist to push out any air pockets; turn dough out.

DOUBLED DOUGH

If you've ever wondered how to tell when yeast dough has doubled, you'll be interested in this simple test. Press the tips of 2 fingers lightly, about ½ inch, into the dough. If an impression remains, the dough has doubled.

SEASONED BUTTERS

To ¼ cup softened butter or margarine add:
- 2 teaspoons chopped parsley.
- 1 teaspoon curry powder.
- 2 teaspoons dillweed and 1 tablespoon lemon juice.
- 1½ teaspoons mixed Italian herbs, crumbled.
- 1 teaspoon basil, crumbled.

BREADSTICK BUNDLES

Bake at 350° for 10 minutes, then at 325° for 15 minutes.
Makes 3 dozen breadsticks.

2 envelopes active dry yeast	**1** egg white
½ teaspoon sugar	**2** tablespoons cold water
1½ cups warm water	**¼** cup sesame seeds or poppy
¼ cup olive oil	seeds
2 teaspoons salt	
4 cups *sifted* all-purpose flour, or as needed	

1. Spinkle yeast and sugar over ½ cup warm water in a large mixing bowl. Stir to dissolve yeast. Let stand until bubbly, about 10 minutes.
2. Beat remaining 1 cup water, oil, salt, and 2 cups of the flour until smooth. Gradually beat in 1½ cups of the remaining flour until well blended.
3. Turn out onto a lightly floured surface; knead until smooth and elastic, about 7 minutes, using as much of the remaining ½ cup flour, or more, if necessary. Form into a ball; place in a large ungreased bowl. Cover; let rise in a warm place.
4. Grease a cookie sheet. Remove dough from bowl; do not punch down. Divide in half. Cover half. Form other half into cylinder 18 inches long; cut into 18 equal pieces. Cover; let rest 5 minutes. Roll and stretch each piece into a rope 15 inches long. Place on prepared cookie sheet, 1 inch apart. Cover; let rise until doubled, 1 hour. Repeat with remaining half of dough.
5. Preheat oven to 350°.
6. Beat egg white and 2 tablespoons cold water until foamy; brush over breadsticks. Sprinkle wiith sesame or poppy seeds.
7. Bake in a preheated moderate oven (350°) for 10 minutes. Lower oven temperature to slow (325°). Bake 15 minutes. Remove to wire racks to cool. Store in an airtight container. The breadsticks freeze well.

FROZEN DOUGH

To 1 pound frozen bread dough, thawed:
• Roll to a 14 x 12-inch rectangle; spread with parsley butter; roll up; bake on a cookie sheet.
• Pat into a 9-inch square pan; top with sautéed onion and basil; bake.

HERB-ONION ROLLS

Bake at 375° for 20 minutes.
Makes 18 rolls.

2	envelopes active dry yeast	½	teaspoon tarragon, crumbled
⅓	cup nonfat dry milk powder	¼	cup vegetable oil
2	tablespoons honey	1	cup very warm milk
1	tablespoon salt	1	cup very warm water
1	small onion, minced (¼ cup)	2	cups whole wheat flour
1	teaspoon basil, crumbled	1½	cups unbleached all-purpose
1	teaspoon oregano, crumbled		flour

1. Combine yeast, dry milk, honey, salt, onion, basil, oregano, tarragon, and oil in a large bowl. Stir in the very warm milk and water. Beat mixture until well blended, about 30 seconds.

2. Blend the whole wheat and all-purpose flours in a medium-size bowl. Stir 2 cups of the mixture into the yeast mixture. Beat with an electric mixer on medium speed for 2 minutes. Stir in another cup of the flour mixture; beat 1 minute. Beat in remaining flour mixture by hand until a heavy, sticky dough forms, about 2 minutes. If dough seems too stiff, beat in 2 extra tablespoons of vegetable oil while adding the remaining flour. Grease 18 muffin pan cups.

3. Fill prepared muffin pan cups, using a wet tablespoon or ice cream scoop. Push dough down, smoothing tops slightly. Cover with a clean cloth, and let rise in a warm place, away from drafts, no longer than 20 minutes. Preheat oven to 375°.

4. Bake in a preheated moderate oven (375°) for 20 minutes or until rolls sound hollow when tapped on their bottoms. Remove from pans; cool on wire racks.

STORING FLOURS AND MEALS

Flours that include the oil-rich germ of the kernel, such as rye and whole wheat, or meals, such as cornmeal and oatmeal, are prone to becoming rancid if stored in a warm or humid environment. Store these flours in airtight containers or heavy-duty plastic bags in the freezer. All-purpose flour may be stored at room temperature.

CINNAMON MUFFINS

Perk up morning appetites with the fragrance of freshly baked cinnamon muffins.

Bake at 400° for 25 minutes.
Makes 12 muffins.

2	cups all-purpose flour	1	egg
¼	cup nonfat dry milk powder	1	cup water
3	tablespoons sugar	¼	cup vegetable oil
3	teaspoons baking powder	½	teaspoon ground cinnamon
¼	teaspoon salt		

1. Stir flour, dry milk, 2 tablespoons of the sugar, baking powder, and salt in a medium-size bowl.

2. Beat egg slightly in a small bowl; stir in water and oil. Add egg mixture all at once to flour mixture; stir with a spoon just until flour is moistened. (Batter will be lumpy.) Grease 12 muffin pan cups. Preheat oven to 400°.

3. Spoon batter into prepared muffin pan cups. Combine the remaining 1 tablespoon of sugar and the cinnamon; sprinkle over top of muffins.

4. Bake in a preheated hot oven (400°) for 25 minutes or until centers spring back when lightly pressed with fingertip. Immediately remove from muffin cups to a wire rack; serve warm.

DOUGH SHORTCUT

If you're pressed for time, take advantage of the convenience of frozen bread dough. Stock up when it's a featured special. Allow dough to thaw in the refrigerator overnight; then turn it into delicious breads, coffee cakes, rolls, pizza crusts, and pastries.

USING UP BREAD

• Roll thinly; place on a cookie sheet; dry in a just-used oven as it cools down.
• Crumble in an electric blender; sprinkle on a jelly roll pan; toast as oven preheats.
• Store different types of bread in a plastic bag in the freezer until ready to make stuffing.

WHOLE WHEAT AND CORN MUFFINS

Two grains give these muffins extra flavor.

Bake at 425° for 25 minutes.
Makes 12 muffins.

½ cup *sifted* all-purpose flour
¼ teaspoon salt
3 teaspoons baking powder
1 cup whole wheat flour
½ cup cornmeal

⅓ cup butter or margarine, softened
¼ cup sugar
1 egg
1¼ cups milk

1. Sift all-purpose flour, salt, and baking powder onto wax paper. Stir in whole wheat flour and cornmeal. Grease well 12 muffin pan cups. Preheat oven to 425°.

2. Combine butter and sugar in a medium-size bowl. Beat until well blended.

3. Beat egg slightly in a small bowl; stir in milk; pour into butter mixture.

4. Add flour mixture to butter mixture. Stir just until flour is moistened. (Batter will be lumpy.) Fill prepared muffin pan cups ⅔ full.

5. Bake in a preheated hot oven (425°) for 25 minutes or until tops are golden brown. Remove from muffin cups to a wire rack; serve warm.

CHEESY SPREADS

Unroll 1 package refrigerated crescent rolls; spread; roll and bake. Add:
- ½ cup shredded Muenster cheese and 1 tablespoon hot dog relish.
- ½ cup shredded Cheddar cheese and 1 tablespoon hot mustard.
- ¼ cup blue and ¼ cup cottage cheeses.

TIDBITS OF MEAT

Hollow out 4 club rolls and fill with:
- 2 cups diced chicken mixed with ½ cup celery and ⅓ cup bottled sandwich spread; heat.
- 1 cup diced ham, 1 cup shredded cabbage, and ⅓ cup bottled cucumber salad dressing.

SWEET BREAKFAST SQUARES

This has a crunchy crumb topping.

Bake at 350° for 35 minutes.
Makes 1 coffee cake.

Topping:
6 tablespoons butter or margarine
½ cup sugar
1 tablespoon grated lemon rind
⅔ cup packaged bread crumbs
½ cup wheat germ

Batter:
1 cup *sifted* all-purpose flour
¾ cup sugar
¼ teaspoon salt
2 teaspoons baking powder
1 cup whole wheat flour
⅓ cup butter or margarine
1 egg
⅔ cup milk
1 teaspoon vanilla

1. To make Topping: Combine 6 tablespoons butter and ½ cup sugar in a small bowl; mix well. Add lemon rind, bread crumbs, and wheat germ. Mix with fork or fingers until crumbly; reserve. Grease a 13 x 9 x 2-inch baking pan. Preheat oven to 350°.
2. Sift all-purpose flour, the ¾ cup sugar, salt, and baking powder into a large bowl. Sitr in whole wheat flour.
3. Cut the ⅓ cup butter into the flour mixture with a pastry blender until fine crumbs form.
4. Beat egg in a small bowl; add milk and vanilla. Pour egg mixture into flour mixture; stir just until ingredients are blended. Turn batter into prepared pan, spreading evenly. Sprinkle topping over batter.
5. Bake in a preheated moderate oven (350°) for 35 minutes or until center springs back when lightly pressed with fingertip. Cut into squares; serve warm.

SEASONED CRUMBS

To 2 cups dry bread crumbs add:
• ¼ cup grated Parmesan cheese and 1 teaspoon basil; sprinkle over a casserole.
• 2 teaspoons sage, crumbled; coat chicken.
• 2 teaspoons grated lemon rind; coat fish fillets.

ORANGE-FLAVORED DOUGHNUTS

Makes about 20 doughnuts and centers.

½ cup (1 stick) butter or margarine
¼ cup granulated sugar
1 tablespoon grated orange rind
¾ cup orange juice

2 envelopes active dry yeast
2 eggs, beaten
4 cups *sifted* all-purpose flour
⅛ teaspoon salt
Vegetable oil for frying
10X (confectioners') sugar

1. Combine butter, granulated sugar, orange rind, and juice in a small saucepan. Heat just until butter is melted; cool to warm. Turn into a large bowl.

2. Sprinkle yeast into orange juice mixture; stir to dissolve. Let stand until bubbly, about 10 minutes. Beat in eggs.

3. Add 3 cups of the flour and the salt; beat until smooth. Add just enough of the remaining flour to make a soft dough.

4. Turn out onto a lightly floured surface; knead until smooth and elastic, about 5 minutes, using only as much flour as needed to prevent dough from sticking.

5. Place in a large greased bowl; turn to coat. Cover; let rise in a warm place, away from drafts, about 30 minutes or until doubled in volume.

6. Punch dough down; knead a few times; let rest 5 minutes. Roll out on floured surface to a ½-inch thickness. Cut out with a 3-inch doughnut cutter. Arrange doughnuts and centers on cookie sheets; cover. Let rise 30 minutes again or until doubled in volume.

7. Heat a 3-inch depth of oil to 360° on a deep-fat frying thermometer in a large, heavy saucepan. Add doughnuts, a few at a time, to make a single layer. (Don't crowd the pan.) Fry, turning once, until golden on both sides, about 3 minutes. Drain on paper toweling. Continue with remaining doughnuts. Toss with 10X sugar.

SERVING SUGGESTION: Mugs of hot spiced cider.

DOUGH IN A TUBE

Toppings for 1 package refrigerated biscuits:
- Brush with oil; sprinkle with sesame seeds.
- Spread with butter; sprinkle with chives.
- Dip in milk; roll in wheat germ and peanuts.

APPLE GRIDDLE CAKES

For a real treat, serve Apple Griddle Cakes for brunch. For an extra protein boost, serve them with a generous dollop of cottage cheese.

Makes 5 servings.

2 cups *sifted* all-purpose flour	1 cup milk
2 tablespoons sugar	1 cup plain yogurt
1 teaspoon baking soda	2 tablespoons vegetable oil
½ teaspoon salt	1 medium-size apple, pared
2 eggs	and finely chopped

1. Sift flour, sugar, baking soda, and salt into a medium-size bowl.
2. Beat eggs lightly in a medium-size bowl; stir in milk, yogurt, and oil.
3. Add milk mixture all at once to dry ingredients; stir just until smooth. Gently stir in apple.
4. Spoon batter onto a hot, lightly greased griddle to form 5-inch circles. Cook over medium heat until brown on underside. Turn; cook until other side is brown. Keep warm in a slow oven until all of the batter is used.

SERVING SUGGESTIONS: Grapefruit sections, maple-flavored syrup (for griddle cakes), cottage cheese, and coffee.

BOOST WITH WHEAT GERM

Give your favorite pancake or waffle recipe a nutrition boost by adding ¼ cup wheat germ (plus ¼ cup additional liquid). You'll also be rewarded with a pleasant nutty flavor.

CASSEROLE TOPPINGS

• Spread dill butter on rye bread; cut into triangles and arrange on a salmon casserole.
• Toss cubed white bread in melted basil butter; arrange, checkerboard-style on top of a casserole.
• Top fingers of bread with cheese and place on a tuna casserole.

2
Soups and Stews

Soups and stews are ideal for anyone on a budget because they allow you to improvise, using ingredients on hand. You can rummage through your refrigerator and freezer and recruit tidbits of vegetables, meats, etc., for your stockpot. Soups and stews are easy to make and require only a minimum of attention. You can also make them in advance and refrigerate or freeze them for future use. This chapter offers homey and soothing soups, such as Herbed Lentil Soup and Italian Vegetable-Bread Soup. Tomato-Orange Soup is nice enough for company. And there's such soul-warming fare as Chicken and Parsleyed-Dumpling Stew and hearty Beef Burgundy.

SOUPE À L'OIGNON GRATINÉE

Bake at 425° for 10 minutes.
Makes 6 servings.

2	large onions chopped (2 cups)
4	tablespoons (½ stick) butter or margarine
¼	cup all-purpose flour
6	cups water
2	tablespoons vinegar
1	chicken bouillon cube
1½	teaspoons salt
¼	teaspoon pepper
12	slices (¼ inch thick) day-old French bread
1	cup shredded Swiss cheese (4 ounces)

1. Sauté onions in 1 tablespoon of the butter in a large heavy saucepan or Dutch oven over low heat until lightly browned, about 15 minutes. Sprinkle flour over onions; toss lightly to coat. Stir in water, vinegar, bouillon cube, salt, and pepper. Bring to a boil. Lower heat; cover; simmer 30 minutes.
2. Melt remaining 3 tablespoons butter in a large skillet. Add bread slices in a single layer; turn to coat with butter. Sauté on both sides over low heat just until bread slices begin to brown. Remove from heat.
3. Preheat oven to 425°.
4. Add 6 slices of the bread and ¼ cup of the shredded cheese to onion soup; stir just until bread begins to soften and cheese begins to melt.
5. Ladle soup with 1 slice softened bread into each of six 8-ounce ovenproof bowls, six 12-ounce custard cups or all of the soup and softened bread into an 8-cup casserole. Arrange remaining bread slices on top; sprinkle with remaining ¾ cup cheese.
6. Heat soup in a preheated hot oven (425°) for 10 minutes. Raise oven temperature to broil. Place soup under broiler; broil until top is bubbly and lightly browned.

SERVING SUGGESTIONS: Tossed green salad and baked custard.

ITALIAN VEGETABLE-BREAD SOUP

Makes 6 servings.

2 large onions, cut into thin wedges

1 pound carrots, pared and cut diagonally into ½-inch slices (2 cups)

2 medium-size ribs celery, cut diagonally into ½-inch slices (1½ cups)

2 medium-size zucchini, halved lengthwise and cut into 1-inch pieces (1½ cups)

2 cloves garlic, minced

½ cup vegetable oil

1 package (10 ounces) frozen chopped spinach, thawed

1 can (14 ounces) Italian-style tomatoes

1 can (1 pound) red kidney beans, drained

2 teaspoons salt

½ teaspoon pepper

½ teaspoon oregano, crumbled

¼ teaspoon basil, crumbled

12 slices (1-inch thick) French bread, toasted

1 can (13¾ ounces) chicken broth

Water

½ cup grated Parmesan cheese

1. Sauté onions, carrots, celery, zucchini, and garlic in oil in a large saucepan or Dutch oven until vegetables are soft, about 5 minutes. Remove vegetables with a slotted spoon to a large bowl. Add spinach, tomatoes with their liquid, beans, salt, pepper, oregano, and basil; stir gently to mix well.

2. Return one third of vegetable mixture to saucepan; top with 6 slices French bread, another third of vegetable mixture, the remaining bread, and remaining vegetable mixture.

3. Pour chicken broth into a 2-cup glass measure; add water to make 2 cups liquid; pour over vegetable-bread mixture. Bring to a boil; lower heat; cover; simmer for 30 minutes or until heated through. Remove from heat; let stand 10 minutes. Sprinkle with Parmesan cheese. Serve in deep bowls, passing additional cheese.

SERVING SUGGESTIONS: Tomato and lettuce salad, anise cookies, and fresh grapes.

TOMATO-ORANGE SOUP

Serve this soup hot or cold.

Makes 6 servings.

1 medium-size onion, chopped (½ cup)	1 cup water
2 tablespoons butter or margarine	1 teaspoon salt
	1 teaspoon sugar
2 tablespoons all-purpose flour	1 cup orange juice
	⅛ teaspoon ground cardamom
1 can (13¾ ounces) chicken broth	½ cup dairy sour cream (optional)
4 medium-size tomatoes, peeled and chopped	Orange slices (optional)
Or: 1 can (16 ounces) tomatoes	

1. Sauté onion in butter in a large saucepan until soft, about 5 minutes. Stir in flour. Gradually stir in chicken broth, tomatoes, water, salt, and sugar.

2. Bring to a boil; lower heat; cover, and simmer for 15 minutes. Press through a food mill or sieve. Wipe out pan with paper toweling. Return soup to pan.

3. Stir in orange juice and cardamom; heat until hot. If serving cold, chill several hours. Garnish with sour cream and orange slices.

HEARTY VEGETABLE SOUP

Beef bones and a little meat bring hearty flavor to this vegetable soup.

Makes 4 generous servings.

Bones and meat from blade chuck steak	1 quart water
	1 teaspoon salt
3 tablespoons vegetable oil	¼ teaspoon pepper
1 small onion, chopped	1 bay leaf
1 large carrot chopped	1 medium-size potato, diced
2 large ribs celery, chopped	3 tablespoons all-purpose flour
1 cup tomato puree	⅓ cup chopped parsley

1. Brown bones and meat on all sides in a medium-size saucepan. Remove from pan; add 1 tablespoon of the oil to saucepan. Add onion, carrot, and celery; sauté, stirring often, until onions are tender, about 3 minutes. Add tomato puree, water, salt, pepper, and bay leaf; bring to a boil. Return meat and bones to pan along with potato. Lower heat; cover; simmer for 30 minutes.

2. Remove bones and meat from pan. When cool enough to handle, cut off meat from bones. Chop meat into small pieces. Return meat to saucepan; cover and simmer 30 minutes longer.

3. Combine remaining 2 tablespoons oil and all of the flour in a small skillet; cook over low heat, stirring constantly, until mixture turns a golden brown. Add to soup, stirring constantly to mix well. Sprinkle with parsley before serving.

SERVING SUGGESTIONS: Warm crusty bread with herb butter and baked apples.

PORTUGUESE BEAN SOUP

Makes 8 servings.

1 **pound dried kidney beans**	1 **large potato, pared and diced**
1 **pound smoked ham hocks**	2 **teaspoons salt**
¼ **cup vegetable oil**	¼ **teaspoon pepper**
1 **large onion, chopped (1 cup)**	1 **quart water**
1 **large clove garlic, minced**	1 **package (10 ounces) frozen**
¾ **cup diced carrots (2 small)**	**chopped spinach**
4 **cups shredded cabbage**	
(about 1 pound)	

1. Pick over and wash beans; place in a kettle or Dutch oven. Add water to cover; bring to a boil; boil 2 minutes. Remove from heat; cover; let stand 1 hour. Check occasionally to make sure beans are covered with water and add more water if needed.

2. Drain beans; return to kettle with ham hocks. Add enough water just to cover beans. Bring to a boil, then cover; simmer 1 hour. Remove ham hocks; cool slightly; cut meat from bones; dice.

3. Heat oil in large skillet; sauté onion and garlic until tender, about 3 minutes. Add meat and carrots; sauté 3 minutes more. Add mixture to kettle with cabbage, potato, salt, pepper, and 1 quart of water.

4. Bring to a boil, then lower heat; cover; simmer for 30 minutes or until vegetables are tender. Add spinach; cook 2 minutes longer. Taste; add salt and pepper if needed.

SERVING SUGGESTIONS: Autumn Barley Loaf■, sliced pears, and Cinnamon-Nut Cookies ■.

SPANISH BEAN SOUP

This hearty soup contains meats and vegetables. It is a superb winter dish that can be served as a soup or over hot cooked rice.

Makes 8 servings.

1 pound dried Great Northern beans	2 tablespoons vinegar
10 cups water	2 tablespoons olive or vegetable oil
1 medium-size piece salt pork, sliced (about ⅓ pound)	1 bay leaf
1 ham bone or ham hock	¼ teaspoon salt
11 medium-size yellow onions (about 3 pounds), chopped	¼ teaspoon pepper
1 green pepper, seeded and chopped	2 large potatoes (about 1 pound), pared and quartered
2 cloves garlic, crushed	1 medium-size cabbage, cored and shredded
½ cup tomato sauce	1 small butternut squash, pared and cubed

1. Pick over and wash beans. Put in a large kettle with the water. Bring to a boil, uncovered, for 2 minutes. Remove from heat; cover and let stand 1 hour.

2. Add salt pork, ham bone, onions, green pepper, garlic, tomato sauce, vinegar, oil, bay leaf, salt, and pepper.

3. Bring back to a boil; cover. Lower heat and simmer about 1½ hours. Remove ham bone from soup and cut meat from bone. Dice meat and return to soup.

4. Add potatoes, cabbage, and squash to soup. Continue cooking, covered, about 25 minutes longer or until vegetables are tender.

SERVING SUGGESTIONS: Serve this robust soup with a light dessert—sliced oranges and vanilla butter cookies.

DRESS IT UP

Soup can be festive and special when served in attractive soup bowls or cups. For best enjoyment, warm the bowls for hot soups and chill them for cold soups. Just before serving, dress up the soup with an attractive garnish, such as a sprinkling of chopped hard-cooked eggs, chives, or parsley. Or top with crisp croutons, thin slices of lemon or lime, or julienne pieces of carrot or celery.

HERBED LENTIL SOUP

Makes 5 servings.

2	large onions, chopped (2 cups)	3	beef bouillon cubes
1	carrot, coarsely grated	1	cup dried lentils, rinsed
½	teaspoon marjoram, crumbled	1	teaspoon salt
½	teaspoon thyme, crumbled	¼	teaspoon pepper
¼	cup olive or vegetable oil	¼	cup dry sherry or dry white wine
1	can (1 pound) tomatoes	¼	cup chopped parsley
5	cups water	1	cup shredded Cheddar cheese (4 ounces)

1. Sauté onions, carrots, marjoram, and thyme in oil in a large kettle or Dutch oven, stirring often, until lightly browned, about 5 minutes.
2. Add tomatoes, water, bouillon cubes, lentils, salt, and pepper, stirring to dissolve cubes; bring to a boil. Lower heat; cover; simmer about 1 hour or until lentils are tender.
3. Add sherry and parsley; simmer for 2 minutes.
4. Serve in soup bowls; garnish with a sprinkling of cheese.

SERVING SUGGESTIONS: Wheat Germ Bread ■, sliced cucumber salad, and Cottage Cheese Pound Cake ■.

NO-COST SOUP

Be clever and thrifty by collecting all the leftover scraps of vegetables, pasta, meats, etc., that usually go to waste. An easy way to do this is to continually add leftovers to a freezer container labeled "Soup Scraps." When enough leftovers are collected, simmer them in water or broth to make a soup. Season to taste. If desired, puree the mixture in a blender or food processor. To thicken, add flour or cornstarch (first made into a paste with a little water), cream, butter, egg yolks, or bread crumbs.

SPEEDY SPLIT PEA SOUP

A hearty pea soup just right for cold winter lunches.

Makes 4 servings.

1 package (6 ounces) split pea soup mix	1 large clove garlic, peeled
5 cups water	¾ teaspoon salt
1 large rib celery, chopped	¼ teaspoon poultry seasoning
1 medium-size carrot, chopped	¾ teaspoon pepper
1 medium-size onion, chopped	2 frankfurters (optional)
1 medium-size potato, pared and diced	

1. Combine split pea soup mix, water, celery, carrot, onion, and potato in a medium-size saucepan; bring to a boil. Lower heat; cover; simmer 1 hour, stirring occasionally.
2. Mash garlic with salt; stir into soup with poultry seasoning and pepper. Simmer for 3 minutes. If you wish slice 2 frankfurters; add to soup while heating.

SERVING SUGGESTIONS: Honey and Cream Cheese Whole Wheat Bread ■ and bananas.

BONUS BROTH

Utilize the bones of your leftover chicken or meat roast to make a flavorful broth. Simmer the bones in water with vegetables and herbs. Cool completely, then store in covered containers in the refrigerator up to 3 days; remove the layer of fat just before using. For longer storage, pour skimmed broth into freezer containers, in family-size portions, allowing ½-inch space at top for expansion in freezing. Seal, label, date, and freeze at 0° for up to 3 months.

HEARTY VEGETABLE STEW

Bake at 350° for 45 minutes, then at 357° for 20 minutes.
Makes 8 servings.

3	large onions, sliced	2	teaspoons salt
2	large cloves garlic, minced	¼	teaspoon pepper
2	tablespoons vegetable oil	1	teaspoon basil, crumbled
2	tablespoons butter or margarine	1	can (13¾ ounces) vegetable juice cocktail
1	pound carrots, pared and cut into 1-inch pieces	1	can (13¾ ounces) beef broth*
1	pound new potatoes, washed and quartered	2	cans (20 ounces each) chick-peas
1	head cauliflower (1 pound) separated into flowerets	2	green peppers, halved, seeded, and cut into strips
½	pound mushrooms, quartered	2	cups fresh bread crumbs (6 slices bread)
½	small cabbage, cored and cut into 8 wedges	½	cup freshly grated Parmesan cheese
		½	cup chopped parsley

1. Sauté onion and garlic in oil and butter in a 4-quart flameproof casserole for 5 minutes. Add carrots, potatoes, cauliflower, mushrooms, and cabbage. Cook, stirring occasionally, 20 minutes.
2. Sprinkle vegetables with salt, pepper, and basil. Add vegetable juice and beef broth. Cover; bring to a simmer. Stir in chick-peas and green peppers. Preheat oven to 350°.
3. Bake, covered, in a preheated moderate oven (350°) for 45 minutes or until potatoes are tender. Remove from oven; raise oven temperature to 375°.
4. Combine bread crumbs, cheese, and parsley in medium-size bowl. Spoon over vegetables, covering entire surface.
5. Bake, uncovered, 20 minutes longer or until crumbs are nicely browned.

SERVING SUGGESTIONS: Breadstick Bundles ■ and baked apples.

---

*An additional 13¾-ounce can of vegetable juice cocktail can be used instead of the beef broth.

CHICKEN IN THE POT

Makes 4 servings.

1	broiler-fryer (about 2¼ pounds), cut up	1	teaspoon salt
1	tablespoon vegetable oil	¼	teaspoon pepper
1	large onion, chopped (1 cup)	1	cup long-grain rice
½	cup chopped celery	⅓	cup chopped fresh dill
1	cup water	⅓	cup plain yogurt

1. Brown chicken on all sides in oil in a large skillet; remove and reserve. Add onion and celery to skillet; cook, stirring often, until onion is tender, about 3 minutes.

2. Return chicken to skillet. Add water, salt, and pepper and bring to a boil. Lower heat; cover; simmer for 15 minutes.

3. Add rice; stir to cover with liquid. Cover; simmer for 20 minutes or until rice is tender. (Check during cooking time to see if more water is needed to cook rice.) Remove chicken; stir dill and yogurt into rice; turn chicken to rice mixture. Serve hot.

SERVING SUGGESTIONS: Marinated string bean salad, Herb-Onion Rolls ■, and Carrot-Nut Cake ■.

LAZY DAY STEW

Take it easy with an oven-baked stew. Use an attractive casserole that can go from the oven to the table. If using a flameproof casserole, you cut down on cleaning chores because you can brown ingredients and do all the preliminary steps in the same casserole. Another bonus is that you can save energy by baking apples or a bread pudding in the oven with your stew.

CHICKEN AND PARSLEYED-DUMPLING STEW

An easy chicken stew with plenty of parsley-speckled dumplings
to help soak up the savory broth.

Makes 6 servings.

1	broiler-fryer (3-pounds), cut up	1	large rib celery, sliced (½ cup)
½	cup all-purpose flour	½	teaspoon salt
¼	teaspoon salt	¼	teaspoon pepper
⅛	teaspoon pepper	1	package (10 ounces) frozen mixed vegetables
3	tablespoons vegetable oil		
1	tablespoon butter or margarine		*Dumplings:*
1	medium-size onion, sliced	1	cup buttermilk baking mix
1	clove garlic, minced	1½	tablespoons chopped parsley
1	can (13¾ ounces) chicken broth	1½	tablespoons rosemary, crumbled
2	cups water	⅓	cup milk

1. Shake chicken with flour, salt, and pepper in a plastic or paper bag until thoroughly coated.

2. Sauté chicken in oil and butter in a large kettle or Dutch oven until lightly browned, about 5 minutes on each side. Add onion and garlic; sauté for 3 minutes or until golden brown.

3. Stir in chicken broth and water; add celery, salt, and pepper. Bring to a boil. Lower heat; cover; simmer for 15 minutes or until chicken is almost tender.

4. Meanwhile, make dumplings: Combine buttermilk baking mix, parsley, and rosemary in a medium-size bowl. Stir in milk until well blended.

5. Uncover stew; bring back to a boil. Add mixed vegetables. Drop dumplings, about 1 inch in diameter, from a wet teaspoon on top of the boiling stew (there should be about 20 dumplings). Cook, uncovered, 5 minutes. Cover; cook 5 minutes longer or until dumplings are firm. Ladle broth, chicken, and dumplings into individual bowls.

SERVING SUGGESTIONS: Tangy Cucumber Salad■ and spiced fruit compote.

SLOW COOKER TIPS

Slow cookers, available in many sizes and shapes, are an ideal way to cook a stew. You can be out of the house all day and be greeted by a perfectly cooked stew when you come home. Slow cookers are also a convenient way to keep foods hot on a buffet table when entertaining informally.

Here are general directions for converting your favorite one-pot recipes for a slow cooker:
• Uncooked meat and vegetable combinations need 8 to 10 hours on low (190° to 200°) or 4 to 5 hours on high (290° to 300°).
• One hour of simmering on the range or baking at 350° in an oven is equal to 8 to 10 hours on low (190° to 200°) or 4 to 5 hours on high (290° to 300°).
• Reduce the amount of liquid in your recipe to 1 cup, since the slow cooker method retains all the natural juices of the food.
• Use canned soups, broths, wine, or water, *but not* dairy products, such as milk, dairy sour cream, or cream, during long cooking. Dairy products can be added during the last 30 minutes.
• Don't peek while the slow cooker is at work. You lose the equivalent of 30 minutes cooking time in heat each time the cover is removed.

BEEF BURGUNDY

This dish can be kept hot in the slow cooker for about 2 hours.

Makes 5 servings.

1½ pounds boneless beef rump, cubed
2 tablespoons all-purpose flour
1 teaspoon salt
½ teaspoon pepper
2 tablespoons margarine
1 tablespoon olive or vegetable oil
2 cups water
2 beef bouillon cubes
1 cup Burgundy or other dry red wine

3 carrots, sliced
2 medium-sized onions, sliced
1 clove garlic, minced
1 bay leaf
¼ teaspoon thyme, crumbled
2 tablespoons cornstarch
2 tablespoons water
⅓ cup drained canned mushroom pieces (½ of a 6-ounce can)
1 tablespoon chopped parsley

1. Shake meat with flour, salt, and pepper in a plastic or paper bag to coat well.

2. Heat margarine and oil in a large skillet. Brown beef on all sides and transfer to a slow cooker.

3. Pour off fat from skillet; add the 2 cups water, stirring to loosen browned bits and deglaze pan. Pour into slow cooker with bouillon cubes, wine, carrots, onion, garlic, bay leaf, and thyme. Stir to combine. Cover; cook on low for 7½ hours.*

4. Mix cornstarch and the 2 tablespoons water until smooth; stir into the beef mixture; add mushrooms and parsley. Cover and cook 30 minutes longer.

SERVING SUGGESTIONS: Tossed green salad, garlic bread, and Orange Chiffon Cake ■.

---

*If you do not have a slow cooker, simmer beef in a kettle or Dutch oven on top of the stove for 2 hours.

QUICK FISH STEW

Your guests will think you've spent hours in the kitchen preparing this 30-minute fish stew.

Makes 6 servings.

1   package (7½ ounces) risotto-style rice mix
1   clove garlic, minced
2   tablespoons vegetable oil
1   can (13¾ ounces) chicken broth
1   can (16 ounces) stewed tomatoes

1   package (10 ounces) Italian-style vegetables in sauce
¼   teaspoon rosemary, crumbled
1   package (1 pound) frozen turbot or cod, slightly thawed
½   cup dry white wine

1. Remove seasoning packet from rice package; reserve. Sauté rice and garlic in oil in a large saucepan or Dutch oven until rice is golden.
2. Pour chicken broth into a 4-cup measure; add water to make 3 cups liquid. Add to rice in saucepan with reserved seasoning packet, stewed tomatoes, vegetables, and rosemary. Cover; bring to a boil.
3. Cut turbot or cod into cubes; add to saucepan with the wine. Cover; lower heat; simmer for 20 minutes or until rice is tender. Transfer to soup tureen. Serve in soup bowls.

SERVING SUGGESTIONS: Baking powder biscuits, lettuce salad with Thousand Island Dressing, and lemon sherbet.

RANGE-TOP TIPS

For range-top casserole cooking, the most energy-efficient materials are heavy metal, porcelain-coated cast iron or flameproof ceramic. Be sure that your Dutch oven or casserole has a tight-fitting cover and that the base fits the size of the burner. This allows more even cooking and efficient energy usage.

3

Salads

Y ou'll find all kinds of tantalizing recipes here—colorful vegetable salads, salad molds, and main-dish spectaculars, such as Rice Salad Niçoise or Chicken and Rotelle Salad. This chapter is also studded with enough tips to make you a salad pro. Remember that salads, like soups and stews, are a great way to use up leftovers and tidbits.

Whether you're preparing a salad as a main dish or as an accompaniment, these points will help you make it tastier and more nutritious:

● When selecting greens, keep in mind that the darker the leaves, the more vitamins A and C they contain.

● The best greens for iron are spinach and beet; spinach is the highest in potassium and calcium content; the top sources for vitamin A are spinach, beet greens, and watercress; for vitamin C, beet greens.

● To boost a healthy green salad, add a sprinkling of nuts or sunflower seeds, raisins, bean sprouts, or avocado slices.

• If you're counting calories, avoid dressings made with sour cream, mayonnaise, or cheese; instead opt for a simple oil and vinegar dressing, or low-fat yogurt-based dressings. Another alternative: Squeeze a fresh lemon over the salad; then add a sprinkling of fresh herbs (tarragon, basil, chives, dill, or parsley) for more flavor.

• Instead of using olive oil in your dressing, try the higher-in-polyunsaturates oils, such as vegetable, peanut, corn, soy, safflower, or sunflower. Note: When using these, the proportion of oil to vinegar should be 4 to 1 instead of 3 to 1.

• Use a wide variety of greens for an interesting flavor. Consider escarole, chicory, red cabbage, or endive mixed with the more traditional Boston, Bibb, iceberg, or romaine lettuces.

• The following can easily be added to any salad to make it more delicious: bean sprouts, grapes, fresh broccoli flowerets, cauliflower flowerets, olives, apples, pimientos, string beans, cooked macaroni.

• To zip up a bland dressing, add a few drops of lemon juice. Or try a dash of dry mustard or finely minced garlic or onion.

CARROT SALAD IN LEMON AND MUSTARD DRESSING

Tender young carrots make a delicious salad or side dish.

Makes 6 servings.

¼ cup lemon juice
2 teaspoons Dijon-style mustard
2 teaspoons sugar
½ cup minced green onions
6 tablespoons olive or vegetable oil
½ teaspoon salt
⅛ teaspoon pepper

2 tablespoons snipped fresh dill
Or: 2 teaspoons dillweed
1 pound carrots, cut in julienne strips
3 cups water
Dash salt
1 teaspoon sugar

1. Combine lemon juice, mustard, the 2 teaspoons sugar, green onions, oil, the ½ teaspoon salt, pepper, and dill in a screw-top jar. Shake until well blended.
2. Combine carrots, water, remaining salt, and sugar in a large saucepan. Bring to a boil, lower heat; cover. Simmer until tender, about 5 minutes. Do not overcook. Drain; cool quickly under cold running water to stop further cooking; drain again. Transfer to a salad bowl.
3. Pour dressing over; toss lightly to coat. Taste; add additional seasoning if needed. Chill until ready to serve.

GRATED ZUCCHINI AND GREEN PEPPER SALAD

Makes 4 servings.

2 medium-size zucchini, coarsely shredded
2 medium-size green peppers, halved, seeded, and diced
1 medium-size cucumber, pared, halved, seeded, and sliced

Bottled Italian salad dressing
1 tablespoon chopped chives
2 tablespoons chopped parsley
¼ teaspoon salt
⅛ teaspoon pepper
Lettuce leaves

1. Combine the zucchini, green peppers, and cucumber in a medium-size bowl. Add enough dressing to moisten.
2. Toss with the chives, parsley, salt, and pepper; refrigerate. Serve in lettuce cups.

CUCUMBER AND TOMATO VINAIGRETTE

Makes 8 servings

2 cucumbers, pared and thinly sliced

2 medium-size ripe tomatoes, thinly sliced

1 red onion, thinly sliced

½ cup bottled vinaigrette salad dressing

1. Combine cucumbers, tomatoes, onion slices, and dressing in a salad bowl; toss until thoroughly coated.

2. Chill until ready to serve. Toss again before serving.

TANGY CUCUMBER SALAD

Makes 6 servings.

3 to 4 small cucumbers (2 pounds), pared and thinly sliced

1 small red onion, thinly sliced

⅔ cup white wine vinegar

⅓ cup vegetable oil

1 tablespoon lemon juice

1 teaspoon dry mustard

¼ teaspoon tarragon, crumbled

½ teaspoon salt

¼ teaspoon white pepper

1 tablespoon chopped parsley

1. Place cucumbers and onion in bowl.

2. Combine vinegar, oil, lemon juice, dry mustard, tarragon, salt, and pepper in a large screw-top jar; cover; shake well. Pour over vegetables; toss. Cover. Chill until ready to serve.

3. To serve, sprinkle with chopped parsley.

CORN SALAD

Makes 12 servings.

3	cans (10½ ounces each) whole kernel corn, drained	½	cup chopped green onions
2	cans (15¼ ounces each) red kidney beans, drained	2	cloves garlic, crushed
		2	tablespoons lemon juice
1	large red pepper, halved, seeded, and chopped	2	tablespoons red wine vinegar
		1	teaspoon dry mustard
1	large green pepper, halved, seeded, and chopped	½	teaspoon salt
		½	teaspoon basil, crumbled
1	cup sliced celery	¼	teaspoon pepper
		1⅓	cups olive or vegetable oil

1. Combine corn, beans, red and green peppers, celery, and green onions in a large salad bowl; toss lightly.

2. Combine garlic, lemon juice, vinegar, dry mustard, salt, basil, pepper, and oil in a screw-top jar; shake well. Pour over vegetables; toss lightly. Chill until serving time.

SERVING SUGGESTIONS: Grilled sausages, Giant Whole Wheat Twists ■, and Fresh Fruit Salad with Sour Cream Dressing ■.

SPROUT SOME BEANS

Perk up your next salad with some bean sprouts. They'll provide visual appeal, crunch, and good nutrition (protein and vitamin C). Because sprouts are also low in calories, they're a calorie counter's dream. If you sprout your own mung beans, you can enjoy them for just pennies a serving! Here's how:

(1) Place beans in a jar and soak in water for 4 to 6 hours.

(2) Cover top of jar with cheesecloth and secure with string or a rubber band.

(3) Drain off water through cloth. Store beans in a dark place, such as below the kitchen sink.

(4) Rinse beans every day to keep them from drying out. Keep beans at room temperature. Continue rinsing procedure until beans have sprouted, about 3 to 4 days, or until they are almost 3 inches long.

(5) Refrigerate sprouts.

POTATO SALAD

Makes 12 servings.

12	hard-cooked eggs	2	to 3 teaspoons salt
12	medium-size potatoes	¼	teaspoon pepper
	(about 4 pounds), cooked,	1	large onion, quartered
	peeled, and diced	¾	cup mayonnaise
½	cup milk	3	tablespoons vinegar
1	tablespoon prepared	¼	cup chopped parsley
	mustard		Paprika (optional)

1. Chop 10 of the eggs; combine with potatoes in a large bowl.

2. Combine milk, mustard, salt, pepper, and onion in the container of an electric blender; cover and whirl until onion is finely chopped. Add mayonnaise and vinegar; whirl just to blend. Pour over potato-egg mixture; mix well.

3. Cover and refrigerate until chilled. When ready to serve, slice the remaining 2 eggs. Sprinkle salad with parsley, garnish with egg slices; sprinkle with paprika if you wish.

SERVING SUGGESTIONS: Alfalfa-Wheat Bread■ and Peanut Butter Brownies ■.

DILLED POTATO AND APPLE SALAD

Makes 8 servings

6	medium-size potatoes	½	cup dairy sour cream
1	apple, pared, cored, and	½	cup mayonnaise
	diced	2	tablespoons chopped dill
½	cup chopped celery	½	teaspoon salt
2	hard-cooked eggs, shelled	¼	teaspoon pepper
	and chopped		Apple slices (optional)
⅓	cup chopped green onions		Fresh dill sprigs (optional)

1. Cook potatoes in boiling salted water in a large saucepan until tender, about 20 minutes; drain. Peel; cut into ½-inch chunks.

2. Combine potatoes, apple, celery, eggs, and green onions; toss.

3. Combine sour cream, mayonnaise, dill, salt, and pepper in a small bowl, blending well. Gently mix with potatoes to coat well. Chill thoroughly. Garnish with apple slices and sprigs of fresh dill if you wish.

SERVING SUGGESTIONS: Carrot Cornbread ■ and No-Fuss Chocolate Chewy Squares ■.

GARDEN SALAD MOLD

Crunchy-fresh vegetables in a refreshing lemony gelatin.

Makes about 6 servings.

1 package (3 ounces) lemon-flavored gelatin	½ cup chopped green pepper
1 envelope unflavored gelatin	1 cup shredded carrots
1 teaspoon salt	1 can (8 ounces) crushed pineapple, drained
1 cup boiling water	2 cups shredded green cabbage
2 cups cold water	Lettuce
⅓ cup vinegar	

1. Combine flavored gelatin, unflavored gelatin, and salt in a medium-size bowl. Add boiling water, stirring until gelatin is dissolved.
2. Add cold water and vinegar; refrigerate until thickened to the consistency of unbeaten egg whites.
3. Divide gelatin mixture equally among 3 medium-size bowls. Add green pepper to one, carrots and pineapple to the second, and cabbage to the third.
4. Pour pepper mixture into mold. Put in freezer for 10 minutes until sticky-firm. Spoon in carrot mixture; freeze until sticky-firm. Spoon in cabbage mixture. Refrigerate until firm, about 4 hours.
5. Unmold; garnish with lettuce. Serve with mayonnaise or bottled dressing if you wish.

PICKLE POWER

When the last pickle has been devoured, don't throw out the juice. It's a great flavor enhancer for salad dressings, marinades, sandwich fillings, etc.

CONFETTI SLAW

Try this slaw instead of sauerkraut to go with frankfurters.
There's enough to serve another day.

Makes about 6 cups.

1	small head cabbage (about 1½ pounds)	⅓	cup mayonnaise
1	small carrot	2	teaspoons sugar
⅓	cup chopped green pepper	2	teaspoons vinegar
¼	cup chopped parsley	½	teaspoon salt
1	tablespoon chopped onion	⅛	teaspoon pepper

1. Shred cabbage and carrot; combine with green pepper, parsley, and onion in a medium-size bowl.
2. Combine mayonnaise, sugar, vinegar, salt, and pepper in a small bowl and mix well. Toss with the slaw. Refrigerate until serving time.

RED CABBAGE AND APPLE SALAD

Makes 6 servings.

1	medium-size head red cabbage (about 1¾ pounds), shredded	⅓	cup vegetable oil
		⅓	cup cider vinegar
2	red Delicious apples, quartered, cored, and thinly sliced	2	tablespoons sugar
		1½	teaspoons ground celery seed
1	medium-size onion, thinly sliced	1	teaspoon salt
		⅛	teaspoon pepper
		1	cup dairy sour cream

1. Combine cabbage, apples, and onion in a salad bowl; toss lightly.
2. Combine oil, vinegar, sugar, celery seed, salt, pepper, and sour cream in a small bowl; stir until blended.
3. Toss dressing with salad until well coated.
4. Just before serving, toss salad again.

SPINACH, CHICK-PEA, AND MUSHROOM SALAD

A lemon-mint dressing coats tender spinach leaves, crunchy chick-peas, and crisp mushroom slices.

Makes 6 servings.

6	tablespoons olive or vegetable oil	**¼**	pound sliced fresh mushrooms
2	tablespoons lemon juice		Or: 1 can (4 ounces) sliced mushrooms, drained
½	teaspoon salt	**4**	cups fresh spinach leaves*
¼	teaspoon pepper		(from a 10-ounce package)
¼	teaspoon dried mint		
1	can (8 ounces) chick-peas, drained		

1. Combine oil, lemon juice, salt, pepper, and mint in bottom of a glass or wooden salad bowl; stir to combine.
2. Add chick-peas; top with mushroom slices and spinach. Toss at the table.

SERVING SUGGESTIONS: Cracked Wheat, Corn, and Sesame Loaf■ and Apricot-Yogurt Whip ■.

---

*Romaine lettuce can be substituted for spinach if you wish.

CABBAGE IS SUPER

The cabbage family is a great friend of the salad lover. Cabbage keeps well and adds crunch to salads. It's also inexpensive and low in calories. Although slightly more expensive, buy red cabbage occasionally for a colorful change of pace. When buying cabbage, look for a head that is solid and heavy for its size, with bright, fresh leaves.

CHEF'S SALAD

Makes 5 servings.

½ head lettuce, torn into bite-size pieces
2 carrots, thinly sliced
1 cup diced zucchini (1 medium size)
1 cup chopped cabbage
½ cup chopped broccoli, with stems
½ cup sliced celery
¼ green pepper, chopped

2 tablespoons chopped onion
Julienned chicken meat (from 2 poached chicken thighs)
1 cup julienned cooked ham
1 cup julienned Cheddar cheese
3 hard-cooked eggs, quartered
½ cucumber, sliced

1. Combine lettuce, carrots, zucchini, cabbage, broccoli, celery, green pepper, and onion in a large bowl.
2. Arrange chicken, ham, cheese, and eggs on top of salad. Arrange cucumber slices around edge of bowl. Serve with your favorite dressing.

SERVING SUGGESTIONS: Mexican Corn Sticks ■ and No-Fuss Chocolate Chewy Squares ■.

PREPARING LETTUCE

Prepare salad greens properly and you will be rewarded with a salad of crisp, fresh-looking lettuce leaves. For lettuce with loose leaves, trim greens of bruised leaves and wash in cold water; drain in a large colander or salad spinner. When thoroughly drained, place in a large plastic bag. To prepare iceberg lettuce, twist out the core and discard it. Rinse under cold running water; drain thoroughly, cored-end down, on a dish rack or in a colander. Place in a plastic bag. Store washed greens in the crisper drawer of a refrigerator; they will stay fresh for several days and will be ready to use immediately.

MARGIE'S SALMON-MACARONI SALAD

Hot or cold, this main-dish salad is a favorite.
It's perfect to bring along to a covered-dish supper.

Makes 4 servings.

1   can (7¾ ounces) salmon, drained and mashed
½   green pepper, chopped (½ cup)
2   tablespoons chopped green onion
2   tablespoons salad dressing
1   teaspoon Worcestershire sauce
1   teaspoon seasoned pepper
1   tablespoon lemon juice
1   package (8 ounces) elbow macaroni or small shells
    Lemon wedges (optional)
    Green pepper slices (optional)
    Tomato wedges (optional)

1. Combine salmon, green pepper, green onion, salad dressing, Worcestershire, seasoned pepper, and lemon juice in a large bowl. Toss gently to mix.

2. Cook 1 package elbow macaroni in a large pot of boiling water following package directions. Drain. Add hot cooked macaroni; toss gently again to coat ingredients with dressing. Salad can be served at once or refrigerated and served cold. Garnish with lemon wedges, green pepper slices, and tomato wedges if you wish.

SERVING SUGGESTIONS: Whole Wheat and Corn Muffins ■, dilled string bean salad, and Apricot-Glazed Peach Cake ■.

SALAD POTPOURRI

Salads provide a wonderful way to use up various leftovers that you may find in your refrigerator. Leftover rice, cooked vegetables, meat, or seafood can add interest to a salad. For instance, last night's leftover corn on the cob can be salvaged when the kernels are removed and added to a tossed salad. The most important guideline to follow is to aim for a contrast of color, flavor, form, and texture when combining salad ingredients.

CHICKEN AND ROTELLE SALAD
WITH PESTO DRESSING

Makes 8 servings.

1 broiler-fryer (about 3 pounds), cut up
1 pound rotelle (spiral pasta)
1 cup olive or vegetable oil
4 cups fresh parsley leaves
¼ cup pine nuts (pignoli) or walnuts
2 large cloves garlic, minced
1½ teaspoons basil
1 teaspoon salt
½ cup grated Parmesan cheese
  Romaine lettuce leaves
2 cups (1 pint-size basket) cherry tomatoes, halved
¼ cup pitted black olives

1. Simmer chicken in water to cover in a large saucepan until tender, about 40 minutes; cool. Skin, bone, and cut into strips. Cover and refrigerate.

2. Cook rotelle following package directions; drain. Rinse with cold water; drain again; turn into a large salad bowl.

3. Combine olive oil, parsley, pine nuts, garlic, basil, and salt in the container of an electric blender; whirl until parsley is finely chopped. Pour into a small bowl; stir in cheese. Arrange the romaine around the edge of the salad bowl.

4. Toss rotelle with half the dressing; mound chicken in center of bowl; surround with tomatoes and olives. Serve at room temperature. Serve with remaining dressing.

SERVING SUGGESTIONS: Breadstick Bundles ■, fried zucchini slices, and Elegant and Easy Peach Dessert ■.

─── SUBTLE OR STRONG GARLIC ───

• If you're aiming for a subtle garlic flavor, rub the inside of your salad bowl with a halved clove of garlic. Then save the garlic for another purpose.

• For a more potent garlic flavor, sprinkle a garlic clove with salt and chop it on a wooden board. The salt will absorb the flavorful garlic juice that would otherwise be wasted. Then add both garlic and salt to the salad bowl.

MAIN-DISH KASHA SALAD

This is an unusual treatment for the nutritious and full-flavored grain kasha (roasted buckwheat groats).
This delicious salad provides 21 grams of protein per serving.

Makes 6 servings.

1	egg	1	large red pepper, halved, seeded, and diced (1 cup)
1¼	cups whole grain kasha		
2	cups boiling water	1	large green pepper, halved, seeded, and diced (1 cup)
2	large cloves garlic		
1¼	teaspoons salt	1	medium-size red onion, diced (½ cup)
⅓	cup olive or vegetable oil		
¼	cup fresh lemon juice	½	cup pimiento-stuffed olives, sliced
2	tablespoons red wine vinegar		
1	teaspoon oregano, crumbled	½	cup minced parsley
¼	teaspoon crushed red pepper flakes	3	cups shredded chicory or escarole
¼	teaspoon pepper	1	pint cherry tomatoes, halved
2	cans (7 ounces each) tuna		

1. Beat egg slightly in a medium-size bowl; stir in kasha, mixing until grains are moistened.

2. Heat a large saucepan (preferably nonstick); add kasha, stirring constantly until grains are separated and dry, about 2 minutes. Carefully add boiling water, garlic, and ½ teaspoon of the salt; cover. Simmer for 15 minutes; remove from heat and let stand, covered, 15 minutes.

3. Combine remaining ¾ teaspoon salt, oil, lemon juice, vinegar, oregano, red pepper flakes, and pepper in a screw-top jar. Shake well to blend.

4. Drain fish. Break fish into large pieces in a bowl; pour half the dressing over fish.

5. Remove garlic cloves from kasha; add kasha to the bowl with fish; mix gently; cool to lukewarm. Add red and green peppers, onion, olives, parsley, and remaining dressing; mix to coat well. Cover with plastic wrap and chill at least 3 hours for flavors to blend.

6. Just before serving, line a salad bowl with shredded lettuce, mound salad in center; border with halved cherry tomatoes.

SERVING SUGGESTIONS: Spiced tomato juice, sesame breadsticks, and fresh fruit compote.

RICE SALAD NIÇOISE

A rice version of the traditional French salad.

Makes 8 servings.

1½ cups long-grain regular rice	2 tomatoes, cut into wedges
1 can (1 pound) cut green beans, drained	1 small red onion, sliced
¾ cup vegetable oil	2 hard-cooked eggs, shelled and sliced
¼ cup red wine vinegar	1 can (2 ounces) rolled anchovies with capers, drained
2 cloves garlic, minced	
1 teaspoon salt	
¼ teaspoon pepper	2 cans (6½ ounces each) tuna, drained
¼ teaspoon thyme, crumbled	
1 medium-size head romaine or iceberg lettuce	1 can (4 ounces) pitted ripe olives, drained

1. Cook rice following package directions.

2. Combine rice, beans, oil, vinegar, garlic, salt, pepper, and thyme in a large bowl; mix gently to coat thoroughly. Cover. Chill several hours, mixing occasionally.

3. To arrange: Line a large salad plate with romaine. Press rice and bean mixture into a 9-inch ring mold, pressing down to fit; turn upside down in center; remove mold. Arrange the tomatoes, onion, eggs, anchovies, the tuna broken into large chunks, and olives around the rice mixture.

SERVING SUGGESTIONS: Herb-Onion Rolls ■ and Glazed Pears ■.

RECYCLED GREENS

Don't despair if the party is over and you are faced with a large bowl of dressed salad greens and/or vegetables. Simply simmer the ingredients in your favorite broth until tender. Whirl in a blender, if you wish. Serve in soup bowls, topped with an attractive garnish. No one will be the wiser!

LAYERED TUNA AND VEGETABLE SALAD

Makes 8 servings.

¾ cup olive or vegetable oil
½ cup red wine vinegar
1 teaspoon dry mustard
½ teaspoon basil, crumbled
Or: 2 teaspoons chopped
fresh basil
1 teaspoon salt
1 package (4 ounces) alfalfa
sprouts
1 pint cherry tomatoes
2 medium-size cucumbers,
quartered lengthwise

2 cans (7 ounces each) solid
tuna, drained and broken
into bite-size pieces
1 can (6 ounces) pitted black
olives, drained and halved
1 can (20 ounces) chick-peas,
drained
1 tablespoon minced chives or
green onion

1. Combine oil, vinegar, dry mustard, basil, and salt in a screw-top jar; shake. Chill.
2. Place sprouts in an even layer on the bottom of a 2½-quart straight-sided clear glass bowl. Cut enough tomatoes in half to form a loosely packed layer over sprouts. Place tomatoes at perimeter, cut side next to glass. Next, add layers of cucumber, tuna, olives, and chick-peas.
3. To make tomato garnish, cut remaining tomatoes into 6 vertical wedges without cutting through. Arrange on top.
4. To serve, sprinkle chives and some of the dressing over top. Pass remaining dressing.

SERVING SUGGESTIONS: Dinner rolls■ and Blender Banana Cake■.

4

Casseroles and One-Dish Meals

Busy homemakers love casseroles and one-dish meals because they're easy to serve. Many are ideal candidates for entertaining. You'll find a tempting assortment of international and regional delights—Canadian Meat Pie and Baked Macaroni à la Grecque to Louisiana Rice Casserole. Best of all, they're based on thrifty ingredients. To make your casseroles a bit more special, our tips give you ideas for casserole toppers and tasty touches like herbs.

BAKED MACARONI À LA GRECQUE

Bake at 375° for 30 minutes.
Makes 6 servings.

1	large onion, chopped (1 cup)	¼	cup all-purpose flour
1	tablespoon vegetable oil	2½	cups milk
1	pound ground lamb	3	tablespoons tomato paste
½	teaspoon ground cinnamon	1	egg
½	teaspoon ground allspice	½	cup grated Parmesan cheese
¾	teaspoon salt	8	ounces *cooked* elbow
½	teaspoon pepper		macaroni
¼	cup (½ stick) margarine		

1. Sauté onion in oil in a large skillet until soft, about 3 minutes. Add lamb; sauté until no longer pink. Remove from heat; stir in cinnamon, allspice, ½ teaspoon of the salt, and ¼ teaspoon of the pepper.

2. Melt margarine in a medium-size saucepan; add remaining salt and pepper; blend in flour until smooth; cook for 1 minute. Stir in milk until smooth. Cook, stirring constantly, until mixture thickens and bubbles. Blend in tomato paste. Lightly grease an 8-cup baking dish. Preheat oven to 375°.

3. Beat egg slightly in a small bowl. Stir a little sauce mixture into egg; return mixture to saucepan. Stir in ¼ cup of the Parmesan.

4. Combine cooked macaroni, lamb mixture, and sauce in a large bowl. Turn into prepared baking dish; sprinkle with remaining Parmesan.

5. Bake in a preheated moderate oven (375°) for 30 minutes or until casserole is piping hot.

SERVING SUGGESTIONS: Tangy Cucumber Salad ■, sautéed eggplant and tomatoes, Parathas ■ with herb butter, and fresh fruit.

TASTY TOUCH

Perk up your casseroles and other dishes by adding a small amount of sausage meat. You'll gain some added protein and a tremendous amount of zesty flavor for very little cost when using sausages such as hot or sweet Italian, chorizo, or kielbasa.

SWEET AND SOUR BEEF AND CABBAGE

All the flavors of stuffed cabbage but with half the work.

Makes 6 servings.

1 pound ground chuck	2 tablespoons lemon juice
3 tablespoons long-grain rice	1 tablespoon honey
2 tablespoons grated onion	1 small cabbage (1 pound), cored and cut into 6 thin wedges
1 egg	
2 tablespoons water	
2 teaspoons salt	2 large carrots, halved lengthwise and cut into 3-inch pieces
½ teaspoon pepper	
¼ teaspoon dillweed	
2 tablespoons vegetable oil	1 can (1 pound) whole potatoes, drained
1 medium-size onion, chopped (½ cup)	
1 can (16 ounces) whole tomatoes	1 tablespoon chopped parsley

1. Mix chuck lightly with rice, grated onion, egg, water, 1 teaspoon of the salt, ¼ teaspoon of the pepper, and dill in a large bowl until well blended. Shape into 16 oval patties.

2. Sauté patties in oil in a large skillet until lightly browned on both sides; remove from skillet and keep warm. Pour off all but 2 tablespoons fat from skillet.

3. Add chopped onion to skillet; sauté until soft, about 5 minutes. Stir in tomatoes with their liquid, breaking up tomatoes with wooden spoon. Stir in lemon juice, honey, and remaining salt and pepper. Bring to a boil; lower heat. Arrange cabbage wedges in sauce; top with meat patties and carrots. Cover; simmer for 20 minutes. Add potatoes, cutting large ones in half. Cover; simmer 10 minutes longer or until potatoes are heated through. Sprinkle with parsley.

SERVING SUGGESTIONS: Challah and Apricot-Glazed Peach Cake ■.

UNSTUFFED CABBAGE

Bake at 375° for 1 hour.
Makes 6 servings.

½	cup long-grain rice	2	tablespoons brown sugar
3	slices bacon	¼	cup vinegar
1	large onion, chopped	½	teaspoon thyme, crumbled
¾	pound ground chuck	1	head cabbage (about 2
1	teaspoon salt		pounds), coarsely shredded
¼	teaspoon pepper	1	bay leaf
1	can (28 ounces) tomatoes in tomato puree		

1. Prepare rice following package directions, but cook only for 5 minutes; drain and reserve.

2. Cook bacon in a large skillet until crisp. Drain on paper toweling; reserve. Pour off all but 1 tablespoon of bacon fat from skillet.

3. Sauté onion in fat until tender. Add chuck to skillet; cook, stirring to break up, until no longer pink. Stir in bacon, rice, ½ teaspoon of the salt, and half of the pepper.

4. Pour tomatoes with the puree into a medium-size saucepan, breaking them up with a spoon. Stir in brown sugar, vinegar, thyme, and the remaining salt and pepper; heat to a boil. Preheat oven to 375°.

5. Arrange one third of the cabbage in a 3-quart baking dish; spoon half the meat mixture over, then half of the sauce. Repeat layering, ending with cabbage and sauce. Poke bay leaf into center. Cover baking dish.

6. Bake in a preheated moderate oven (375°) for 1 hour or until cabbage is tender.

SERVING SUGGESTIONS: White Honey Bread■, baked potatoes, lemon-glazed carrots, and spiced poached peaches.

SAVE PAPER TOWELS

Bet you never thought of this one before, but here's a good tip: When draining fried foods, such as French fries, bacon, or sausages, you can cut down on paper toweling by using only 1 layer on top of many thicknesses of newspaper.

LIMA BEAN CASSEROLE

Bake at 350° for 1 hour and 30 minutes.
Makes 6 servings.

1   **pound dried large lima beans**
4   **medium-size onions, chopped (2 cups)**
1   **medium-size carrot, chopped**
2   **tablespoons vegetable oil**
1   **can (16 ounces) tomatoes, broken up**

2   **tablespoons dark brown sugar**
2   **teaspoons salt**
¼   **teaspoon pepper**
½   **teaspoon ground cloves**
1   **bay leaf, crumbled**
1½   **pounds smoked ham hocks**

1. Pick over and wash beans. Place in a kettle or Dutch oven. Add water to cover and bring to a boil; boil 2 minutes. Remove from heat; cover; let stand 1 hour. Check occasionally to make sure beans are covered with water.

2. Drain beans, then add fresh water to cover. Bring to a boil; lower heat; cover. Simmer for 1 hour or until tender. Drain; set aside beans. Reserve liquid.

3. Sauté onions and carrots in oil in the kettle, stirring often, until lightly browned. Stir in tomatoes, sugar, salt, pepper, cloves, and bay leaf. Preheat oven to 350°.

4. Place ham hocks in a 3-quart baking dish; add beans; pour in tomato mixture. Add enough of the reserved bean cooking liquid to barely cover beans.

5. Bake in a preheated moderate oven (350°) for 45 minutes. Remove ham hocks; cut meat from bones and dice. Return meat to beans; stir to mix. Bake, uncovered, 45 minutes longer.

SERVING SUGGESTIONS: All-American Coleslaw ■, Whole Wheat and Corn Mufffins ■, and raisin-stuffed baked apples.

LOUISIANA HOT POT

Leftover pork, frankfurters, or sliced bologna can be substituted for the slab bacon in this recipe.

Bake at 325° for 2 hours.
Makes 6 servings.

3	large yams or sweet potatoes	1	package (10 ounces) frozen
1	pound slab bacon, cooked		lima beans
	and drained	1½	cups boiling water
	Or: 6 ounces sliced	2	teaspoons curry powder
	boiled ham	2	chicken bouillon cubes
1	large onion, sliced	1	teaspoon salt

1. Pare yams and cut into thin slices. Layer yams with cooked bacon, onion rings, and lima beans in an 8-cup casserole, beginning and ending with yams. Preheat oven to 325°.
2. Combine boiling water, curry powder, bouillon cubes, and salt in a 2-cup measure; stir and crush bouillon cubes with the back of a spoon until the cubes are dissolved. Pour into casserole and cover.*
3. Bake in a preheated slow oven (325°) for 2 hours or until vegetables are tender.**

SERVING SUGGESTIONS: Tossed green salad, Carrot Cornbread ■, and Gingercake with Hot Lemon Drizzle ■.

---

*You can prepare and refrigerate this dish the night before; then the first one home places it in the oven. It will take and extra ½ hour to cook.
**If you cook in an electric slow cooker, set on low (190°) and cook 8 to 10 hours.

VERSATILE RICE

Few ingredients are as versatile as rice, which is used all over the world. The most popular type is long-grain rice, a polished rice, whose grains remain separate and fluffy when cooked. Although rice is inexpensive, there are even greater savings when you buy it in quantity. Buy 5-pound (or larger) bags and store them in a dry place.

One cup of uncooked rice will yield about 4 cups of cooked rice. You can reheat leftover rice easily by placing it in a sieve or colander set over simmering water. Cover with a towel and steam for 10 minutes. Fluff it up with a fork before serving. Leftover rice may be used for soups, salads, casseroles, puddings, etc.

TUNA-RICE CASSEROLE

This casserole is made extra special by using reduced-salt tuna. If you are watching your sodium intake, you can enjoy this delicious casserole because of its low-sodium ingredients.

Bake at 450° for 10 minutes.
Makes 6 servings.

1	cup long-grain rice	½	teaspoon pepper
½	pound small mushrooms, sliced (1½ cups)	2	cans (6½ ounces each) water-packed chunk tuna with reduced salt, drained and flaked
2	medium-size onions, chopped (1 cup)		
6	tablespoons (¾ stick) unsalted butter or margarine	⅓	cup chopped parsley
3	tablespoons all-purpose flour	½	cup shredded low-sodium cheese of your choice (2 ounces)
1½	cups water		
½	cup dry white wine		Chopped parsley and parsley sprigs
½	cup heavy cream		
2	packets low-sodium instant chicken-flavored broth		

1. Preheat oven to 450°. Grease a 10-cup soufflé dish, casserole, or baking dish.

2. Cook rice following package directions.

3. Sauté mushrooms and onion in butter in a large skillet until onion is soft, about 3 minutes. Stir in flour; cook for 1 minute. Stir in water, wine, heavy cream, instant broth, and pepper. Cook, stirring constantly, 5 minutes or until mixture thickens slightly. Stir in cooked rice, tuna, and the ⅓ cup chopped parsley. Cook for 1 minute or until some of the liquid is absorbed. Spoon into prepared dish. Sprinkle the shredded cheese over the top.

4. Bake in a preheated very hot oven (450°) for 10 minutes or until mixture is heated through and cheese is melted. Garnish with chopped parsley and parsley sprigs.

SERVING SUGGESTIONS: Tossed green salad, herbed string beans, and melon wedges (or sliced oranges).

RAGOUT OF CHICKEN WITH GARLIC

Makes 4 servings.

2   tablespoons olive or vegetable oil
20   cloves unpeeled garlic (1 large or 2 small bulbs)
½   teaspoon thyme, crumbled
½   teaspoon rosemary, crumbled
1   bay leaf
½   cup dry white wine

½   cup chicken broth or water
4   carrots (about ½ pound)
9   small new red potatoes (about ½ pound)
1   barbecued or roasted chicken from deli department (about 1½ to 2 pounds)
1   tablespoon chopped parsley

1. Heat oil in large deep skillet or Dutch oven. Add garlic, thyme, and rosemary; sauté 1 minute. Add bay leaf, wine, and chicken broth. Cover; simmer over low heat while preparing vegetables.
2. Pare carrots; cut on a diagonal into 1-inch lengths; add to skillet. Scrub potatoes; cut into half; add to skillet. Cook, covered, until tender, about 25 minutes.
3. Meanwhile, cut chicken into quarters. Add to skillet 5 minutes before end of cooking time.
4. Arrange chicken and vegetables in serving dish; garnish with parsley. To eat garlic, press purée from skin with fork; spread on toast.

CHICKEN HASH

A moist chicken hash that's unmolded and topped with tomato wedges and green peas.

Makes 4 servings.

1½   pounds potatoes (4 medium-size)
1   medium-size onion, chopped (½ cup)
¼   cup chopped green pepper
3   tablespoons reserved chicken fat (from roast chicken)
2   cups chopped, cooked chicken (from unstuffed roast chicken)

2   tablespoons nonfat dry milk powder
⅓   cup water
1   teaspoon salt
⅛   teaspoon pepper
1   tomato, cut in wedges
½   10-ounce package frozen green peas, cooked

1. Pare potatoes; halve. Cook in boiling salted water in a large saucepan until just tender, about 15 minutes. Drain. When cool enough to handle, shred coarsely; reserve.

2. Sauté onion and green pepper in 1 tablespoon of the chicken fat in a large skillet until soft, about 3 minutes. Combine with potatoes, chicken, dry milk, water, salt, and pepper in a large bowl.

3. Melt remaining 2 tablespoons chicken fat in the skillet; spoon in hash mixture. Pat down mixture in skillet; cook, uncovered, 10 minutes over moderate heat without stirring. Cover and cook over low heat for 5 minutes. Loosen from bottom with a pancake turner; flip over onto serving platter. Arrange tomato wedges to make a circle on top of hash; fill center with cooked green peas.

SERVING SUGGESTIONS: Lettuce wedges with dressing and Glazed Pears ■.

CASSEROLE TOPPERS

Change the look and taste of your family's favorite casseroles by topping them with one of the following. To add extra crispness, our toppings are baked at high temperatures.

• Trim 4 slices whole wheat bread and spread with softened butter or margarine and sprinkle with sesame seeds and seasoned black pepper. Cut into 1-inch pieces with a sharp knife. Arrange on the tray of a toaster oven. Bake in a preheated hot oven (425°) for 8 to 10 minutes or until seeds are golden and bread is crisp.

• Toss 2 cups popcorn with 3 tablespoons melted butter or margarine, 1 teaspoon garlic salt, and 3 tablespoons grated Parmesan cheese. Spread on the tray of a toaster oven. Bake in a preheated hot oven (425°) for 5 minutes or until very hot.

• Cut Italian or French bread into very thin slices. Beat 1 egg white until stiff in a small bowl; add ¼ cup mayonnaise or salad dressing, and ¼ cup shredded Cheddar or Swiss cheese. Spread on bread and arrange on the tray of a toaster oven. Bake in a preheated hot oven (425°) for 5 minutes or until topping turns golden.

CURRIED CHICKEN AND VEGETABLES IN PUFF RING

Bake at 375° for 50 minutes.
Makes 4 servings.

½	chicken breast (about 8 ounces)	2	tablespoons margarine
1	cup water	2	teaspoons curry powder
½	cup (1 stick) margarine	1	tablespoon all-purpose flour
¼	teaspoon salt	¾	cup water
1	cup all-purpose flour	¼	cup milk
4	eggs	1	chicken bouillon cube
1	rib celery, chopped	1	package (10 ounces) frozen mixed vegetables, cooked following package directions
1	small onion, chopped (¼ cup)		

1. Cook chicken, covered, in a small amount of water in a medium-size saucepan until tender, about 25 minutes. Cool; skin and bone. Dice the meat and reserve.

2. Preheat oven to 375°.

3. Combine the 1 cup water, the ½ cup margarine, and salt in a medium-size saucepan. Bring to a boil; lower heat. Add the 1 cup flour all at once, stirring quickly until mixture forms a ball; remove from heat. Add eggs, 1 at a time, beating well after each addition. Drop dough by rounded teaspoonfuls around the edge of a 10-inch skillet with an ovenproof handle.

4. Bake in a preheated moderate oven (375°) for 40 minutes. Quickly cut a slit in each puff; bake 10 minutes longer.

5. While puff ring is baking, sauté celery and onion in the 2 tablespoons margarine until soft, about 3 minutes. Stir in curry and the 1 tablespoon flour until smooth; cook 1 minute. Stir in the ½ cup water, milk, and bouillon cube. Cook, stirring constantly, until mixture thickens and bubbles. Add reserved chicken and vegetables. Taste; add salt and pepper if needed. Spoon mixture into center of ring. Serve hot.

SERVING SUGGESTIONS: Warm French bread, shredded carrot salad, and Gingered Grapefruit ∎.

RISOTTO WITH CHICKEN LIVERS

An easy, simple-to-prepare main dish of rice,
vegetables, and chicken livers.

Makes 4 servings.

1 **pound chicken livers, halved**	1 **cup long-grain rice**
¼ **cup all-purpose flour**	1 **can (4 ounces) mushroom**
1 **teaspoon salt**	**stems and pieces**
¼ **teaspoon pepper**	2 **envelopes or cubes instant**
¼ **cup (½ stick) margarine**	**chicken broth**
1 **medium-size onion, chopped**	½ **teaspoon salt**
(½ cup)	¼ **teaspoon pepper**
½ **cup diced carrot**	2½ **cups boiling water**
½ **cup sliced celery**	**Chopped parsley (optional)**

1. Shake chicken livers with flour, salt, and pepper in a plastic or paper bag until coated.

2. Melt margarine in a large skillet. Brown livers over low heat on both sides about 3 minutes total. (Be careful not to overcook them.) Remove with a slotted spoon; keep warm.

3. Sauté onion, carrot, and celery in same skillet until crisp-tender, about 5 minutes. Add rice, mushrooms with liquid, instant chicken broth, salt, pepper, and boiling water.

4. Bring to a boil; lower heat; stir rice mixture well; cover. Simmer for 15 minutes. Spoon browned chicken livers over rice; cover. Simmer 15 minutes longer or until liquid is absorbed and rice is tender. Fluff up rice. Garnish with chopped parsley if you wish.

SERVING SUGGESTIONS: Warm French bread, Grated Zucchini and Green Pepper Salad ■, and Vanilla Pudding ■ with sliced peaches.

SAVE $ WITH LIVER

Chicken livers are a wonderful way to economize. They're packed with nutrients, have no waste, cook quickly, and are absolutely delicious. Use beef liver also—it's half the price of calves' liver. To keep beef liver tender, braise it or broil just until a bit of pink remains.

POLENTA WITH CHICKEN LIVERS

Bake at 350° for 10 minutes.
Makes 6 servings.

1 quart water	1½ pounds chicken livers
1 teaspoon salt	1 cup plus 2 tablespoons water
1 cup yellow cornmeal	2 chicken bouillon cubes
2 green peppers, halved, seeded, and cut into strips	1 tablespoon tomato paste
2 medium-size onions, sliced	¼ teaspoon pepper
4 tablespoons (½ stick) margarine	2 teaspoons cornstarch

1. Lightly grease a 13 x 9 x 2-inch baking dish, or six individual baking dishes. Bring the 1 quart water with salt to a boil in a medium-size saucepan; sprinkle in cornmeal, stirring constantly to prevent lumping. Lower heat; cook, stirring often, until thickened, about 30 minutes. Spread mixture in prepared baking dish or evenly among the individual dishes, if using them.
2. Sauté peppers and onions in 2 tablespoons of the margarine in a large skillet until crisp-tender. Remove vegetables with a slotted spoon; reserve. Preheat oven to 350°.
3. Add the remaining 2 tablespoons margarine to skillet. Sauté chicken livers until browned, about 3 minutes total. (Be careful not to overcook them.) Add the 1 cup water, bouillon cubes, tomato paste, and pepper; bring to a boil, stirring to dissolve cubes. Blend cornstarch and the remaining 2 tablespoons water in a cup until smooth; stir into skillet mixture. Cook, stirring often, until thickened. Return sautéed vegetables to skillet.
4. Top polenta with chicken liver mixture; cover.
5. Bake in a preheated moderate oven (350°) until bubbly hot, about 10 minutes.

SERVING SUGGESTIONS: Red Cabbage and Apple Salad ∎ and Mousse de Bananes ∎.

CALIFORNIA CASSEROLE

String beans, carrots, or sweet red or green peppers can be substituted
for the zucchini and yellow squash.

Bake at 325° for 50 minutes.
Makes 6 servings.

2 **pounds zucchini and/or yellow squash**	3 **eggs**
1 **large onion**	1½ **cups reconstituted nonfat dry milk**
¼ **cup (½ stick) margarine**	1 **cup shredded Monterey Jack or Muenster cheese (4 ounces)**
2 **tablespoons all-purpose flour**	
1 **teaspoon dillweed**	1 **cup crushed cracker crumbs**
1 **teaspoon salt**	2 **tablespoons margarine, melted**
¼ **teaspoon pepper**	

1. Trim squash and cut into thin slices; cut onion into slices and separate into rings. Preheat oven to 325°.

2. Sauté squash and onion in the ¼ cup margarine in a large skillet until soft; stir in flour, dill, salt, and pepper until well blended. Spoon into an 8-cup shallow casserole.

3. Beat eggs in a medium-size bowl; add milk. Pour over vegetables; sprinkle cheese over.

4. Bake in a preheated slow oven (325°) for 40 minutes. Toss cracker crumbs with the 2 tablespoons melted margarine in a small bowl; sprinkle over casserole. Bake 10 minutes longer or until crumbs are golden and custard is set. Let stand on a wire rack for 10 minutes before serving.

SERVING SUGGESTIONS: Mexican Corn Sticks ■, Tangy Coleslaw ■, and Rice Pudding ■ topped with fresh fruit.

TRY TOFU

If you've never tried tofu, you should. It's a white, custard-like food that is sold in Oriental food shops and some supermarkets. Also known as soybean curd, tofu is an excellent source of protein and calcium, low in calories, and inexpensive. Shop for unbroken cakes of tofu that are well covered with water. Keep tofu in the refrigerator covered with water until you are ready to use it. Drain tofu before using. If cubes or slices of tofu are needed, firm up the texture first by pressing out some of the water. Place tofu between several sheets of paper towels, press gently to remove as much moisture as possible, then cut into desired shapes. Or try some of these variations:

• TOFU GARNI: Place chilled tofu in individual bowls. Serve with a platter of assorted garnishes, such as chopped red and green onion, grated gingerroot, shredded carrot and radish, bean sprouts, sesame seeds, and diced pepper. Pass soy sauce.

• TOFU DIP: Use this as a dip with raw vegetables and breadsticks, or as a creamy salad dressing. Combine ⅔ cup (6 ounces) tofu, 2 tablespoons vegetable oil, 2 tablespoons lemon juice or vinegar, 1 clove garlic, quartered, and soy sauce or Worcestershire sauce to taste in the container of an electric blender; cover and process on high for 1 minute or until smooth. Refrigerate before serving. Makes 1 cup.

• BROILED TOFU: Press tofu until firm, then slice into ¾-inch-thick pieces. Marinate in bottled teriyaki sauce 15 minutes. Broil, 4 inches from heat, brushing once or twice with sauce, 5 minutes on each side, or until brown and crusty. Serve over brown rice, garnished with green onion fans and tomato slices.

• TOFU SHAKE: Combine ½ cup tofu, 1 small banana, ⅓ cup plain or fruit yogurt, 1 tablespoon honey, and 1 tablespoon orange juice in the container of an electric blender; cover and process on high for 30 seconds or until smooth. Add more juice if too thick.

STIR-FRIED VEGETABLES AND TOFU IN OYSTER SAUCE

This colorful Oriental main dish tastes best
when served soon after cooking.

Makes 6 servings.

1   pound soybean curd or tofu, preferable firm-style

⅔   to 1 cup water or beef broth

⅓   cup oyster-flavored sauce* (optional)

3   tablespoons soy sauce

2   tablespoons freshly grated gingerroot

2   tablespoons cornstarch

3   tablespoons vegetable oil

3   cups broccoli flowerets (about ½ bunch)

1   large red pepper, halved, seeded, and sliced

¼   pound mushrooms, sliced (about 1 cup)

⅓   cup sliced green onions

½   cup sliced water chestnuts

½   pound mung bean sprouts

1. Press bean curd between several sheets of paper toweling to remove as much moisture as possible. Cut into ½- to ¾-inch cubes.

2. Mix ⅔ cup of the water with the oyster sauce, soy sauce, gingerroot, and cornstarch.

3. Heat oil in a large skillet. Add broccoli, red pepper, mushrooms, and green onions. Stir-fry for 3 to 4 minutes or until vegetables are almost tender. Add water chestnuts, bean sprouts, and tofu. Stir soy sauce mixture and pour, all at once, into vegetable mixture. Stir gently until sauce thickens and tofu is hot. If sauce is too thick, add remaining water to thin.

SERVING SUGGESTIONS: Hot and sour soup, vegetable eggrolls, hot cooked rice, and gingered orange slices.

---

* Oyster-flavored sauce is available in Oriental food stores or in the gourmet section of your supermarket.

POLISH POTATO PIE

Spicy sausage tempered by creamy herbed potatoes need only
a simple pastry topping.

Bake at 400° for 45 minutes.
Makes 6 servings.

Flaky pastry (recipe below)
1 pound kielbasa sausage
6 medium-size potatoes
   (2 pounds)
2 medium-size onions,
   chopped (1 cup)
2 cloves garlic, minced
1 tablespoon all-purpose flour
1½ teaspoons salt

1 teaspoon minced chives
1 teaspoon minced parsley
½ teaspoon pepper
¼ teaspoon ground mace
¼ cup (½ stick) butter or
   margarine
⅔ cup heavy cream
1 egg

1. Prepare Flaky Pastry; reserve. Skin sausage; cut into ⅓-inch-thick
slices.
2. Cook potatoes in boiling salted water in a large saucepan until
partially cooked, about 15 minutes. Drain; shake in pan over low heat
to dry; peel and slice thinly.
3. Combine onions, garlic, flour, salt, chives, parsley, pepper, and
mace in a small bowl; mix well.
4. Roll out two thirds of the pastry on a floured surface to a 14-inch
round; fit into a 10-inch pie plate.
5. Arrange half the potatoes in pasty-lined plate. Sprinkle with half
the onion-garlic mixture; top with half the sausage. Dot with half the
butter. Repeat layering, using remainder of ingredients. Pour ⅓ cup of
the cream over the layers.
6. Preheat oven to 400°.
7. Roll out remaining pastry to a 13-inch round. Cut a ¾-inch vent
hole in the center. Cover pie; trim and seal edges; flute.
8. Beat egg slightly in a small bowl; stir in remaining ⅓ cup cream.
Brush pastry with mixture, reserving remainder.
9. Bake in a preheated hot oven (400°) for 35 minutes. Carefully pour
remaining egg-cream mixture into pie through vent hole. Bake 10
minutes longer or until pastry is golden brown. Cool pie on a wire rack
about 10 minutes before cutting into wedges to serve.

Flaky Pastry: Combine 3 cups *sifted* all-purpose flour and 1 teaspoon
salt in a medium-size bowl. Cut in 1 cup vegetable shortening with a

pastry blender or 2 knives until mixture is crumbly and texture is size of peas. Sprinkle ½ cup ice water over mixture, stirring with a fork just until it holds together and leaves side of bowl clean. Gather into a ball. Wrap in wax paper or plastic wrap and refrigerate until ready to use.

SERVING SUGGESTIONS: Garden Salad Mold ■, String Beans with Water Chestnuts ■, and pineapple chunks with vanilla yogurt.

CHICKEN POT PIE

Bake at 425° for 15 minutes.
Makes 6 servings.

1	whole broiler-fryer (about 3 pounds)	⅛	teaspoon pepper
2	cups water		Cornmeal Cheese Biscuits (recipe below)
2	carrots, sliced	¼	cup (½ stick) margarine
2	ribs celery, sliced	¼	cup all-purpose flour
1	medium-size onion, cut in wedges	1	package (10 ounces) frozen peas
2	envelopes instant chicken broth		

1. Combine chicken, water, carrots, celery, onion, instant broth, and pepper in a medium-size saucepan; bring to a boil. Lower heat; cover; simmer until chicken is tender, about 30 minutes. Prepare Cornmeal Cheese Biscuits.

2. Remove chicken; cool; skin and bone. Cut meat into bite-size pieces; reserve. Strain cooking liquid, reserving both the liquid and vegetables.

3. Lightly grease a 10-cup baking dish. Preheat oven to 425°.

4. Melt margarine in a medium-size saucepan; blend in flour until smooth. Stir in reserved cooking liquid. Cook over medium heat, stirring constantly, until sauce thickens and bubbles. Add peas; bring to a boil. Taste; add salt and pepper if needed.

5. Stir in reserved chicken and vegetables. Turn mixture into prepared baking dish. Top with Cornmeal Cheese Biscuit wedges.

6. Bake in a preheated hot oven (425°) for 15 minutes or until biscuits are golden brown and chicken mixture is bubbly-hot.

Cornmeal Cheese Biscuits: Heat ¾ cup milk in a small saucepan until bubbles appear around edge, but do not boil; stir in ½ cup cornmeal; cool. Sift 1 cup *sifted* all-purpose flour, 3 teaspoons baking powder, and ¼ teaspoon salt into a medium-size bowl. Cut in 3 tablespoons margarine with a pastry blender until crumbly. Stir in ½ cup shredded Cheddar cheese and the milk-cornmeal mixture until dough is smooth. Turn out on a lightly floured surface; knead 5 times. Pat out into a circle 2 inches smaller in diameter than top of baking dish. Cut into 6 wedges.

SERVING SUGGESTIONS: Garden Salad Mold ■, fresh fruit salad, and Oatmeal-Raisin Cookies ■.

VEGETABLE-HAM SOUFFLÉ PIE

Bake at 425° for 10 minutes, then at 375° for 20 minutes.
Makes 6 servings.

1 cup *sifted* all-purpose flour	½ teaspoon salt
¼ teaspoon salt	¼ teaspoon pepper
⅓ cup vegetable shortening	½ teaspoon marjoram, crumbled
2 to 3 tablespoons ice water	
1 cup sliced carrots (about 4 small)	3 tablespoons butter or margarine
3 small onions, each cut into 6 wedges	3 tablespoon all-purpose flour
	¾ cup water
1 cup sliced mushrooms (¼ pound)	3¾ tablespoons nonfat dry milk powder
1 medium-size zucchini, cut into 2 x ¼-inch sticks	½ cup shredded Swiss cheese (2 ounces)
¼ pound cooked ham, cut into 1 x ¼-inch strips	3 eggs, separated

1. Preheat oven to 425°.

2. Sift the 1 cup flour and the ¼ teaspoon salt into a medium-size bowl; cut in shortening with a pastry blender until mixture is crumbly. Sprinkle ice water over mixture; mix lightly with a fork just until pastry holds together and leaves side of bowl clean.

3. Roll out pastry to a 12-inch round on a lightly floured surface. Fit into a 9-inch pie plate. Trim overhang to ½ inch; turn edge under; pinch to make a stand-up edge; flute. Prick shell well all over with a fork.

4. Bake shell in a preheated hot oven (425°) for 10 minutes. (Check shell after 5 minutes. If bubbles have formed, prick again.) Cool on wire rack. Lower oven temperature to 375°.

5. Cook carrots, onions, mushrooms, and zucchini in boiling salted water for 5 minutes or until crisp-tender; drain. Turn into a large bowl; add ham, the ½ teaspoon salt, pepper, and marjoram; mix lightly.

6. Melt margarine in a medium-size saucepan; blend in flour; cook 1 minute. Stir the ¾ cup water into dry milk in a small bowl; stir mixture into saucepan. Cook, stirring constantly, until mixture thickens and bubbles. Remove from heat; stir in cheese until melted. Let sauce cool.

7. Meanwhile, beat egg whites in a small bowl with an electric mixer until soft peaks form.

8. Beat egg yolks until light in a medium-size bowl with same beaters. Beat in cooled cheese sauce. Measure ¼ cup of the cheese mixture; stir into vegetables. Fold remaining cheese mixture into beaten egg whites until no streaks of white remain.

9. Spoon vegetable mixture into cooled pastry shell. Carefully spoon soufflé mixture over vegetables, spreading to edge of pastry to seal in vegetables.

10. Bake in a preheated moderate oven (375°) for 20 minutes or until soufflé top has puffed and is lightly browned. Serve at once.

SERVING SUGGESTIONS: Tomatoes vinaigrette, crusty brown rolls, and spice layer cake.

STORING HERBS

Dried herbs keep their color and flavor best when stored in a cool, dry place. Do not keep them near your stove.

Fresh herbs can be enjoyed year-round if properly prepared for the freezer. Wash herbs and drain them thoroughly. Spread out on a tray on several layers of paper toweling until dry. Chop herbs or leave whole and place in containers and freeze. Use scissors to snip as much as needed from whole herbs, such as parsley.

NEW ENGLAND TUNA PIE

Thrifty Yankee cooks have always known how to serve satisfying meals while keeping the costs low.

Bake at 400° for 55 minutes.
Makes 6 servings.

Flaky Pastry (recipe below)
1 can (6½ ounces) chunk light tuna
3 large potatoes, pared and thinly sliced
2 large onions, thinly sliced
2 tablespoons margarine
2 tablespoons chopped parsley
1½ teaspoons salt
¼ teaspoon freshly ground pepper
Creamy Pea Sauce (recipe below)

1. Prepare Flaky Pastry.
2. Roll out half the pastry on a lightly floured pastry cloth or board to a 12-inch round. Fit into a 9-inch pie plate. Preheat oven to 400°.
3. Flake tuna into pie plate; layer potato and onion slices over tuna, dotting each layer with part of the margarine and seasoning with the parsley, salt, and pepper.
4. Roll out remaining pastry to an 11-inch round; cut some slits in center of pastry; transfer over rolling pin to top of pie; turn under rim and flute edge.
5. Bake in a preheated hot oven (400°) for 55 minutes or until pastry is golden and potato slices are tender. Cut into wedges and serve with Creamy Pea Sauce.

Flaky Pasty: Cut ⅔ cup vegetable shortening into 2 cups all-purpose flour and 1 teaspoon salt with a pastry blender, until mixture is as crumbly as cornmeal. Stir in ⅓ cup ice cold water with a fork, just until mixture forms a ball. Makes enough for a two-crust 9-inch pie.

Creamy Pea Sauce: Melt ¼ cup margarine in a medium-size saucepan; stir in ¼ cup all-purpose flour, 1 teaspoon salt, and ¼ teaspoon ground allspice and cook 1 minute; stir in 1¾ cups reconstituted nonfat dry milk; cook, stirring constantly, until sauce thickens and bubbles 3 minutes; add 1 package (10 ounces) frozen peas, cooked and drained. Serve hot over wedges of New England Tuna Pie.

SERVING SUGGESTIONS: Confetti Slaw ■ and pear cobbler.

CANADIAN MEAT PIE (Tourtière)

Bake at 450° for 10 minutes, then at 350° for 40 minutes.
Makes 6 servings.

Filling:

2 large onions, finely chopped (2 cups)
1 clove garlic, minced
2 tablespoons vegetable oil
1 cup water
1½ pounds ground lean pork
2 medium-size tomatoes, peeled, seeded, and chopped Or: 1 can (8 ounces) tomatoes, drained, and chopped

½ teaspoon salt
½ teaspoon savory, crumbled
¼ teaspoon pepper
⅛ teaspoon ground cloves
⅛ teaspoon ground cinnamon
¼ cup chopped parsley
¼ cup water
¼ to ½ cup packaged bread crumbs

Wrapper:
1 package piecrust mix

1. Prepare Filling: Sauté onions and garlic in oil in a large skillet about 3 minutes. Add the 1 cup water; bring to a boil. Cook, stirring often, until water has evaporated and onions are tender.

2. Add pork; cook, breaking up with a spoon, until meat is no longer pink. Stir in tomatoes, salt, savory, pepper, cloves, cinnamon, parsley, and ¼ cup water. Lower heat to medium; cook mixture, stirring often, until it is almost dry. Remove from heat; stir in ¼ cup of the bread crumbs; let stand for 10 minutes. Add remaining crumbs if mixture is still moist. (Makes about 6 cups filling.)

3. Preheat oven to 450°.

4. For Wrapper: Prepare piecrust mix following package directions for a 2-crust pie. Line a 9-inch pie plate with half the rolled-out pastry. Spoon filling into pastry-lined pie plate.

5. Roll out remaining pastry; cut vents for steam to escape. Top pie; flute edge.

6. Bake in a preheated very hot oven (450°) for 10 minutes. Lower oven temperature to moderate (350°). Bake an additional 40 minutes or until pastry is golden brown. Cool slightly.

SERVING SUGGESTIONS: Lettuce wedges with herb dressing, Stir-Fried Corn and Peppers ■, and Mousse de Bananes ■.

OLD ENGLISH MEAT PIE

Thrifty beef liver stars in a tempting supper dish. Leftover beef, pork, or turkey can be substituted for the liver.

Bake at 400° for 40 minutes.
Makes 6 servings.

1	pound beef liver	2	large onions, sliced
¼	cup all-purpose flour		Water
1	teaspoon salt	2	envelopes or teaspoons
¼	teaspoon pepper		instant beef broth
¼	cup vegetable oil	1	teaspoon sage or leaf thyme,
4	large carrots		crumbled
2	large potatoes		Flaky Pastry (recipe below)

1. Cut beef liver into 1½-inch squares; coat with a mixture of flour, salt, and pepper on wax paper.

2. Brown beef liver, a bit at a time, in hot oil in a large skillet; remove with a slotted spoon to an 8-cup casserole.

3. Pare and slice carrots and potatoes; cook in salted boiling water in a small saucepan for 10 minutes or just until tender; remove with slotted spoon to casserole. Reserve cooking liquid.

4. Sauté onions in drippings in skillet until soft. Add enough water to vegetable cooking liquid to make 2 cups; stir into skillet with beef broth and sage. Cook, stirring constantly, until sauce thickens and bubbles; pour over vegetables and liver in casserole. Preheat oven to 400°.

5. Roll out Flaky Pastry to a round 1-inch wider than diameter of casserole on a lightly floured pastry cloth or board; make slits in pastry in a pretty pattern to allow steam to escape. Place on rolling pin and transfer to top of casserole, turning under pastry around edge and fluting.

6. Bake in a preheated hot oven (400°) 40 minutes or until pastry is golden brown.

Flaky Pastry: Cut ⅔ cup vegetable shortening into 2 cups all-purpose flour and 1 teaspoon salt with a pastry blender until mixture is as crumbly as cornmeal. Stir in ⅓ cup ice cold water with a fork, just until mixture forms a ball. Makes enough for a two-crust 9-inch pie.

SERVING SUGGESTIONS: Warm buttermilk biscuits, mixed green salad with creamy garlic dressing, and fresh fruit compote.

5

Beans, Grains, Pasta, and Rice

I f your family has been on a meat and potato routine, they are in for a treat! Entice them with exciting dishes based on grains, beans, pasta, and rice. They can lunch heartily on a Rice and Lentil Salad or enjoy Mexican Bean Pot for dinner. The recipes in this chapter are good for your health *and* your pocketbook.

LEGUMES

Americans have been enjoying legumes since the days of the American Indians. Just in case you're not familiar with the term, legumes is another name for dried beans and peas.

Enjoy legumes in many ways. They're inexpensive, versatile, and a nutritional powerhouse. They contain no cholesterol and almost no fat. Their subtle flavor can be enhanced with stronger ones, such as sausage, garlic, onions, fiery spices, tangy tomato sauces, and pungent cheeses.

Selecting Legumes
● Choose legumes that are uniform in color, size, and shape. Pale color indicates long storage; uniform size and shape is necessary for even cooking. Avoid open packags and those that contain cracked or pin-hole-marked beans, and foreign matter, such as very small bits of pebbles.

Cooking Legumes
● Wash peas, beans, and lentils; pick out foreign matter. Pre-soak all legumes, except split peas for soup, and lentils, in one of two ways: Boil 2 minutes in water to cover, then soak overnight; or boil 2 minutes, remove from heat, soak 1 hour. (Note: You can buy canned beans that don't need pre-soaking, for just pennies more.) Now cook in a pot on top of the stove, in a slow cooker, or pressure cooker (don't cook lentils, split peas, or black-eyed peas in the pressure cooker), or in the oven: Use soaking liquid in cooking to preserve vitamins; add onions, herbs, and spices, but not salt or acidic tomatoes or wine— they'll toughen skins. Simmer or slow-bake, stirring only occasionally, until beans are tender; skins should burst when you blow on a few or gently rub a couple between your fingers.

Varieties of Legumes
● Baby Limas—The dry form of the fresh bean; serve in main dishes, soups, or simply buttered.
● Black Beans (Turtle Soup Beans)—Use in sauces, soups, and salads, especially those with an Oriental or Mediterranean flavor.
● Black-eyed Peas—Oval with a black speck, a traditional ingredient in soul food; serve with pork and chicken.
● Garbanzos (Chick-peas)—Beige and nutty in flavor, add to minestrone or marinate for a hearty salad.
● Great Northern—Good baking beans; use in cassoulet, stew, chowder, or salads.
● Kidney Beans—Light or dark red, this bean stands up to the hottest chili recipe. Use in salads and soups, too.
● Large Limas (Butter Beans)—Cook with smoked meats and cheese for main-dish casseroles and substantial side dishes.
● Lentils—Quick to prepare; excellent in soups and curries.
● Navy Beans—General term for Great Northern and small-white beans.
● Peas—Available split or whole, yellow or green. Use split peas in soups and croquettes, whole peas in casseroles.

- Pintos—Speckled and succulent; serve in Tex-Mex dishes, such as refried beans, and spicy chili.
- Small-Whites (Pea Beans)—Farm beans that keep their shape, even after long simmering. Bake or use in soup.
- Soybeans—The only bean to contain all 8 essential amino acids, they rival meat in high-quality protein. Mix their unusual flavor and texture with other, more familiar beans in salads and chili.

Serving Legumes
- 1 cup of dried legumes expands anywhere from 2½ to 4½ cups cooked, depending on the type of dried bean; this makes enough to serve 3 to 4 people. Prepare a large batch and refrigerate leftovers for up to 1 week, or freeze 4 to 6 months. Reheat gently to retain shape.

Storing Legumes
- Keep in a closed jar or plastic bag in a cool, dry place.
- Peanuts are legumes, too! They share the same nutritive qualities as other peas and beans.
- Buy canned beans when you want instant soups, casseroles, and salads. They're more expensive than dry ones, but still a good food buy.

RICE AND LENTIL SALAD

Makes 4 servings.

¾	cup lentils	¼	cup chopped radishes
¾	cup long-grain rice	¼	cup vegetable oil
¾	cup chopped leftover ham	¼	cup red wine vinegar
1	cup thinly sliced celery	1	teaspoon dillweed
⅔	cup sliced green onions	¼	teaspoon pepper

1. Cook lentils following package directions. Cook rice following package directions, but use only ½ teaspoon salt.
2. Combine lentils, rice, and ham in a large bowl; stir to mix. Add celery, green onions, and radishes.
3. Combine oil, vinegar, dill, and pepper in a cup; pour over lentil mixture. Mix gently but well. Cover; refrigerate at least 3 hours.

SERVING SUGGESTIONS: Tomato and lettuce salad, cheese biscuits, and frozen yogurt.

LENTIL-CHEESE LOAF

Bake at 350° for 25 minutes.
Makes 4 servings.

1   package (8 ounces) American
    cheese
2   cups cooked drained lentils
    (¾ cup raw)
½   small onion, finely chopped
¼   teaspoon thyme, crumbled
½   teaspoon salt

¼   teaspoon pepper
1   cup fresh bread crumbs
    (2 slices bread)
1   egg, slightly beaten
1   tablespoon margarine,
    softened
    Tomato sauce (optional)

1. Grease a 9-inch pie plate. Preheat oven to 350°. Cut half the cheese into 3 slices. Cut each slice in half to make 6 strips. Set aside. Shred the remaining cheese.
2. Mash the hot lentils with the back of a wooden spoon or potato masher. Cool. Combine lentils with onion, thyme, salt, pepper, bread crumbs, egg, margarine, and shredded cheese. Mix well. Spread evenly in prepared pie plate.
3. Bake in a preheated moderate oven (350°) for 20 minutes.
4. Arrange cheese strips on top of the lentil mixture in a spoke pattern and bake 5 minutes or more. Serve in wedges with tomato sauce if you wish.

SERVING SUGGESTIONS: Crisp brown rolls, marinated vegetable salad, and apple crisp.

SPECIAL BAKED BEANS

Small bowls of these beans, cold, make a wonderful snack.
Refrigerate up to 4 days, or freeze.

Bake at 300° for 3 hours.
Makes 12 large servings.

2   pounds dry navy beans
    (4 cups)
    Water
    Ham bone
2   cups sugar
½   cup molasses

1   tablespoon salt
1   teaspoon dry mustard
½   teaspoon ground ginger
¼   teaspoon pepper
1   cup catsup

1. Pick over beans and rinse under running water. Combine beans and enough water to cover in a large saucepan or kettle. Cover pan and bring to a boil over medium heat; boil gently 2 minutes. Remove from heat; let stand, covered, 1 hour.

2. Add ham bone to saucepan; add additional water to cover beans completely, if necessary. Return beans to heat; bring to a boil; lower heat; cover, and simmer about 1½ hours or until beans are tender but before skins burst. Add more water as needed to cover beans.

3. Preheat oven to 300°.

4. Drain beans, reserving liquid. Turn beans into a 4-quart bean pot or baking dish. In a small bowl, combine sugar, molasses, salt, dry mustard, ginger, pepper, catsup, and 1 cup hot bean liquid. Stir into beans. If necessary, add just enough hot bean liquid to cover beans; cover.

5. Bake in a preheated slow oven (300°) for 2 hours. Uncover; bake 1 hour longer to brown the top.

SERVING SUGGESTIONS: Cracked Wheat, Corn, and Sesame Loaf ■, grilled frankfurters, and seasonal fresh fruit.

LENTILS

Lentils—a small, flat, round legume—are among nature's most inexpensive and nourishing foods. They offer a concentrated source of protein and can be used year-round in salads, soups, main dishes, stews, and more. Lentils offer a distinctive flavor of their own and can be served simply with some melted butter. However, they are also enhanced with additions of pork, mushrooms, onions, cheese, nuts, herbs, or sour cream. Experts advise that lentils should not be soaked, as many recipes instruct. The procedure is unnecessary and results in the loss of valuable nutrients. To prepare 1 pound of lentils (2⅓ cups), wash them with cold water and drain them in a colander. Place them in a large, heavy saucepan and add 5 cups water and 2 teaspoons salt. (Don't use a pressure cooker.) Bring lentils to a boil; reduce heat and simmer, covered, for 30 minutes. You'll have almost 7 cups of cooked lentils and 1 cup liquid. The liquid can be used for stews, soups, or gravies. Store extra lentils in a covered container in the refrigerator for several days. For longer storage, place in freezer.

MEXICAN BEAN POT

Beans are great eating all year round, but especially in summer, when they are an easy portable supper for patio, picnic, or beach.

Bake at 325° for 2 hours.
Makes 6 servings.

1	package (1 pound) dried large lima, pinto, or Great Northern beans	2	to 4 teaspoons chili powder, according to taste
6	cups water	2	teaspoons salt
½	pound hot Italian sausage Or: 6 ounces domestic salami	1	teaspoon basil, crumbled
		2	envelopes or teaspoons instant beef broth
1	large onion, chopped (1 cup)		
2	large green peppers, halved, seeded, and cut into large pieces		

1. Pick over and wash beans. Place in a large saucepan and add water to cover and bring to a boil. Lower heat; cover saucepan; simmer for 1 hour.

2. While beans cook, cut sausage into small pieces; brown in a small skillet; remove with slotted spoon and reserve. Sauté onion until soft; stir in peppers and sauté 2 minutes longer; add chili powder, salt, basil, and instant beef broth. Cook, stirring constantly, 2 minutes. Preheat oven to 325°.

3. Transfer cooked beans with a slotted spoon to a 10-cup casserole; add sausage pieces and sautéed vegetables to cooked beans and mix until well blended. Add enough bean cooking liquid to cover beans.

4. Bake in a preheated slow oven (325°)* for 2 hours or until beans are tender and liquid thickens. (If the beans seem too dry, add more cooking liquid.)

SERVING SUGGESTIONS: Mexican Corn Sticks ■, Confetti Slaw ■, and mocha custard.

---

*This recipe can be cooked in an electric slow cooker set at low (190°) for 8 to 10 hours.

CASTILLIAN BEANS

Bake at 350° for 40 minutes.
Makes 8 servings.

¼ pound piece pepperoni, sliced
1 large onion, chopped (1 cup)
1 clove garlic, minced
1 teaspoon salt
1 teaspoon thyme, crumbled
¼ teaspoon pepper

3 cans (1 pound each) cannellini or white kidney beans, drained
1 cup chicken broth
1 can (4 ounces) jalapeño peppers, drained, seeded, and diced

1. Preheat oven to 350°. Sauté pepperoni in a large skillet 5 minutes; remove with a slotted spoon and reserve.

2. Sauté onion and garlic in pan drippings until soft; stir in salt, thyme, and pepper; add drained cannellini beans, chicken broth, reserved sautéed pepperoni slices, and diced jalapeño peppers. Bring to a boil, stirring once or twice; spoon into an 8-cup casserole.

3. Bake in a preheated moderate oven (350°) for 40 minutes or until bubbly hot.

SERVING SUGGESTIONS: Grilled pork sausages, tomatoes vinaigrette, and sliced oranges spiced with cinnamon.

DRIED BEANS ARE SUPER

It's high time for dried beans to be used frequently because they have so many advantages:
- Inexpensive—a fraction of the price of animal protein
- Tremendous variety of dried beans available
- Wide variety of uses—appetizers, soups, stews, salads, casseroles, main-dish meals, sandwich spreads, and more
- No waste—beans offer fully usable protein
- Provide complete protein when teamed with rice, grains, wheat products, eggs, milk, or cheese
- Nutritional powerhouse—beans contain thiamine (vitamin B), riboflavin, niacin, iron, and calcium
- No cholesterol and almost no fat
- Long shelf-life—will keep for a year or longer if stored properly in an airtight container in a cool, dry place

BULGUR-CHICK-PEA SALAD

Makes 8 servings.

1 cup uncooked bulgur (cracked wheat)
2 cups boiling water
½ cup sunflower or vegetable oil
½ cup fresh lemon juice
1 cup sliced green onions
1 can (20 ounces) chick-peas, drained
1 cup finely chopped parsley
1 cup diced carrots

1. Place bulgur in a large heatproof bowl; pour boiling water over; mix to moisten. Let stand 1 hour at room temperature. (Bulgur will expand to 3½ cups.) Drain in a colander. Return to bowl.

2. Beat oil and lemon juice in a cup and pour over the bulgur; mix with a fork.

3. Place bulgur in bottom of a 2-quart glass jar with a tight-fitting lid, or a bowl with a cover. Layer each vegetable in this order: green onions, chick-peas, parsley, carrots. Cover; refrigerate. Toss the salad to mix just before serving.

SERVING SUGGESTIONS: Crusty French bread and fruit compote with custard.

HOT COOKED CEREALS

For a change of pace, serve hot, cooked cereals. They're nutritious and less expensive than cold cereals. The good news for weight-conscious people is that cooked cereals are very filling and most do not contain sugar. To add some interest, serve with sliced fruit, applesauce, honey, or spices.

ITALIAN-STYLE DUMPLINGS

Bake at 350° for 20 minutes.
Makes 6 servings.

1½ cups water
1½ cups milk
1 teaspoon salt
1 cup regular enriched farina
½ cup (1 stick) butter or margarine
3 eggs, well beaten

2 cups grated Parmesan cheese (about 6 ounces)
Or: 2 cups shredded Swiss cheese (8 ounces)
1 tablespoon chopped parsley (optional)

1. Combine water, milk, and salt in large saucepan. Bring to a boil. Gradually stir in farina, stirring constantly to prevent lumping. Lower heat to medium; cook, stirring constantly, 5 to 7 minutes or until mixture becomes very thick and begins to pull away from side of pan.
2. Remove from heat. Stir in half the butter until well blended.
3. Stir in eggs very slowly; then stir in 1 cup of the cheese. Rinse a cookie sheet or shallow baking pan with cold water; drain, but do not dry. (This will prevent mixture from sticking.) Spread farina mixture onto sheet in ¼-inch-thick layer. Smooth top evenly with a metal spatula dipped in cold water. Cool completely on a wire rack.
4. Butter a 12 x 8 x 2-inch baking dish. Preheat oven to 350°. Cut cooled farina mixture with a 1½ to 2-inch cookie cutter or water glass into as many circles as possible. Transfer the scraps with the point of a wet knife to the prepared baking dish; arrange in 1 layer. Melt the remaining ¼ cup butter in a small saucepan; drizzle half over pieces in baking dish. Sprinkle with half the remaining cheese. Arrange the circles in overlapping rows over the scraps. Drizzle remaining butter over all; sprinkle with remaining cheese.
5. Bake in a preheated moderate oven (350°) for 20 minutes or until golden. Sprinkle with parsley.

SERVING SUGGESTIONS: Tomato sauce (for dumplings), chilled broccoli vinaigrette, and zabaglione.

PASTA

People are enjoying pasta, in its myriad forms, all over the world. It's inexpensive, cooks quickly, is easy to store, and is just plain delicious. Best of all, you can stretch a meager amount of meat or cheese and have a scrumptious, satisfying dish.

Varieties

- Durum wheat pasta—Most pasta is made from durum wheat flour and water. Experiment with the enormous range of shapes and sizes, from barley-like orzo to tubular manicotti.
- Egg noodles—A bit richer with egg yolks added; serve with spicy ground meat mixtures and stroganoffs.
- Spinach pasta—Adds garden-patch color and flavor. Toss with regular pasta, melted butter, and grated cheese, for "straw and hay." Serve with a medley of vegetables in cream sauce.
- Whole wheat pasta—Available in the health food section of your market; a chewy pasta with nutty flavor and whole grain nutrients. Toss with spicy tomato sauce and chunks of cheese.
- High-protein pasta—A new-comer to the world of pasta, this product was developed as a low-cost, low-cholesterol alternative to meat.
- Oriental noodles—Found in Oriental food shops, they add exotic texture and taste to soups and main dishes. Chinese cellophane noodles, clear when cooked, are delicious in vegetable soup. Japanese buckwheat noodles are tasty when served with chopped green onions and soy sauce.

Selecting:

Buy pasta in well-wrapped packages and avoid those with many broken pieces.

Cooking:

Cooking time varies with the size, shape, and type of pasta, as well as its freshness. Be sure to read individual package or recipe directions and watch the kettle carefully.

PERCIATELLI WITH EGGPLANT AND TOMATOES

Rich fried eggplant and perciatelli, a thick tubular spaghetti, make this a very hearty meatless dish.

Makes 4 servings.

1	medium-size eggplant (about 1½ pounds)	1	teaspoon rosemary or basil, crumbled
½	cup olive or vegetable oil	¼	cup chopped parsley
1	onion, thinly sliced	1	package (1 pound) perciatelli or spaghetti
2	cloves garlic, minced		Grated Parmesan cheese
1	can (16 ounces) tomatoes		
1	teaspoon salt		
¼	teaspoon crushed red pepper flakes		

1. Pare eggplant; cut into ½-inch-thick slices, then into cubes.

2. Heat half the oil in a large skillet. Add half the eggplant, stirring and tossing until browned. Remove eggplant with a slotted spoon; repeat with remaining oil and eggplant.

3. Return all of the eggplant to skillet; add onion and garlic. Cook, stirring constantly, until onion is tender, about 1 minute. Add tomatoes, salt, red pepper flakes, and rosemary. Bring to a boil, stirring and breaking up tomatoes with a spoon. Lower heat; simmer for 2 minutes or until eggplant is tender and liquid in skillet is reduced slightly. Stir in parsley; remove from heat.

4. Bring 4 to 6 quarts of water to a boil in a large, covered kettle. Cook pasta following package directions. Drain and return to kettle. Reheat the sauce; add half the sauce to the pasta; toss. Divide mixture among 4 heated bowls; top with remaining sauce. Serve with Parmesan cheese.

SERVING SUGGESTIONS: Garlic bread, herbed string bean salad, and sliced peaches.

THIRTY-SIX
SUPER PASTA RECIPES

Glorious, glorious pasta! Now you can cook it to your heart's content. The chart gives 36 tempting combinations. Each dish is such a snap to make that you'll have dinner ready in a twinkling. To use the chart, just pick 8 ounces of pasta. Then choose one of the four basic sauces, listed below. To complete the pasta dish, prepare one of the delicious special touches from the following columns. When the pasta is cooked, drain, and toss with the sauce and special touch. To round out the menu, serve with bread sticks or crusty bread, a crisp green salad, and some fresh fruit.

Classic Cream and Egg Sauce

Melt ¼ cup (½ stick) butter or margarine in a small saucepan. Sauté 1 large onion, chopped (1 cup) until soft; remove pan from heat. Beat 2 egg yolks slightly in a small bowl with a fork; beat in 1 cup light cream or milk; stir into butter-onion mixture and return pan to burner. Heat slowly, stirring often, but *do not boil*. Season with 1 teaspoon salt and a dash of ground nutmeg. Pour over pasta and add 1 cup Parmesan cheese.

20-Minute Tomato Sauce

Heat ¼ cup olive or vegetable oil in a medium-size saucepan. Stir in 1 medium-size onion, chopped (½ cup), 2 medium-size carrots, pared and finely chopped, and 1 clove garlic, minced. Cook, stirring, 10 minutes or until vegetables are soft. Stir in 1 can (1 pound) stewed tomatoes, 2 teaspoons salt, 1 teaspoon mixed Italian herbs, crumbled, and ¼ teaspoon freshly ground black pepper. Bring to boil; lower heat and simmer for 10 minutes or until pasta has been drained.

Garlicky Butter and Oil Sauce

Melt ¼ cup (½ stick) butter or margarine in a small saucepan. Sauté 1 large onion, chopped (1 cup) and 2 cloves garlic, minced, in butter until onion is soft, *but not brown*. Add ½ cup chicken or beef broth or clam juice and ¼ cup olive or vegetable oil and heat slowly for 3 minutes. Stir in ¼ cup chopped parsley, 1 teaspoon salt, and ¼ teaspoon freshly ground pepper. (Note: You can substitute 1 bunch leeks or green onions, trimmed, washed well, and sliced, for the onion.)

Velvety Béchamel Sauce

Melt ¼ cup (½ stick) butter or margarine in a small saucepan; sauté 1 small onion, chopped (¼ cup), in butter until soft; stir in 3 tablespoons all-purpose flour, 1 envelope or teaspoon instant chicken broth, and ¼ teaspoon pepper with a wire whisk. Cook, stirring constantly, until mixture bubbles 3 minutes. Stir in 2 cups milk with a wooden spoon and cook, stirring constantly, until sauce thickens and bubbles 3 minutes.

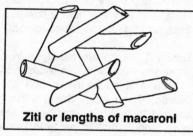

Ziti or lengths of macaroni

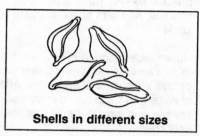

Shells in different sizes

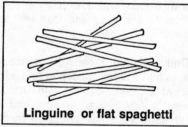

Linguine or flat spaghetti

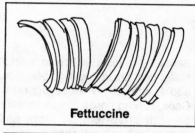

Fettuccine

Egg noodle bow-ties

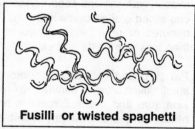

Fusilli or twisted spaghetti

Very thin spaghetti

Rigatoni or wide macaroni

Cook ¼ cup sliced almonds in 2 tablespoons butter or margarine in a small skillet until golden; push to one side; add 2 cups thinly sliced raw broccoli and sauté 3 minutes or until crisp-tender; add 1 cup julienne pieces baked ham and cook 2 minutes. Add with sauce to pasta in kettle.

Heat 1 tablespoon olive or vegetable oil in a small skillet; sauté 3 minutes or until zucchini is crisp-tender. Add to kettle with 1 cup cubed mozzarella cheese and tomato sauce and toss until cheese melts.

Sauté 1 cup diced salami in a small skillet until brown; push to one side; add 2 cups thinly sliced eggplant. Cook, stirring constantly, 5 minutes or until crisp-tender; taste and season with salt and pepper. Add ¼ cup sliced stuffed olives and heat 2 minutes or until pasta is cooked; then toss with pasta and sauce.

Pat ½ pound bulk sausage into a small skillet; brown 5 minutes on one side; turn and brown 5 minutes on other side; drain off fat; crumble sausage; stir in ¼ teaspoon sage, crumbled. Cook, stirring often, 3 minutes longer. Toss well with pasta, sauce, and ¼ cup shredded Swiss cheese.

Cook 1 package (9 ounces) frozen artichoke hearts in a small saucepan following package directions; drain, cool slightly, then cut each artichoke into quarters. Return to saucepan and add 1 cup diced ham bologna and ¼ cup finely chopped parsley. Heat over very low heat 2 minutes. Toss with pasta and sauce to coat.

Brown 3 hot Italian sausages in a small skillet; cut into thin slices; add ¼ pound string beans, tipped and halved, if too long. Cook, stirring often, 10 minutes or until beans are crisp-tender. Add to pasta in kettle with sauce and 1 cup shredded Provolone cheese and toss well to blend.

Drain oil from 1 can (6½ ounces) tuna into a small saucepan and add 2 tablespoons capers with liquid. Heat slowly, just until warm. Add 2 tablespoons finely chopped fresh basil or 1 teaspoon dried basil, crumbled. Add with sauce to pasta in kettle and toss to coat the pasta well.

Cut 1 package (12 ounces) frozen fish fillet of cod into small blocks with a sharp chef's knife. Place on top of 1 package (9 ounces) frozen Italian green beans in a small saucepan. Cook, following bean package directions, 10 minutes. Remove with slotted spoon to kettle with pasta; toss gently with sauce to coat.

Wash and trim 1 package (10 ounces) fresh spinach; place in a large skillet with water clinging to leaves; cover. Bring to boil, turn off heat and let stand 2 minutes; drain very well. Chop coarsely. Add to pasta with sauce and ½ cup crumbled Gorgonzola cheese and toss until cheese melts.

Melt 1 tablespoon butter or margarine in a small skillet; add 1 cup cubed cooked beef and 1 large green pepper, halved, seeded and diced. Cook, stirring often, until pepper is crisp-tender and meat is heated through. Add to kettle with sauce and 1 cup shredded Fontina cheese.

Halve and seed 2 sweet red peppers; broil, skin side up, 4 inches from heat, 10 minutes or until skin blisters. Peel off skin; cut pepper into 1-inch pieces. Drain 1 can (2 ounces) anchovy fillets and add with peppers and 1 lemon, quartered and thinly sliced, to pasta and sauce in kettle.

Sauté ½ pound chicken livers, halved, in 2 tablespoons butter or margarine in a medium-size skillet 5 minutes; push to one side. Cut ½ pound trimmed fresh string beans into 1-inch pieces; add to skillet and cook 5 minutes or until crisp-tender. Toss with pasta and sauce in kettle.

Combine 1 package (10 ounces) frozen peas with 2 tablespoons butter or margarine and 1 tablespoon water in a small saucepan; bring to a boil; cover; simmer 5 minutes. Stir in 1 cup finely diced boiled ham and 1 teaspoon basil, crumbled, and sauté 3 minutes. Add to pasta with sauce and toss.

Cook 1 package (9 ounces) frozen cut green bean with sliced mushrooms following label directions; drain vegetables and return to saucepan; add 1 can (6½ ounces) chopped clams and liquid and heat slowly. Add to kettle with sauce and ½ cup grated Romano cheese and toss well until cheese melts.

Wash and trim 1 package (10 ounces) fresh spinach. Place in a large skillet with water clinging to leaves; cover; steam 2 minutes. Drain well and chop coarsely; return to skillet with 1 cup diced cooked pork and 2 tablespoons white wine. Heat, but do not boil. Add to pasta and sauce.

Sauté 1 cup (thawed) frozen peas and 1 large tomato, peeled and chopped, in 2 tablespoons butter or margarine in medium-size skillet. Cook, stirring frequently, for 5 minutes. Add to pasta with sauce; toss. Top with 4 sliced warm hard-cooked eggs.

Cook 1 package (10 ounces) frozen chopped spinach in a medium-size saucepan following package directions; drain well and return to saucepan. Add 1 cup diced knockwurst and 2 tablespoons brandy or Marsala wine. Heat slowly, but do not boil. Add after sauce to pasta in kettle and toss until mixed.

Shape ½ pound ground pork into a large patty in a small skillet; brown 5 minutes on one side; turn; brown 5 minutes on second side; crumble and push to one side; stir in 1 small yellow squash, diced, and cook 3 minutes; add 1 can (1 pound) red kidney beans, drained, and heat 5 minutes. Add to pasta with sauce and toss until well blended.

Heat 2 tablespoons olive or vegetable oil in a small skillet; add 1 large red pepper, halved, seeded, and diced; sauté 3 minutes; add 1 cup diced leftover meat loaf or pork roast and heat slowly for 5 minutes. Add to kettle with sauce and ½ cup shredded Provolone cheese and toss just until cheese melts.

Brown 3 sweet Italian sausages in a small skillet; cut into thin slices; add 1 large zucchini, diced, and cook 8 minutes or until sausage is cooked and squash is crisp-tender; stir in 1 teaspoon oregano, crumbled. Add with sauce to pasta in kettle; toss well.

Sauté 1 cup sliced pepperoni in a small skillet 5 minutes; push to one side. Add 1 cup halved cherry tomatoes and 2 tablespoons capers with liquid. Heat slowly, stirring several times, just until heated through. Add to kettle with sauce and toss gently to coat.

Place 1 package (10 ounces) frozen chopped broccoli in a medium-size saucepan. Cut 1 package (12 ounces) frozen haddock fillets into 1-inch blocks with a heavy knife; place on top of broccoli. Cook, following broccoli package directions. Remove with slotted spoon to kettle and toss gently with sauce to mix well.

Halve, seed and dice, 1 red and 1 green pepper. Drain oil from 1 can (6½ ounces) tuna into a small skillet; sauté diced pepper in oil 5 minutes, or just until crisp-tender; flake tuna into skillet and heat 2 minutes. Add to kettle with ½ cup grated Parmesan cheese and toss well with sauce.

Heat 2 tablespoons olive or vegetable oil in a small skillet; add 2 cups thinly sliced cauliflower flowerets and sauté 5 minutes or until crisp-tender; stir in 1 cup diced cooked kielbasa and heat for 3 minutes. Add to kettle with ¼ cup chopped parsley and toss with sauce to coat.

Prepare 1 package (9 ounces) frozen French green beans with toasted almonds following package directions; drain off liquid and keep for a soup or sauce. Add 1 cup diced cooked chicken to saucepan and heat slowly 3 minutes. Add to pasta with sauce and ½ cup sliced pitted ripe olives.

Sauté 1 cup julienne pieces salami in a small skillet 5 minutes; push to one side; add 1 cup sliced fresh mushrooms, or 1 can (6 ounces) sliced mushrooms and liquid, and cook 3 minutes. Add to pasta in kettle with sauce and ½ cup grated Romano cheese and toss over low heat to blend.

Drain liquid from 1 can (7 ounces) salmon into a small skillet. Pare and thinly slice 1 medium-size cucumber; add to skillet and cook, stirring often, 5 minutes; flake salmon into skillet, removing skin and bones. Heat slowly with ¼ cup pine nuts 3 minutes. Add to pasta with sauce and toss to blend. Sprinkle with ground black pepper.

Place 1 package (10 ounces) frozen peas with pearl onions into a medium-size saucepan; add 1 package (8 ounces) frozen shelled, deveined shrimp; add ½ cup water; cover pan; bring to a boil and steam 8 minutes. Add to pasta and sauce with slotted spoon; add 1 tablespoon lemon juice. Toss well to coat.

Cook 1 package (8 ounces) brown-and-serve pork sausages in a medium-size skillet following package directions; cut into small pieces. Sauté 1 cup cubed zucchini or yellow squash in pan drippings 5 minutes or until crisp-tender. Add to pasta with sauce and toss to coat well.

Drain liquid from 1 can (10 ounces) whole oysters or clams into a small saucepan. Pare and thinly slice 2 large carrots; add to saucepan; cover and steam 10 minutes. Add oysters or clams and turn off heat; cover pan and let stand 2 minutes. Toss with pasta and sauce; add 1 cup shredded Swiss.

Pour 1 can (1 pound) chick-peas and liquid into a medium-size saucepan; drain liquid from 1 can (1 pound) red kidney beans and add beans to chick-peas with 1 tablespoon chopped fresh oregano, or 1 teaspoon dried oregano, crumbled. Heat slowly. Remove with slotted spoon to pasta with sauce and toss to mix well.

Sauté 4 sliced frankfurters in 2 tablespoons butter or margarine in a medium-size skillet; add 1 package (10 ounces) frozen lima beans and 2 tablespoons water; cover skillet; cook 5 minutes. Add to pasta and sauce with 1 cup cubed white process American cheese and toss until cheese melts.

SPAGHETTI PRIMAVERA

Makes 4 servings.

¾ pound high-protein spaghetti
¼ pound carrots, cut into matchstick-size pieces (1 cup)
¼ cup chopped green onions
3 tablespoons vegetable oil
2 cups fresh broccoli flowerets
1 small red pepper, cut into thin strips
½ pound mushrooms, halved or quartered
1 cup low-fat skim milk
½ teaspoon Worcestershire sauce
Few drops liquid red pepper seasoning
2 ounces sharp American cheese, diced

1. Bring 4 quarts of water to a boil in a large, covered kettle. Cook spaghetti following package directions, but adding only ½ teaspoon salt to water. Drain.
2. While spaghetti is cooking, stir-fry carrots and green onions in 2 tablespoons of the oil in a large skillet for 2 minutes. Add broccoli and red pepper; stir-fry 2 minutes longer. Add the remaining tablespoon of oil and the mushrooms; stir-fry 2 minutes longer; keep warm.
3. Combine milk, Worcestershire, and the red pepper seasoning in a cup; stir into spaghetti along with the cheese.
4. Place spaghetti mixture on a serving platter; top with vegetables.

SERVING SUGGESTIONS: Crusty whole wheat rolls, tomatoes vinaigrette, and baked custard topped with fresh fruit.

STIR-FRIED THIN SPAGHETTI WITH TOMATO SAUCE

Makes 4 servings.

3½ teaspoons vegetable oil
1¼ teaspoons salt
1 package (8 ounces) thin spaghetti
¼ cup grated Parmesan cheese
1 cup cottage cheese
2 tablespoons chopped parsley
2 cans (1 pound each) tomatoes
¼ teaspoon pepper
½ teaspoon mixed Italian herbs

1. Bring 3 quarts of water to a boil in a large, covered kettle; add ½ teaspoon of the oil and ¼ teaspoon of the salt. Add spaghetti slowly, so water continues to boil. Boil rapidly for 5 minutes or just until slightly firm to the bite. Drain; place in a large bowl with 1 teaspoon of the oil. Keep warm.

2. Combine Parmesan and cottage cheese, parsley, and ½ teaspoon of the salt in a small bowl.

3. Heat a wok or skillet over high heat; add the remaining 2 teaspoons of oil, tomatoes, breaking them up with a spoon, the remaining ½ teaspoon of salt, pepper, and Italian herbs.

4. Add spaghetti; stir and lift to mix well. Stir in cheese mixture quickly.

SERVING SUGGESTIONS: Sesame breadsticks, Grated Zucchini and Green Pepper Salad ■, and lemon sherbet.

PASTA WITH GARDEN VEGETABLES

Try tossing linguine with a colorful collection of fresh vegetables for a truly Italian treat.

Makes 8 servings.

1½ **pound linguine or thin spaghetti**	2 **medium-size zucchini, washed and sliced**
¼ **cup olive or vegetable oil**	1 **large red pepper, halved, seeded, and diced**
¼ **cup (½ stick) butter or margarine**	½ **pound fresh mushrooms, washed and sliced**
1 **clove garlic, minced**	**Freshly grated Parmesan cheese**
1 **pound thin asparagus, washed, trimmed, and cut into 1-inch pieces**	**Freshly ground black pepper**

1. Bring 4 to 6 quarts of salted water to a boil in a large, covered kettle. Cook pasta following package directions. Drain and return to kettle.

2. While pasta cooks, heat oil and butter in a large skillet; add garlic and cook 2 minutes.

3. Add asparagus pieces, zucchini slices, diced red pepper, and mushroom slices to skillet. Stir-fry for 3 minutes or until crisp-tender.

4. Pour vegetables and sauce over pasta in kettle and toss to coat evenly. Spoon into a heated serving platter; sprinkle with Parmesan cheese and freshly ground pepper. Serve at once.

SERVING SUGGESTIONS: Autumn Barley Loaf ■ with herb butter and Spiced Peach Cake ■.

STUFFED SHELLS MARINARA

Great Italian cooks have always known the art of stretching a little meat or fish into a marvelous main dish.

Bake at 350° for 45 minutes.
Makes 8 servings.

1 package (12 ounces) large shells*	2 teaspoons basil, crumbled
	½ teaspoon pepper
1 can (7 ounces) chunk light tuna in oil	1 package (10 ounces) frozen chopped spinach
1 large onion, chopped (1 cup)	2 eggs
1 clove garlic, minced	1 cup fresh bread crumbs (2 slices bread)
2 cans (15 ounces each) tomato sauce	
3 teaspoons salt	1 cup cream-style cottage cheese

1. Bring 4 quarts of water to a boil in a large, covered kettle. Cook shells following package directions, for 9 minutes. Drain and place in a large bowl of cold water.

2. While pasta cooks, drain oil from tuna into a large skillet. Heat oil and sauté onion and garlic until soft. Stir in tomato sauce, tuna, 2 teaspoons of the salt, basil, and ¼ teaspoon of the pepper; simmer 15 minutes to blend flavors. Add 1 cup pasta cooking water to sauce if it gets too thick.

3. Cook spinach following package directions; drain well. Beat eggs in a medium-size bowl with a wire whisk; add cooked spinach, bread crumbs, cottage cheese, the remaining 1 teaspoon salt, and remaining ¼ teaspoon pepper; stir until well blended. Preheat oven to 350°.

4. Drain shells on paper towels. Fill each shell with a teaspoon of the spinach-cheese mixture. Spoon a generous half of the sauce in a 12-cup shallow casserole.** Arrange stuffed pasta shells over sauce; drizzle remaining sauce over. Cover casserole with aluminum foil.

5. Bake in a preheated moderate oven (350°) for 45 minutes or until shells are tender and casserole is bubbly hot.

SERVING SUGGESTIONS: Crusty Italian bread and tossed green salad.

---

*You can use elbow macaroni or ziti instead of shells; spoon half the cooked pasta over sauce; then top with a layer of spinach-cheese filling, remaining pasta, and, finally, sauce.

**This recipe can be easily divided, with half spooned into a 9x9x2-inch ovenproof casserole, lined with heavy-duty aluminum foil. Seal, package, date, and freeze. When solid, remove foil package from casserole. When ready to serve; peel foil from frozen pasta; place in original casserole. Bake in a preheated moderate oven (350°) for 1 hour.

JAVANESE CURRIED NOODLES AND BEEF

Makes 4 servings.

¼ teaspoon salt
3½ teaspoons vegetable oil
2½ cups curly broad noodles
½ cup catsup
2 tablespoons soy sauce
¼ teaspoon black pepper
¼ cup water

2 to 3 teaspoons curry powder
½ cup chopped green onions
1 pound ground chuck
1 cup bean sprouts
Or: Finely shredded romaine lettuce

1. Bring 3 quarts of water to a boil in a large, covered kettle; add salt and ½ teaspoon of the oil. Add noodles slowly so that water continues to boil. Boil about 5 minutes or until noodles are still slightly firm. Drain; place in large bowl; toss with 1 teaspoon of the oil. Keep warm.
2. Combine catsup, soy sauce, pepper, and water in a small bowl. Reserve.
3. Place a large wok or large skillet over low heat; add curry, heating until fragrant, 1 minute. Add remaining 2 teaspoons oil. Increase heat; add onions; stir-fry 1 minute. Add meat; stir-fry until no longer pink.
4. Stir in reserved catsup mixture; bring to a boil. Add noodles and bean sprouts. Stir and mix until hot.

SERVING SUGGESTIONS: Cucumbers vinaigrette, Stir-Fried Broccoli ■, and sliced pineapple.

FRIED RICE MAIN DISHES—
HEARTY & THRIFTY

Yes—you *can* still feed your family a hearty meal without going broke. These fried rice main dishes are a great way to loosen a tight budget without skimping on flavor or nutrition. Look over the chart below, select your favorite variation, then give your family (and budget) a real treat.

BASIC FRIED RICE (BFR)

1 tablespoon vegetable oil; 1 small green pepper, chopped (½ cup); ½ cup chopped green onions; 2 tablespoons soy sauce; 3 cups cold Easy-to-Cook Rice.*

1. Heat oil in large skillet. Stir-fry pepper and onion 1 minute.

2. Add soy sauce and cold rice. Cook and stir until hot.

*EASY-TO-COOK RICE: 1 teaspoon salt; 1 cup converted or long-grain rice; 2 cups boiling water. Add salt and rice to water in medium-size saucepan. Lower heat; cover; simmer 20 minutes. Remove from heat. Let stand 5 minutes. Cool; chill. (Makes 3 cups.)

BFR WITH PORK

½ pound cooked pork, beef, or lamb, cut into strips 1 x ¼-inch long (about 1½ cups); 2 eggs, lightly beaten.

1. Proceed with Step 1 in Basic Fried Rice.

2. In Step 2, add meat with soy sauce and rice. Stir-fry until hot. Pour eggs over and stir until eggs are set. (Makes 4 servings.)

BFR WITH SAUSAGE AND PEPPERS

¾ pound hot Italian sausage (pricked with fork); 2 medium-size green peppers, seeded and cut into thin strips; ½ teaspoon mixed Italian seasoning; 1 can (1 pound) tomatoes, cut up with juice; 1 teaspoon salt; grated Parmesan cheese

1. Place sausage in boiling water; simmer 15 minutes. Drain; cut into ¼-inch slices. In Step 1 of Basic Fried Rice, substitute green pepper strips for chopped green pepper and add with Italian seasoning to green onions.

2. In Step 2 *omit* soy sauce. Add sausages; stir-fry 1 minute. Stir in tomatoes and salt with rice. Cook and stir until hot. Sprinkle with cheese. (Makes 6 servings.)

BFR WITH BEEF AND PEAS

¾ pound ground beef; 1 tablespoon catsup; 1 teaspoon wine vinegar; 1 teaspoon sugar; ⅓ cup water; 1 package (10 ounces) frozen peas, thawed; ½ cup sliced water chestnuts; ½ cup bean sprouts, drained and rinsed.
1. In Step 1 of Basic Fried Rice, stir-fry beef with vegetables until meat loses pink color.
2. In Step 2, combine soy sauce with catsup, vinegar, sugar, and water. Add to meat with peas, water chestnuts, and rice. Cook and stir until hot. Stir in bean sprouts. (Makes 6 servings.)

BFR WITH BACON AND BROCCOLI

½ pound bacon, cooked until crisp; 1 package (10 ounces) frozen chopped broccoli, thawed; 1 tablespoon additional soy sauce; ½ cup sliced water chestnuts; 1 egg, lightly beaten; Chinese noodles.
1. Drain bacon and crumble. Remove all but 1 tablespoon fat from pan. In Step 1 of Basic Fried Rice *omit* oil; cook broccoli with other vegetables.
2. In Step 2, add 3 tablespoons soy sauce, water chestnuts, and bacon with the rice. Cook and stir until hot. Stir in egg; cook until set. Serve with Chinese noodles. (Makes 5 servings.)

BFR WITH LENTILS AND SALAMI

½ cup thinly sliced celery; 1 small clove garlic, minced (¼ teaspoon); 1 package (8 ounces) sliced cotto salami, cut into thin strips; 1½ cups cooked lentils (start with ⅔ cup raw lentils and 1 quart water and save the liquid); 1 cup finely shredded romaine lettuce.
1. In Step 1 of Basic Fried Rice, cook celery and garlic with other vegetables.
2. In Step 2, *omit* soy sauce. Add salami, cooked lentils, and 2 tablespoons of the cooking liquid with the rice. Cook and stir 5 minutes. Stir in lettuce just before serving. Season with salt and pepper. (Makes 6 servings.)

BFR WITH CURRIED CHICKEN

½ teaspoon chili powder; 2 teaspoons curry powder, 1 cup thinly sliced celery; 1 small tart apple, pared, cored, and chopped; ½ pound cooked, cubed chicken or turkey (1½ cups); ¼ cup dry sherry; ¼ cup chicken broth; ¼ cup raisins; ¼ cup slivered almonds.
1. In Step 1 of Basic Fried Rice, cook chili powder, curry powder, celery, and apple with vegetables.
2. In Step 2, *omit* soy sauce. Add chicken or turkey to skillet. Stir in sherry and chicken broth with the rice. Cook and stir until almost all the liquid is evaporated. Stir in raisins and almonds. (Makes 4 servings.)

FRIED RICE

Makes 5 generous servings.

2 cups long-grain rice
2 cups chicken broth
2 cups water
2 tablespoons Worcestershire sauce
1 tablespoon margarine
2 teaspoons salt
2 cloves garlic, minced
3 tablespoons vegetable oil
3 cups assorted chopped fresh vegetables (carrots, onions, green pepper, zucchini)
5 eggs, lightly beaten
1 cup diced leftover ham

1. Combine rice, broth, water, Worcestershire, margarine, salt, and garlic in a large saucepan and bring to a boil. Lower heat; cover; simmer 15 minutes.

2. Heat 1 tablespoon of the oil in a large skillet or wok. Add vegetables; stir-fry until crisp-tender. Remove with a slotted spoon to a medium-size bowl.

3. Add 1 more tablespoon of the oil to the skillet. Scramble eggs, breaking them up into small pieces. Remove from skillet and add to vegetables.

4. Add remaining 1 tablespoon oil to skillet; stir in rice, ham, vegetables, and eggs. Stir until heated through. Serve at once with soy sauce if you wish.

SERVING SUGGESTIONS: Broccoli vinaigrette, fortune cookies, and melon.

SPANISH-STYLE RICE

Makes 4 servings.

1 medium-size onion, finely chopped (½ cup)
½ green pepper, seeded and chopped
1 tablespoon vegetable oil
1 can (28 ounces) whole tomatoes, undrained
⅔ cup long-grain rice
1 cup shredded American cheese

1. Sauté onion and pepper in oil in a medium-size skillet until tender. Add tomatoes, breaking them up with a spoon, and rice; mix well.

2. Bring to a boil; lower heat; cover. Cook slowly, about 30 minutes or until rice is cooked. Stir in cheese until melted. Serve at once.

SERVING SUGGESTIONS: Whole wheat rolls, buttered broccoli, and baked custard.

RICE AND BEANS WITH SAUSAGES

Makes 6 servings.

½ pound hot or sweet Italian sausage (or a combination), cut into ¼-inch slices

1 large onion, chopped (1 cup)

1 medium-size green pepper, halved, seeded, and diced (¾ cup)

1 medium-size red pepper, halved, seeded, and diced (¾ cup)

1 clove garlic, minced

1 medium-size tomato, chopped (½ cup)

1½ teaspoons salt

½ teaspoon oregano, crumbled

¼ teaspoon liquid red pepper seasoning

2 cups water

2 cups packaged precooked rice

1 can (1 pound) black beans, drained

1. Cook sausage in a large skillet over moderate heat until browned on both sides. Remove with a slotted spoon to paper toweling; keep warm. Do not drain off fat.

2. Add the onion, green and red peppers, and garlic, and sauté in sausage fat until tender, about 10 minutes. Add tomato, salt, oregano, red pepper seasoning, and water.

3. Bring to a boil. Stir in rice and beans. Remove from heat; cover; let stand 8 minutes or until liquid is absorbed. Fluff up rice.

4. Spoon mixture onto a serving plate and arrange sausage on top.

SERVING SUGGESTIONS: Carrot Cornbread ■ and Mudpie Chocolate Cake ■.

LAYERED BROWN RICE, CHEESE, AND SPINACH

Firm-textured brown rice is topped with a savory combination of herbed spinach and cheese.

Bake at 425° for 30 minutes.
Makes 6 servings.

1	can condensed chicken broth	1	teaspoon salt
1¼	cups brown rice	¼	teaspoon pepper
2	packages (10 ounces each) frozen chopped spinach, thawed	1	teaspoon tarragon, crumbled
		1¼	cups milk
1	medium-size onion, finely chopped (½ cup)	1	cup cottage cheese
		1	cup shredded Jarlsberg or Swiss cheese, lightly packed (2½ ounces)
3	tablespoons butter or margarine		
2	tablespoons all-purpose flour		

1. Pour broth into a 4-cup glass measure; add water to make 2⅓ cups liquid. Combine with rice in a large saucepan; bring to a boil; lower heat. Cover; simmer for 35 minutes. Remove from heat and let stand, covered, 30 minutes.

2. Place spinach in a strainer. With the back of a wooden spoon, press spinach against strainer until as dry as possible. Preheat oven to 425°.

3. Sauté onion in butter in a medium-size saucepan until soft; add spinach and cook for a few minutes, stirring constantly. Add flour, salt, pepper, and tarragon; toss to coat; gradually stir in milk and cook over low heat, stirring constantly, until mixture thickens, about 5 minutes.

4. Butter a 2-quart shallow baking dish. Spread rice in dish in an even layer. Combine cottage cheese with half of Jarlsberg cheese and dollop mixture evenly over rice, then spread to make an even layer. Spread spinach mixture evenly over top; sprinkle with remaining shredded cheese.

5. Bake in upper third of a preheated hot oven (425°) for 30 minutes or until hot and bubbly.

SERVING SUGGESTIONS: Crusty rolls, baked tomatoes, and sliced pineapple.

NUTTED ZUCCHINI-RICE LOAF WITH CHEDDAR CHEESE SAUCE

Bake at 350° for 55 minutes.
Makes 6 servings.

1 cup brown rice
1¾ cups water
1 teaspoon salt
1 pound small zucchini, washed and trimmed
3 eggs
3 green onions, sliced
1 cup finely chopped walnuts
½ teaspoon sage, crumbled
½ teaspoon thyme, crumbled
¼ teaspoon pepper

Cheddar Cheese Sauce:
1 tablespoon butter or margarine
1 tablespoon plus 2 teaspoons cornstarch
2 teaspoons sharp prepared mustard
¼ teaspoon salt
1¼ cups milk
4 ounces sharp Cheddar cheese, shredded (1 cup)
½ cup buttermilk

1. Combine rice, water, and ½ teaspoon of the salt in a medium-size saucepan; bring to a boil over high heat; cover. Lower heat; simmer 35 minutes. Remove from heat and let stand, covered, for 20 minutes.

2. Meanwhile, shred zucchini into a large sieve or colander placed over a medium-size bowl; add remaining ½ teaspoon salt; let stand 30 minutes while rice cooks. With the back of a wooden spoon press liquid from zucchini until dry. Butter an 8½ x 4½ x 2⅝-inch glass or aluminum baking dish. (Do not use tin as it will discolor the loaf.) Preheat oven to 350°.

3. Beat eggs in a large bowl; add zucchini, mixing well to separate strands. Add rice, green onions, walnuts, sage, thyme, and pepper; mix well to moisten thoroughly (use hands, if necessary).

4. Spoon mixture into prepared baking dish. Spread evenly in pan; cover with aluminum foil.

5. Bake in a preheated moderate oven (350°) for 45 minutes. Remove foil and continue baking an additional 10 minutes. Remove from oven to a wire rack. Let stand 15 minutes. Run a small sharp pointed knife around edges of pan to loosen zucchini-rice loaf; place serving dish on top and invert loaf onto dish.

6. While loaf rests, make Sauce: Melt butter in a saucepan; stir in cornstarch, mustard, and salt and continue stirring over medium heat until frothy. Remove from heat. Gradually add milk, stirring with a wire whisk until mixture is smooth. Return to heat. Cook over low heat, stirring constantly, until mixture thickens. Add cheese; continue to cook until cheese melts; stir in buttermilk. Spoon some sauce over loaf; pour remaining sauce into sauceboat to pass at table.

SERVING SUGGESTIONS: Sautéed green peppers and onions, baked tomatoes, and spiced poached pears.

BROWN RICE

Brown rice is unpolished rice that retains the bran and many valuable nutrients. You'll enjoy its characteristic nutty flavor. Brown rice absorbs more liquid during cooking and will take longer to cook; 1½ cups uncooked rice yields about 4 cups cooked. Use brown rice in many of the same ways you use white rice: for casseroles, stuffed vegetables, salads, pilaf, poultry or meat stuffing, soups, and puddings.

6

Eggs and Cheese

Eggs provide consumers with a perfectly packaged, highly nutritious, inexpensive food, untouched by human hands or additives. Once removed from its shell, all of the egg is usable—there is no waste. Eggs are extremely versatile and can be used in countless ways, from the simplest poached egg to the most elegant meringue.

Eggs provide high-quality protein and contain all of the essential amino acids, 13 minerals, and all of the vitamins, except vitamin C. Furthermore, eggs can be enjoyed by almost everyone because they are easy to digest. Finally, hard-cooked eggs can be the basis of a quick lunch—as a sandwich filling or in a salad—and supper is a snap when you add sliced hard-cooked eggs to a cream sauce or a can of creamed soup and serve over baked potatoes or toast.

Cheese, too, is a wonderfully versatile and relatively inexpensive source of complete proteins. This chapter's recipes feature eggs and cheese in appetizers, frittatas, soufflés, pizza, salads, casseroles, and more.

FOUR-CHEESE-STUFFED SHELLS

Bake at 350° for 15 minutes.
Makes 6 servings.

Four-Cheese Filling:
1   egg
¼   cup chopped parsley
½   teaspoon salt
⅛   teaspoon ground nutmeg
¼   teaspoon pepper
½   cup grated Romano cheese
½   cup shredded Swiss cheese
½   cup shredded mozzarella
    cheese

½   cup ricotta cheese
¼   cup heavy cream
1   can (15 ounces) tomato sauce

Wrapper:
1   package (12 ounces) jumbo
    pasta shells, cooked,
    following package directions

1. Preheat oven to 350°. Prepare Filling: Beat egg lightly in a medium-size bowl. Stir in parsley, salt, nutmeg, and pepper until blended. Stir in Romano, Swiss, mozzarella, and ricotta cheeses until thoroughly combined. Stir in heavy cream. (Makes 1¾ cups filling.)
2. Fill cooled pasta shells; arrange in a shallow baking dish. Pour tomato sauce over.
3. Bake in a preheated moderate oven (350°) for 15 minutes or until bubbly hot.

SERVING SUGGESTIONS: Green peppers and zucchini vinaigrette, sesame breadsticks, fresh fruit, and Cinnamon-Nut Cookies ■.

SAVE $ ON CHEESE

• Slice your own cheese and save money. (If you have a large family or entertain frequently, consider buying a slicing machine.) Another plus is that a whole piece of cheese is less likely to dry out and can be kept longer.
• Don't toss away small pieces of cheese. Save them all in a covered container in the refrigerator. When you've collected enough, grate the cheese, either by hand or with a food processor. Store in a container in the freezer (you can mix different types of cheese together). The frozen grated cheese will melt quickly and can be used for soufflés, casseroles, omelets, etc.

CHEESE-LASAGNE ROLLUPS

Bake at 350° for 35 minutes.*
Makes 8 servings.

16 lasagne noodles
   (about ¾ pound)
2 packages (10 ounces each)
   frozen chopped spinach,
   thawed
1 container (1 pound) cream-
   style cottage cheese (2 cups)
2 cups shredded Cheddar
   cheese (8 ounces)

1 egg
2 teaspoons salt
¼ teaspoon pepper
1 teaspoon mixed Italian herbs
¼ cup (½ stick) margarine
3 tablespoons all-purpose flour
2 cups water
10 tablespoons nonfat dry
   milk powder

1. Cook noodles following package directions for minimum amount of cooking time; drain well.

2. Place spinach in a colander; press out excess liquid by pressing against side of colander with a wooden spoon (or squeeze spinach between hands). Turn into a large bowl; with a fork blend in the cottage cheese, ½ cup of the Cheddar, egg, 1½ teaspoons of the salt, the pepper, and Italian herbs. Place 2 tablespoons spinach-cheese filling along length of lasagne noodles; roll up, jelly roll style. Preheat oven to 350°.

3. Melt margarine in a medium-size saucepan. Blend in flour and remaining ½ teaspoon salt; cook, stirring constantly, just until bubbly. Stir water into dry milk in a small bowl. Stir mixture into saucepan. Continue cooking and stirring until mixture thickens and bubbles. Add remaining Cheddar, stirring until cheese is melted.

4. Spread ½ cup cheese sauce in bottom of an 11¾ x 7 x 1-inch baking dish; arrange lasagne rollups in dish; pour remaining sauce over rollups, covering completely.

5. Bake in a preheated moderate oven (350°) for 35 minutes or until bubbly and brown.

SERVING SUGGESTIONS: Crisp Italian bread, broccoli with herb butter, and lemon pound cake.

---

*Prepared dish can be made ahead and refrigerated. Increase baking time to 1 hour.

EASY SPICY CHEESE SQUARES

Remember all those quiches?
This is a small, sure variation designed for snacking.

Bake at 350° for 40 minutes.
Makes 9 servings.

5 eggs	1 can (4 ounces) chopped
¼ cup (½ stick) butter or	green chilies, drained
margarine, melted	1 medium-size tomato, diced
¼ cup all-purpose flour	(½ cup)
½ teaspoon baking powder	1 small onion, chopped
¼ teaspoon salt	(¼ cup)
¼ teaspoon cayenne pepper	¼ cup chopped parsley
2 cups shredded Cheddar	(optional)
cheese (8 ounces)	

1. Grease an 8 x 8 x 2-inch baking pan. Preheat oven to 350°.
2. Beat eggs in a medium-size bowl. Add butter, flour, baking powder salt, and cayenne; beat until smooth.
3. Stir in cheese, chilies, tomato, and onion; blend well. Pour into prepared baking pan.
4. Bake in a preheated moderate oven (350°) for 40 minutes or until golden brown. Let stand 5 minutes. Sprinkle with chopped parsley if you wish.
5. Cut into 9 squares; serve warm.

FETTUCCINE WITH CHEESE, GREEN ONIONS, AND DILL

If fresh dill is unavailable, fresh parsley is a good alternative.

Makes 4 servings.

1 container (1 pound)	½ teaspoon pepper
cream-style cottage cheese	1 package (12 ounces)
½ cup grated Parmesan cheese	fettuccine
¾ cup green onions, minced	¼ cup (½ stick) butter or
¼ cup chopped dill or parsley	margarine
1 teaspoon salt	⅓ cup heavy cream

1. Combine cottage cheese, Parmesan, onions, dill, salt, and pepper in a medium-size bowl; blend well.

2. Bring 4 quarts of water to a boil in a large, covered kettle. Cook pasta following package directions. Heat butter with cream in a small saucepan until butter is melted. Drain pasta; return to kettle; add butter and cream; toss to coat. Add cheese mixture; toss gently over low heat until well blended and piping hot.

SERVING SUGGESTIONS: Garlic toast, Stir-Fried Broccoli ■, Herbed Carrots ■, and lemon butter cookies.

CHEESE 'N' HAM PUFF

Bake at 325° for 1 hour.
Makes 6 servings.

½ loaf (8 ounces) Italian or French bread	1½ cups diced Muenster cheese (6 ounces)
¼ cup (½ stick) margarine	½ cup diced ham (4 ounces)
1 small onion, chopped (¼ cup)	4 eggs
2 tablespoons prepared mustard	2 cups reconstituted nonfat dry milk

1. Cut bread into small chunks.
2. Melt margarine in a small saucepan; sauté onion until soft; stir in mustard.
3. Layer one third of the bread chunks in a 10-cup casserole; drizzle one third of the margarine-mustard mixture over; top with half the cheese and ham. Repeat layering, ending with bread chunks and margarine-mustard mixture.
4. Beat eggs in a medium-size bowl with a wire whisk; add milk, pour over bread in casserole, pushing down bread to soak in custard. Cover casserole and refrigerate overnight.
5. Preheat oven to 325° when ready to bake casserole. Bake, uncovered, in a preheated slow oven (325°) 1 hour or until golden and puffed. Serve immediately.

SERVING SUGGESTIONS: Tossed green salad, tomatoes vinaigrette, and tapioca pudding.

ITALIAN CHEESE-RICE BALLS

Makes 8 servings.

2 cups long-grain rice	¼ cup (½ stick) margarine
4 eggs, separated	¼ cup all-purpose flour
1 cup grated Parmesan cheese	1 teaspoon salt
1 package (8 ounces) mozzarella, cut into 24 cubes	⅛ teaspoon pepper
	2 cups reconstituted nonfat dry milk
1 cup packaged Italian bread crumbs	Chopped parsley (optional)
1½ cups vegetable oil	

1. Cook rice following package directions, but eliminating the butter. Cool slightly. Lightly beat egg yolks in a medium-sized bowl. Fold in rice and ½ cup of the grated Parmesan cheese, mixing thoroughly.
2. When cool enough to handle, shape mixture into 24 balls, using about ¼ cup for each, and placing a cube of mozzarella cheese in the center of each ball. (Make sure the rice completely covers the cheese.) Lightly moisten palms of hands for easier shaping.
3. Beat egg whites slightly with a fork in a pie plate; place bread crumbs on a piece of wax paper. Gently roll rice balls in egg whites, then in bread crumbs. Place on a jelly roll pan. Refrigerate for 1 hour or until firm. Preheat oven to 250°.
4. Heat vegetable oil in a 1-quart saucepan to 350° on a deep-fat frying thermometer.
5. Fry rice balls, 3 at a time, turning once, about 4 minutes on each side or until golden. Drain on paper toweling. Keep warm in a preheated slow oven (250°).
6. While rice balls are frying, prepare sauce: Melt margarine over low heat in a medium-size saucepan. Stir in flour, salt, and pepper. Cook, stirring constantly, just until it bubbles. Stir in milk slowly. Continue cooking and stirring just until sauce thickens and bubbles. Remove from heat; stir in remaining ½ cup Parmesan. Arrange rice balls on serving dish; pour sauce into a small serving bowl; pass at table. Garnish each serving with chopped parsley if you wish.

SERVING SUGGESTIONS: Cucumber and Tomato Vinaigrette ■, Herbed Spinach Ring ■, and Bavarian cream.

CHEESE, RICE, AND SPINACH BAKE

Green chili peppers add pep to this rice dish.

Bake at 350° for 30 minutes.
Makes 6 servings.

1 cup brown rice	1 package (6 ounces) Monterey
2 cups (1 pound) cottage cheese, sieved	Jack cheese, cubed (1 cup)
2 eggs	1½ teaspoons salt
1 package (10 ounces) frozen chopped spinach, thawed	⅛ teaspoon pepper
1 can (4 ounces) green chili peppers, seeded and chopped	

1. Cook rice following package directions. Preheat oven to 350°.

2. Combine cottage cheese, eggs, spinach, green chili peppers, ½ cup of the Monterey Jack cheese, salt, and pepper in a large bowl. Stir in cooked hot rice.

3. Spoon into a 2-quart shallow baking dish. Dot with remaining ½ cup cheese.

4. Bake in a preheated moderate oven (350°) for 30 minutes or until bubbly hot and cheese has melted on the top.

SERVING SUGGESTIONS: Cracked wheat rolls, herbed string beans, and peach fritters.

STORING CHEESE

• Preserve the quality of your cheese by storing it properly. Once you have removed the original wrapping from the cheese, be sure to rewrap it in plastic wrap, then foil, to keep air out. (Firm cheeses, such as Swiss, will keep for several months, if unopened. Once opened, these cheeses should be used within a month.) Soft cheeses, such as cream cheese, should be used within several weeks. Pay close attention to the date on your cottage cheese container and try to use it up within a few days of that date.

• If the surface of your hard cheese has become moldy, do not throw out the cheese. You can salvage it by simply scraping off the mold. The mold is harmless and won't impair the flavor or quality of the cheese.

EGGS DIVAN

Bake at 375° for 10 minutes, then at 400° for 10 minutes.
Makes 4 servings.

½	cup long-grain rice	¼	teaspoon Worcestershire
1	package (10 ounces) frozen		sauce
	broccoli spears		Dash cayenne pepper
1	tablespoon margarine	¾	cup milk
1	tablespoon all-purpose flour	1	cup shredded Cheddar
¼	teaspoon salt		cheese (4 ounces)
¼	teaspoon dry mustard	4	hard-cooked eggs

1. Cook rice following package directions; reserve. Cook broccoli, following package directions; reserve. Preheat oven to 375°.

2. Melt margarine in a small saucepan; blend in flour, salt, dry mustard, Worcestershire sauce, and cayenne; cook 1 minute. Stir in milk. Cook, stirring constantly, until mixture thickens and bubbles. Remove from heat; add cheese, stirring until melted.

3. Spread rice over bottom of a 10-inch pie plate or quiche pan. Arrange broccoli over rice. Top with two thirds of the cheese sauce. Slice eggs; arrange over sauce; cover.

4. Bake in a preheated moderate oven (375°) for 10 minutes. Remove from oven; top with remaining sauce.

5. Increase oven temperature to hot (400°); bake, uncovered, 10 minutes longer.

SERVING SUGGESTIONS: Crisp whole wheat rolls and poached gingered plums.

COOK CHEESE GENTLY

High heat or an excessively long cooking period causes cheese to become tough and stringy. When cooking a cheese mixture on top of the range, use low heat and add the cheese near the end of the cooking period, stirring just until the ingredients are blended. When using cheese as a casserole topping, add it a few minutes before the end of the baking period and remove the casserole from the oven as soon as the cheese melts.

DOUBLE DEVILED EGGS

Tuna, salmon, or leftover chicken can be substituted
for the deviled ham in this recipe.

Bake at 350° for 20 minutes.
Makes 6 servings.

1	cup long-grain rice	2	tablespoons mayonnaise or salad dressing
1	tablespoon margarine		
1	envelope or teaspoon instant chicken broth	2	teaspoons prepared mustard
2¼	cups water	1	package (10 ounces) frozen cut green beans, cooked and drained
6	hard-cooked eggs		
1	can (3 ounces) deviled ham or luncheon meat		Rich Cheese Sauce (recipe below)

1. Combine rice with margarine, instant chicken broth, and water in a medium-size saucepan. Bring to a boil; lower heat; cover saucepan. Simmer for 25 minutes or until water is absorbed and rice is tender. Preheat oven to 350°.

2. While rice cooks, shell and halve eggs; press yolks through a sieve into a small bowl; add deviled ham, mayonnaise, and mustard; mix to blend well; spoon into egg whites.

3. Toss cooked green beans with rice and spoon into an 8-cup shallow casserole; arrange stuffed eggs over rice. Pour Rich Cheese Sauce over.

4. Bake in a preheated moderate oven (350°) for 20 minutes or until bubbly hot.

Rich Cheese Sauce: Melt ¼ cup margarine in a medium-size saucepan; stir in ¼ cup all-purpose flour and 1 teaspoon salt; cook 1 minute; stir in 2 cups reconstituted nonfat dry milk; cook, stirring constantly, until sauce thickens and bubbles 3 minutes.

SERVING SUGGESTIONS: Warm biscuits and spiced fruit compote.

CHUTNEY-STUFFED EGGS

Makes 6 servings.

6	hard-cooked eggs, shelled	2	teaspoons curry powder
3	tablespoons mayonnaise	1	teaspoon Dijon-style mustard
1	tablespoon finely chopped drained chutney	½	teaspoon salt
1	tablespoon finely chopped green onion	¼	teaspoon pepper
			Green onion, sliced (optional)

1. Halve eggs lengthwise; scoop out yolks into a small bowl. Mash yolks thoroughly. Stir in mayonnaise, chutney, chopped green onion, curry, mustard, salt, and pepper, blending well.

2. Refill whites with yolk mixture. Garnish with a small slice of green onion if you wish.

SERVING SUGGESTIONS: Paratha ■, cold rice and celery salad, string beans vinaigrette, and spiced poached fruit.

EGG KNOW-HOW

- Eggs will separate more easily when cold.
- When separating a large quantity of eggs, separate the white from the yolk, one egg at a time, over a small bowl. Then add the yolk and white to their respective bowls. This prevents the possibility of getting any egg yolk into a bowl of egg whites. If you separate each egg over a small bowl and a tiny bit of yolk accidentally gets into the white, you can remove it with a spoon. However, if too much of the yolk has mixed with the white, you have not "ruined" a whole bowlful of whites—you can use that egg for another purpose.
- Eggs will beat up to their greatest volume when at room temperature.
- Choose a large, deep bowl when beating egg whites because they will increase many times in volume. And keep your hand beater moving in and around the bowl to get the best volume.
- Make sure your bowl and beaters are sparkling clean when beating egg whites; the slightest trace of grease will prevent the whites from beating to their greatest volume.
- The basic rule for cooking eggs on the range-top or in the oven, is to use low to moderate heat and precise timing. If eggs are cooked at too high a temperature or too long, they will become tough and rubbery.

DILLED CREAMED EGGS
IN A PUFFY PANCAKE

Bake at 500° for 5 minutes, then at 450° for 10 minutes.
Makes 4 servings.

10 eggs	½ teaspoon dry mustard
8 slices bacon	½ teaspoon dillweed
¼ cup (½ stick) butter or margarine	Or: 1½ teaspoons chopped fresh dill
¾ cup milk	1½ cups milk
¾ cup all-purpose flour	Dash liquid hot pepper seasoning
¾ teaspoon salt	
2 tablespoons all-purpose flour	

1. Cover 8 of the eggs with cold water in a large saucepan. Bring to a boil. Remove from heat. Cover; let stand 15 minutes. Drain; rinse with cold water and peel.

2. Cook bacon until crisp in a large skillet. Drain on paper toweling and, while still warm, roll up 2 slices into a roll that resembles a rose; make 3 more. Preheat oven to 500°.

3. Melt butter in a medium-size saucepan. Remove from heat. Pour half the butter into a 9-inch pie plate; swirl to coat bottom and side. Beat remaining 2 eggs in a small bowl with an electric mixer on high speed until light and fluffy. Beat in ¾ cup milk, ¾ cup flour, and ¼ teaspoon of the salt on low speed. Pour into buttered pie plate.

4. Bake in very hot oven (500°) for 5 minutes. Lower oven temperature to 450° and bake 10 minutes longer or until pancake is puffy around edges and golden brown. Keep warm in oven.

5. Stir 2 tablespoons flour, remaining ½ teaspoon salt, dry mustard, and dill into butter remaining in saucepan. Cook until bubbly. Gradually stir in milk. Cook until thickened and bubbly, stirring constantly. Stir in hot pepper seasoning. Remove from heat.

6. Cut 2 hard-cooked eggs into quarters; coarsely chop remainder and add to dill sauce. Spoon egg mixture into center of pancake; top with bacon roses and quartered eggs.

SERVING SUGGESTIONS: Citrus fruit compote and Sweet Breakfast Squares ■.

PORK OMELETS (Tan Chiao)

The shape and color of these tiny omelets resemble gold nuggets and are a symbol of wealth for the New Year. This is a simplified version of the traditional dish from the Far East.

Makes 4 servings.

1	pound Chinese cabbage	3	to 4 tablespoons vegetable
4	eggs		oil
¼	pound ground pork or beef	1	cup chicken broth
1	teaspoon cornstarch	1	teaspoon salt
1	tablespoon soy sauce	½	teaspoon sugar
1	tablespoon dry sherry		
1	green onion, finely chopped		
	(2 teaspoons)		

1. Cut cabbage into 2 x 1-inch strips (about 4 cups)

2. Beat eggs in a large bowl with a rotary beater until frothy. Add pork, cornstarch, soy sauce, sherry, and green onion. Stir with fork to make sure pork is in very small pieces.

3. Heat a large skillet; add 1 tablespoon of the oil. Pour egg mixture by tablespoonsful into skillet to make 2½-inch omelets. Make 4 or 5 at a time. Cook about 2 minutes or just until most of the egg is set. While omelets are still soft, fold in half, using a small spatula. Press lightly, then turn and cook 1 more minute. Remove to a platter. Continue with remaining mixture and use as much oil as is necessary. (Makes about 24 omelets.)

4. Wipe skillet clean; reheat and add 2 tablespoons of the oil. Stir-fry cabbage for 2 minutes. Add chicken broth, salt, and sugar. Stir well.

5. Arrange omelets on top of cabbage. Cover; cook until cabbage is just tender, about 5 minutes.

SERVING SUGGESTIONS: Stir-fried celery, hot cooked rice, and gingered pineapple chunks.

PARTY POTATO AND ZUCCHINI OMELET

This hearty, impressive, main-dish omelet is perfect for brunch or a light dinner. Surround it with crisp watercress and sliced ripe tomatoes.

Bake at 375° for 20 minutes.
Make 6 servings.

8	eggs	2	zucchini (about 12 ounces), thinly sliced
2	tablespoons milk		
¾	teaspoon salt	1	tablespoon butter or margarine
⅛	teaspoon pepper		
4	tablespoons vegetable oil	½	cup grated Parmesan cheese
1	small onion, chopped (¼ cup)	1	large tomato, sliced and each slice cut in half
2	large all-purpose potatoes (about ¾ pound), pared and grated	1	bunch watercress

1. Preheat oven to 375°. Beat eggs, milk, salt, and pepper in a bowl.
2. Heat 3 tablespoons of the oil in a large skillet with an ovenproof handle.* Add onion and potatoes and cook, stirring constantly, until potatoes are almost tender, about 3 minutes. Stir into egg mixture. Wipe skillet clean.
3. Add remaining 1 tablespoon oil to skillet and sauté zucchini until tender. Remove from skillet; wipe pan clean.
4. Melt butter in skillet. Add egg-potato mixture and sprinkle with about ⅓ cup of the cheese. Top with zucchini and then the remaining cheese.
5. Bake in a preheated moderate oven (375°) for 20 minutes or until a knife inserted in the center of the omelet comes out clean. Loosen around edges with metal spatula and slide omelet onto serving plate, zucchini side up. Garnish with tomatoes and watercress.

SERVING SUGGESTIONS: Autumn Barley Loaf ■, sliced orange and onion salad, and toasted pound cake.

---

*Or wrap handle in several thicknesses of aluminum foil.

POTATO AND CHORIZO FRITTATA

Bake at 350° for 10 minutes.
Makes 6 servings.

¼ pound chorizo (Spanish sausage) or smoked garlic sausage, sliced (1 cup)

1 can (8¼ ounces) whole potatoes, drained and sliced

1 medium-size green pepper, halved, seeded, and chopped (½ cup)

1 medium-size onion, chopped (½ cup)

6 eggs

3 tablespoons milk

½ teaspoon salt

¼ teaspoon pepper

¼ teaspoon basil, crumbled

¼ cup (½ stick) butter or margarine

1 tablespoon chopped parsley

1. Preheat oven to 350°. Reserve ½ cup sliced sausage and ½ cup sliced potatoes for garnish; chop remaining suasage and potatoes separately.

2. Sauté chopped sausage in an 8-inch skillet with an ovenproof handle over very low heat until some of the fat is rendered, about 1 minute. Add green pepper and onion; cook until vegetables are soft, about 5 minutes. Remove sausage mixture with slotted spoon to small bowl; set aside.

3. Beat eggs with milk, salt, pepper, and basil in a medium-size bowl until foamy.

4. Swirl butter over bottom and side of skillet over low heat. Pour in eggs. Cook over very low heat, stirring with flat side of fork and shaking pan back and forth, until frittata is firm on bottom and almost set on top. Remove from heat. Spread reserved chopped sausage mixture and chopped potatoes over top. Arrange reserved slices of sausage and potato over all.

5. Bake in a preheated moderate oven (350°) for 10 minutes or until eggs are set and chorizo slices are heated through. Sprinkle with parsley just before serving. Cut into wedges.

SERVING SUGGESTIONS: Stir-fried zucchini, baked tomatoes, and Apricot-Yogurt Whip ■.

CORN FITTATA

Quick and easy for lunch, brunch, or supper.

Bake at 350° for 10 minutes.
Makes 8 servings.

6	tablespoons (¾ stick) butter	10	eggs
1	small onion, chopped	½	cup heavy cream
	(¼ cup)	1¼	teaspoons salt
2	medium-size zucchini, sliced	1	teaspoon basil, crumbled
2⅔	cups corn kernels	1	teaspoon pepper
	(from 4 large ears)	2	large ripe tomatoes, sliced

1. Preheat oven to 350°. Melt 3 tablespoons of the butter in a 10-inch skillet with an ovenproof handle. Sauté onion, zucchini, and corn just until tender. Remove with a slotted spoon to bowl; reserve.

2. Beat eggs in a large bowl until frothy. Beat in heavy cream, salt, basil, and pepper until well blended. Melt remaining 3 tablespoons butter in same skillet. Pour eggs into skillet; sprinkle reserved vegetables evenly over eggs; cover.

3. Cook over low heat for 20 minutes or until eggs are partially set. Arrange tomato slices around outer edge of skillet.

4. Bake in a preheated moderate oven (350°) for 10 minutes or until center is set.

SERVING SUGGESTIONS: Cheese bread, tossed green salad, and banana pudding.

ARE YOUR EGGS FRESH?

A simple method will indicate how fresh or stale your eggs are. Simply put the eggs in a bowl of cold water. If the eggs sink, they are fresh. If the eggs are partially stale, they will bob up on one end. If the eggs float, they are very stale and possibly rotten and should be discarded.

PEPPER FRITTATA

Bake at 350° for 20 minutes.
Makes 8 servings.

12	eggs	1	large red onion, coarsely
2	teaspoons salt		chopped
¼	teaspoon white pepper	¼	cup (½ stick) butter or
½	cup water		margarine
2	red peppers, halved, seeded,	¼	cup chopped parsley
	and diced		(optional)
2	green peppers, halved,		
	seeded, and diced		

1. Beat eggs with salt, pepper, and water in a large bowl until foamy and well blended. Preheat oven to 350°.

2. Sauté peppers and onion in butter in a large skillet with an oven-proof handle,* until tender, about 5 minutes. Pour egg mixture over sautéed vegetables; stir gently to mix.

3. Bake in a preheated moderate oven (350°) for 20 minutes or until firm and puffed. Remove from oven; cool. Cut into wedges; garnish with chopped parsley.

SERVING SUGGESTIONS: Corn muffins, spinach-bacon salad, and Raisin Bread Pudding ■.

---

*Use a 10 x 10 x 2-inch porcelainized cast iron skillet, or a 9 x 9 x 2-inch baking pan. If using baking pan, sauté vegetables in a large skillet; transfer to pan.

CHILIES RELLENOS AND CHILI SAUCE

This is an interesting version of the well-known Southwestern dish
featuring cheese-filled green chilies.

Makes 8 servings.

1	can (7 ounces) green chilies	¾	teaspoon salt
	(8 chilies)	¼	cup vegetable oil
5	ounces American cheese, cut		Chili Sauce (recipe below)
	into 3x½-inch sticks	1½	cups shredded iceberg
4	eggs, beaten		lettuce
1	tablespoon all-purpose flour	1	medium-size tomato,
½	cup evaporated milk		chopped (1 cup)

1. Drain chilies and rinse in cold water. Cut a slit down side of each; remove seeds.
2. Fill each chili center with cheese sticks. Fold over edges of chili to cover cheese.
3. Combine eggs, flour, milk, and salt in a shallow dish. Beat with a fork or whisk until batter is smooth.
4. Dip each cheese-filled chili in batter to coat evenly on all sides.
5. Heat the oil in a large skillet. Fry chilies in hot oil, turning once. Pour remaining batter over chilies. Tip skillet to spread evenly. Cook, covered, 7 minutes or until batter is set.
6. Divide mixture into 8 wedge-shaped portions, allowing 1 chili with batter per portion; remove with a spatula to a warm plate. Serve topped with Chili Sauce, lettuce, and tomatoes.

Chili Sauce: Combine 1 can (8 ounces) tomato sauce, ¼ cup canned hot taco sauce. 1 teaspoon chopped onion, 1 clove garlic, minced, 1 teaspoon crumbled oregano, and ¾ teaspoon salt in a small saucepan. Heat 5 minutes.

SERVING SUGGESTIONS: Pinto beans, cornbread, and fruit-topped custard.

LEFTOVER EGG YOLKS & WHITES

If you have just a few leftover egg yolks or whites, you'll find that you can probably use them in many ways in just a few days. For instance, you could use them in a milk shake, scrambled eggs, pudding, or fried rice. Leftover egg whites or yolks will keep well in a covered jar in the refrigerator. For longer storage, freeze them.

Egg whites are easy to freeze and require no added ingredients; just pour them into freezer containers. Label with the number of whites and the date. For easier measuring and use, you can freeze each egg white in a section of an ice cube tray and then transfer to a freezer container. Large quantities of egg whites can be used in recipes such as meringues and angel food cake.

Egg yolks can be frozen but require added ingredients to keep them smooth. Beat ⅛ teaspoon salt, or 1½ teaspoons sugar, or 1½ teaspoons corn syrup into 4 egg yolks. Label the container with the number of yolks and the added ingredient. When making up a recipe, adjust it by keeping in mind the added ingredient. Leftover egg yolks can be used in recipes such as yellow cakes, custard (sauces), puddings, and pie fillings.

MACARONI AND EGG SALAD

Makes 6 servings.

1½ cups elbow macaroni
   (about 6 ounces)
8   hard-cooked eggs, shelled
    and chopped
½   cup chopped celery
½   cup chopped green pepper

⅔   cup mayonnaise
2   teaspoons prepared spicy
    brown mustard
1   teaspoon salt
⅛   teaspoon pepper

1. Cook macaroni following package directions. Drain; rinse with cold water; drain again. Combine with eggs, celery, and green pepper in a large bowl.
2. Combine mayonnaise, mustard, salt, and pepper in a cup; gently stir into macaroni. Cover; chill until serving time. If you wish, use this mixture to stuff 6 large hollowed-out tomatoes.

SERVING SUGGESTIONS: Herb-Onion Rolls■ and peanut butter cookies.

CHEESE AND SAUSAGE PIZZA

Bake at 425° for 50 minutes.
Makes 12 servings.

1½ packages active dry yeast
½   cup very warm water
¼   cup vegetable shortening
1½ tablespoons sugar
2¼ teaspoons salt
1   cup cold water
¾   cup yellow cornmeal
3   to 3½ cups all-purpose flour
1   pound mild Italian sausage
1   small onion, finely chopped
    (¼ cup)
1   small green pepper, halved,
    seeded, and finely chopped
    (⅓ cup)

1   clove garlic, minced
¾   teaspoon oregano, crumbled
½   teaspoon fennel seed
½   teaspoon salt
¼   teaspoon pepper
1   can (35 ounces) Italian-style
    tomatoes, drained, chopped,
    and drained again
1   can (4 ounces) sliced
    mushrooms, drained
1   package (8 ounces)
    mozzarella cheese, thinly
    sliced
⅓   cup grated Parmesan cheese

1. Sprinkle yeast over very warm water in a large bowl. Stir until yeast dissolves.

2. Heat shortening, sugar, salt, and the 1 cup water in a small saucepan until shortening is melted. Cool to lukewarm. Stir into yeast mixture.

3. Preheat oven to 425°.

4. Beat in cornmeal and 2 cups of the flour until smooth. Stir in enough of the remaining flour to make a soft dough.

5. Turn out onto a lightly floured surface; knead until smooth and elastic, adding only enough additional flour to keep dough from sticking.

6. Lightly brush a 14-inch round pizza pan with oil. Press pizza dough evenly over bottom and up side of pan.

7. Bake in a preheated hot oven (435°) for 5 minutes. Remove from oven.

8. Remove sausage from casing; brown slowly in a large skillet, breaking up with a fork. Remove to paper toweling to drain. Remove all but 2 tablespoons fat from skillet.

9. Sauté onion, green pepper, garlic, oregano, fennel seed, salt, and pepper in fat just until onion and green pepper are soft, about 5 minutes. Stir in well-drained tomatoes, mushrooms, and cooked sausage; heat thoroughly.

10. Spread prebaked pizza shell with tomato-sausage mixture; arrange mozzarella slices over top; sprinkle with Parmesan.

11. Bake in a hot oven (425°) for 45 minutes or until crust is golden brown and cheese has melted. Remove from oven; let stand 5 minutes. Cut into wedges to serve.

CHEESE SOUFFLÉ

Preheat oven to 400°, then bake at 375° for 30 minutes.
Makes 6 servings.

6 tablespoons (¾ stick) butter or margarine	**1¾** cups milk
6 tablespoons all-purpose flour	**6** eggs, separated, at room temperature
½ teaspoon salt	**1¼** cups shredded Swiss cheese (5 ounces)
¼ teaspoon white pepper	**¼** teaspoon cream of tartar
¼ teaspoon dry mustard	

1. Melt butter in a medium-size saucepan. Blend in flour, salt, pepper, and dry mustard; cook, stirring constantly, until bubbly. Stir in milk;

continue cooking and stirring until mixture thickens and bubbles for 1 minute.

2. Beat egg yolks lightly in a small bowl; spoon a few tablespoons of the hot sauce into yolks, blending well.

3. Slowly pour yolk mixture back into sauce in pan. Stir constantly with wire whisk until well blended. Remove from heat. Cool slightly; stir in cheese. Lightly butter an 8-cup soufflé dish. Preheat oven to 400°.

4. Beat egg whites with cream of tartar in a large bowl just until they form firm peaks. Scoop one quarter ot the beaten whites from side of bowl and fold into cheese sauce to lighten.

5. Slowly pour cheese sauce into remaining egg whites. Fold in cheese sauce until no streaks of yellow remain. Pour into prepared soufflé dish.

6. Make a deep circle 1 inch from edge of dish with the tip of a spatula or knife. Place in a preheated hot oven (400°). Immediately reduce to moderate (375°). Bake 35 minutes or until golden and puffed, and center jiggles only slightly when shaken. Serve at once.

SERVING SUGGESTIONS: Breadsticks, tossed green salad, and apple cobbler.

"HIGH-HATTED" SOUFFLÉ

If you've always been impressed by a "high-hatted" soufflé, you'll be glad to know it's produced by an easy technique. Just run the tip of your knife around the inside of the soufflé dish, below the rim, before baking. You will be rewarded with a billowing "high hat."

7

Meats and Poultry

Meat and poultry have been the traditional and most expensive sources of protein for Americans. We still love them, but we have had to learn to make them go further. This chapter gives many specific pointers to "stretch" these proteins. For instance, you'll learn how to extend a meat loaf and how to cut up a whole chicken like a pro.

With spectacular entrées like Chicken Normandy Style and Quick Beef Stroganoff, no one will guess you're on a budget. These and many other exciting dishes follow.

MAKE YOUR BARBECUE SPECIAL

Enhance your barbecued foods with these special touches. Simple fare becomes outstanding when treated to one of the marinades, bastes, butters, sauces, or toppings that follow. Take your pick!

MARINADES

Marinades are thin sauces based on wine, vinegar, or lemon juice with herbs and condiments. They are used to tenderize and flavor food before it is cooked. Food to be marinated should be placed in a non-metal container and covered with the sauce. Turn the food several times and marinate a minimum of 1 hour. The longer it marinates, the more tender and flavorful the food.

Cranberry-Soy Marinade

Combine 1 jar (14 ounces) cranberry-orange relish, ¾ cup dry white wine, ½ cup soy sauce, 2 tablespoons vegetable oil, 1 large onion, chopped (1 cup), 1 clove garlic, crushed, 2 teaspoons ground ginger, and 2 teaspoons dry mustard; blend well. Makes 3 cups.

Pimiento-Garlic Marinade

Combine 1 large onion, chopped (1 cup), 1 can (4 ounces) pimiento, drained and chopped, 2 cloves garlic, crushed, ½ cup dry white wine, ¼ cup vegetable oil, 1 teaspoon salt, and ¼ teaspoon pepper; blend well. Makes 2 cups.

Gingered Yogurt Marinade

Combine 1 cup plain yogurt, 1 medium-size onion, chopped (½ cup), 1 clove garlic, crushed, 1 teaspoon chopped, peeled, fresh gingerroot, ½ teaspoon ground nutmeg, ¼ teaspoon ground cardamom, ¼ teaspoon salt, ⅛ teaspoon ground cloves, and ⅛ teaspoon pepper; blend well. Makes 1¼ cups.

Bourbon-Mustard Marinade

Combine 1 cup water, 1 cup soy sauce, 1 tablespoon dry mustard, 3 cloves garlic, crushed, ¼ cup bourbon, and 6 tablespoons light brown sugar; blend well. Makes 2½ cups.

Red Wine Marinade

Combine 1 cup dry red wine, 2 cloves garlic, crushed, 1 teaspoon salt, ½ teaspoon *each* basil and oregano, crumbled, and 1 can (6 ounces) tomato paste; blend well. Makes 1½ cups.

BUTTERS

Butters are flavored butters, savory and sweet. They are good for "seasoning to taste"—just add a pat to grilled foods, breads, and vegetables.

Basil Butter

Combine ½ cup (1 stick) softened butter, 1 tablespoon minced fresh basil, and 2 tablespoons minced fresh parsley, 1 tablespoon lemon juice, and ¼ cup grated Parmesan cheese; blend well. Makes ½ cup.

Mustard Butter

Combine ½ cup (1 stick) softened butter, 2 tablespoons Dijon-style mustard, 2 teaspoons lemon juice, 2 teaspoons dried parsley flakes, ¼ teaspoon salt, and a dash of pepper; blend well. Makes ½ cup.

Ginger-Orange Butter

Combine ½ cup (1 stick) softened butter, 2 tablespoons light brown sugar, 1 teaspoon ground ginger, and 1 teaspoon grated orange rind; blend well. Makes ½ cup.

Fines Herbes Butter

Combine ½ cup (1 stick) softened butter, 2 tablespoons chopped fresh parsley, 1 tablespoon chopped fresh chives, ½ teaspoon *each* tarragon and chervil, crumbled, ¼ teaspoon salt, and a dash of pepper; blend well. Makes ½ cup.

BASTES

Bastes are thick sauces that are brushed on the food during grilling to give it a special flavor on the outside while retaining the juiciness of the meat.

Curried Honey Baste

Combine ¼ cup honey, 2 tablespoons vegetable oil, 2 tablespoons lemon juice, 1 tablespoon curry powder, and ½ teaspoon salt; blend well. Makes ½ cup.

Chutney Baste

Combine ½ cup chutney, ¼ cup chili sauce, 1 tablespoon soy sauce, 2 tablespoons vegetable oil, 4 drops liquid red pepper seasoning in the container of an electric blender; whirl until smooth. Top basted and grilled meats with chopped, salted peanuts if you wish. Makes 2 cups.

Herb-Sherry Baste

Combine ½ cup dry sherry, ¼ cup vegetable oil, and 4 teaspoons *fines herbes*, crumbled. Marinate meat of your choice. Add ½ cup chili sauce, ¼ cup dry red wine, 1 can (6 ounces) tomato paste, ½ teaspoon salt, and 1 clove garlic, crushed, to reserved marinade for basting. Makes 2 cups.

SAUCES AND TOPPINGS

Sauces and toppings are flavor enhancers served with grilled foods.

Salsa with Chilies

Combine 4 peeled and chopped ripe tomatoes, 1 can (4 ounces) green chilies, drained and chopped, ¼ teaspoon salt, a dash of pepper, 2 tablespoons cider vinegar, and a dash of liquid red pepper seasoning; blend well. Makes 4 cups.

Dilled Cukes

Combine 3 pared and chopped cucumbers, ½ cup vegetable oil, 1 tablespoon cider vinegar, 1 tablespoon lemon juice, 1 teaspoon dillweed, ½ teaspoon salt, ¼ teaspoon pepper, 1 clove garlic, crushed, 1 medium-size onion, chopped (½ cup), and ½ teaspoon dry mustard, mix well. Makes 6 cups.

Guacamole Sauce

Combine 1 peeled and pitted avocado, 1 clove garlic, ¼ teaspoon chili powder, 1 teaspoon lemon juice, 1 small onion, and 1 teaspoon salt in the container of an electric blender. Whirl until smooth. Add 3 slices cooked and crumbled bacon if you wish. Makes 1 cup.

CHICKEN PROVENÇAL

Makes 4 servings.

2 whole chicken breasts (14 ounces each), split
2 tablespoons all-purpose flour
½ teaspoon salt
⅛ teaspoon pepper
1 tablespoon butter or margarine
1 tablespoon vegetable oil
1 clove garlic, crushed
1 small onion, chopped (¼ cup)
1 can (8¼ ounces) tomatoes, drained and chopped
½ cup dry white wine or chicken broth
¼ cup sliced pitted ripe olives
2 tablespoons chopped parsley

1. Skin and bone chicken. Flatten slightly between sheets of wax paper with a rolling pin or flat side of meat mallet. Combine flour, salt, and pepper on wax paper. Turn chicken in flour to coat on all sides.
2. Heat butter and oil in a large skillet. Sauté chicken for 3 minutes on 1 side only; remove to a plate.
3. Sauté garlic and onion in the skillet until onion is softened, about 3 minutes. Stir in tomatoes and wine.
4. Return chicken to skillet, uncooked side down. Spoon some sauce over chicken. Lower heat and simmer until sauce is slightly thickened, about 5 minutes. Add olives; heat 1 more minute. Sprinkle with parsley.

SERVING SUGGESTIONS: Rice pilaf, buttered string beans, and grape-peach compote.

FREE BONUS

Save and freeze the giblets from whole chickens or turkeys. When you've saved enough, make up a pot of tasty spaghetti sauce, a risotto, an omelet, or a casserole. The backs and necks are great for a hearty pot of soup. Or you might want to store livers in a separate container, and save for making sautéed chicken livers or a pâté.

CHICKEN PARMESAN

Makes 4 servings.

2 whole chicken breasts (14 ounces each), split	2 tablespoons grated Parmesan cheese
1 tablespoon all-purpose flour	1 tablespoon butter or margarine
½ teaspoon salt	
⅛ teaspoon pepper	1 tablespoon vegetable oil
1 egg	½ cup dry white wine or chicken broth
1 tablespoon water	
½ cup packaged bread crumbs	1 tablespoon drained capers
	4 thin lemon slices

1. Skin and bone chicken. Flatten slightly between sheets of wax paper with a rolling pin or flat side of meat mallet. Combine flour, salt, and pepper on wax paper. Turn chicken in flour to coat on all sides.
2. Beat egg slightly in a shallow dish; stir in water. Combine bread crumbs and cheese on wax paper. Dip chicken in egg mixture, then in crumbs, repeating until coating mixtures are used up. Chill coated cutlets for 5 minutes.
3. Heat butter and oil in a large skillet. Sauté chicken 3 minutes on each side. Remove to a serving platter; keep warm.
4. Add wine to skillet, stirring and scraping up brown pieces, about 3 minutes. Stir in capers, cooking 1 more minute. Spoon sauce over chicken; top each with a slice of lemon.

SERVING SUGGESTIONS: Brown rice, dilled cucumbers, buttered broccoli, and spiced stewed plums.

CHICKEN NORMANDY STYLE

Makes 4 servings.

2 whole chicken breasts (14 ounces each), split	1 tablespoon vegetable oil
2 tablespoons all-purpose flour	3 tablespoons chopped onion
	½ teaspoon thyme, crumbled
½ teaspoon salt	¼ cup dry white wine or chicken broth
⅛ teaspoon pepper	
1 tablespoon butter or margarine	1 medium-size apple, cored and sliced (16 slices)
	½ cup light cream

1. Skin and bone chicken. Flatten slightly between sheets of wax paper with a rolling pin or flat side of meat mallet. Combine flour, salt, and pepper on wax paper. Turn chicken in flour to coat on all sides.
2. Heat butter and oil in a large skillet. Sauté chicken 3 minutes on 1 side; turn chicken; stir in onion, thyme, and wine. Cook for 3 minutes. Remove chicken to aluminum foil and keep warm.
3. Add apple slices; lower heat; cover and simmer for 2 minutes to soften apples.
4. Return chicken to pan. Stir in cream, spooning over chicken pieces. Remove from heat. Serve immediately.

SERVING SUGGESTIONS: Dinner rolls ■, whipped potatoes, herbed, buttered string beans, and raisin pound cake.

HOW TO BONE A CHICKEN BREAST

1. Slip fingers between skin and meat and gently, but firmly, pull off skin.

2. With a sharp paring knife, cut meat away from rib bones with little strokes.

3. Continue boning, cutting around and removing small bone at top.

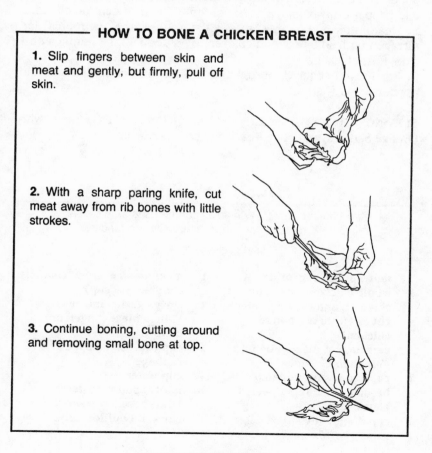

CHICKEN TARRAGON

Makes 4 servings.

2	whole chicken breasts (14 ounces each), split	½	cup chopped leek (white part) Or: ½ cup chopped green onions
2	tablespoons all-purpose flour		
½	teaspoon salt	¼	pound fresh mushrooms, chopped
⅛	teaspoon pepper		
1	tablespoon butter or margarine	½	teaspoon tarragon, crumbled
1	tablespoon vegetable oil	½	cup dry white wine or chicken broth

1. Skin and bone chicken. Flatten slightly between sheets of wax paper with a rolling pin or flat side of meat mallet. Combine flour, salt, and pepper on wax paper. Turn chicken in flour to coat on all sides.
2. Heat butter and oil in a large skillet. Sauté leek, mushrooms, and tarragon until softened. Add chicken to pan. Sauté for 3 minutes on 1 side; turn chicken.
3. Stir in wine; cook 3 more minutes. Taste and add more salt and pepper if you wish.

SERVING SUGGESTIONS: Bread stuffing (for chicken), Beets with Orange Sauce ■, and sliced fresh peaches (or bananas).

CHICKEN STIR-FRY

Any combination of vegetables can be used in this dish;
the secret is to cook them just until crisp-tender.

Makes 5 servings.

4	tablespoons vegetable oil	1	medium-size onion, coarsely chopped (½ cup)
1	whole chicken breast, boned, skinned, and cut into ¾-inch cubes (from a 4-pound chicken)	2	cloves garlic, minced
		1	½-inch piece gingerroot, minced
4	carrots, cut diagonally into ¼-inch-thick slices	1	cup coarsely chopped cabbage
2	cups coarsely chopped broccoli, including peeled stems	1	cup water
		1	tablespoon cornstarch
1	cup diagonally sliced celery	2	tablespoons soy sauce
1	small zucchini, cut into slices	1	chicken bouillon cube

1. Heat 1 tablespoon of the oil in a wok or large skillet over medium-high heat. Add chicken; stir-fry until pieces turn white. Remove with slotted spoon to a small bowl.

2. Add 1 tablespoon of the oil to wok. Add carrots; stir-fry 3 minutes.

3. Add remaining 2 tablespoons oil, the broccoli, celery, zucchini, onion, garlic, and ginger. Stir-fry 3 to 4 minutes until vegetables are crisp-tender. Add chicken and cabbage. Stir-fry until cabbage softens slightly.

4. Mix water and cornstarch in a small bowl until smooth. Add to wok with soy sauce and bouillon cube. Bring to a boil, stirring constantly to dissolve cube; lower heat; simmer 1 minute.

SERVING SUGGESTIONS: Wonton soup, hot cooked rice, and orange sherbet.

CHICKEN WITH HOT PEPPER
(Kung Pao Chi Ting)

This type of dish predominates in the Western region of China where the weather is hot and humid.

Makes 4 servings.

4 chicken legs with thighs (about 2 pounds), skinned and boned	4 tablespoons vegetable oil
1 tablespoon cornstarch	1 large green pepper, halved, seeded, and cut into ½-inch pieces
1 tablespoon soy sauce	1 clove garlic, minced
2 tablespoons water	1 teaspoon crushed red pepper flakes
Sherry Sauce (recipe below)	

1. Cut boned chicken into ½-inch cubes (about 2 cups). Combine cornstarch, soy sauce, and water in a medium-size bowl. Add chicken; toss to coat. Refrigerate at least 30 minutes or up to 24 hours.

2. Prepare Sherry Sauce.

3. Heat a wok or skillet; add oil. Add chicken to wok; stir-fry 2 minutes or until chicken changes color and cubes separate. Return to bowl, using a slotted spoon.

4. Reheat wok; add pepper; stir-fry 2 minutes; add garlic and red pepper flakes. Stir-fry 1 minute.

5. Return chicken to wok; stir Sherry Sauce to combine. Add to chicken; cook and stir until sauce thickens and coats chicken with clear glaze, 1 to 2 minutes.

Sherry Sauce: Combine 1 teaspoon sugar, 1 teaspoon cornstarch, 2 tablespoons soy sauce, 1 tablespoon dry sherry, 1 tablespoon water, and 1 teaspoon vinegar in a cup. Stir well.

SERVING SUGGESTIONS: Hot cooked rice, stir-fried broccoli, and gingered pineapple chunks.

GLAZED CHICKEN WINGS

Makes 6 servings.

12	chicken wings (about 3 pounds)	⅛	teaspoon cayenne pepper
2	tablespoons peanut or vegetable oil	1	cup water
		2	tablespoons soy sauce
1	teaspoon ground ginger	2	tablespoons white vinegar
½	teaspoon ground cinnamon	1	tablespoon sugar
½	teaspoon curry powder		Parsley sprigs (optional)

1. Cut tips from chicken wings and save for soup. Separate each wing at joint.
2. Heat oil in a large skillet; add chicken wing pieces, one third at a time, in a single layer. Brown on both sides, turning once; remove to a bowl. Repeat with remaining pieces. Drain pan drippings into a cup; return 2 tablespoons to skillet.
3. Add ginger, cinnamon, curry, and cayenne to skillet; cook 1 minute. Gradually stir in water, soy sauce, and vinegar. Turn heat to medium; cook for 15 minutes. Add chicken, turning to coat. Lower heat; cover; simmer for 15 minutes. Remove cover; sprinkle with sugar. Turn heat to high. Stir constantly as the sauce becomes syrupy and coats chicken. Serve warm over hot rice. Garnish with parsley, if you wish. To serve cold: Remove from refrigerator about 30 minutes before serving. To reheat: Replace chicken wings in skillet in 1 layer. Add ½ cup water. Turn heat to moderately high and cook, stirring constantly, until wings are hot and sauce has thickenened.

SERVING SUGGESTIONS: Spring rolls, hot cooked rice, stir-fried peppers, and melon.

CHICKEN PRIMAVERA

A quick, easy dinner for 8, cooked in 30 minutes, and in one skillet. Golden-brown pieces of chicken and crisp-tender chunks of vegetables are deliciously seasoned with a light soy-sherry sauce.

Makes 8 servings.

1 broiler-fryer (3 pounds), cut into 8 pieces	2 medium-size zucchini (about ¾ pound)
½ cup all-purpose flour	2 yellow squash (about ¾ pound)
1 teaspoon ground ginger	2 medium-size red peppers
1 teaspoon salt	½ pound fresh mushrooms, sliced
¼ teaspoon pepper	
¼ cup vegetable oil	¼ cup soy sauce
3 cloves garlic, finely chopped	3 tablespoons dry sherry
½ cup chicken broth	½ teaspoon ground ginger
1 pound asparagus spears Or: 1 package (10 ounces) frozen asparagus spears	

1. Shake chicken in a plastic or paper bag with flour, ginger, salt, and pepper until coated.

2. Heat the oil in a large skillet. Fry chicken, turning frequently, about 5 minutes or until golden brown. Add garlic and chicken broth to skillet. Cover; simmer for 15 minutes.

3. Meanwhile, trim, peel, and cut asparagus into 1-inch pieces. (If using frozen, just cut into 1-inch pieces.) Cut zucchini and yellow squash into 1-inch chunks. Halve and seed peppers; cut into 1-inch pieces.

4. Add asparagus, zucchini, squash, red pepper, and mushrooms to skillet. Add soy sauce, sherry, and ginger. Stir gently to mix. Cover; simmer for 10 minutes or until vegetables are crisp-tender.

SERVING SUGGESTIONS: Hot cooked rice, seasonal fresh fruit, and chocolate chip cookies.

SHEARS CAN SAVE $

Invest in good poultry shears. It is cheaper to cut up a whole broiler-fryer at home than to buy chicken parts.

CUTTING A WHOLE CHICKEN

• Whole chickens are the best friend a budget can have. This is especially true when whole birds are "on special" and packed two or three to a bag. Not only its great taste, but its ease of cooking, and low-fat content make it the perfect meat for your family. Chicken also makes for good practice at being a butcher. Start with a good sharp knife and invest in a pair of poultry shears. Follow the simple steps below to cut chickens or small turkeys into your family's favorite parts of the bird.

• Start with a very cold bird. Make a cut with a sharp knife, at one side of the wishbone and up to the neck, pulling skin taut with your fingers as you work.

• Follow knife cut with sharp poultry shears, cutting through bones until bird is split. Remove excess pockets of fat and extra skin; discard.

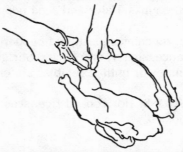

• Turn chicken over and flatten along backbone with palm of hand; make a cut along skin down one side of the backbone with knife, then cut through bone with poultry shears. (Split small birds are great for broiling as are split Rock Cornish hens, when on special. Brush with butter and lemon juice and broil, turning often, for 40 minutes or until tender.)

• Cut along split bird following natural separation of breast and thigh, first with sharp knife, then with poultry shears, to separate chicken into quarters. (Arrange, skin side up, in a shallow roasting pan; sprinkle with seasoned salt and pepper, top with onion rings. Bake at 350° for 1 hour or until chicken is tender)

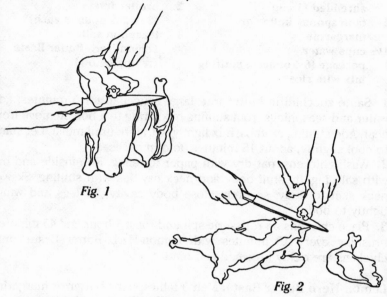

Fig. 1

Fig. 2

• For drumsticks and thighs, first bend leg and thigh quarters; feel with fingers for the joint. Cut through at this point (Fig. 1); separate into drumsticks and thighs. To bone thighs, cut along and against bone, following the direction of the bone.

• To prepare the wings and breast; bend wing and breast quarter and feel with fingers for joint. Cut through at this point (Fig. 2) and separate quarter into wing and breast. Wings are great for stir-fry cooking and also served as an appetizer. To skin halved chicken breasts, slip index finger between skin and meat and pull away skin in one piece with your fingers.

• For chicken cutlets, start at wishbone end and cut with short, quick strokes, using a sharp knife and finger to guide knife away from breast meat. Keep bones for soup kettle and use cutlets in any recipe that calls for veal cutlets. When chicken is on special, it's a great time to make up a batch of cutlets. Just wrap them in heavy-duty aluminum foil, label, date, and freeze. Come party time, you have a supply of budget-pleasing treats.

STUFFED TWIN CHICKENS

Roast on a rotisserie for 1 hour, 45 minutes.
Makes 8 servings.

1 medium-size zucchini, shredded (1 cup)	¾ cup shredded Swiss cheese
2 tablespoons butter or margarine	2 broiler-fryers (2 to 2½ pounds each)*
1½ cups water	1 teaspoon salt
1 package (6½ ounces) stuffing mix with rice	Lemon-Herb Butter Baste (recipe below)

1. Sauté zucchini in butter in a large saucepan for 5 minutes; add water and seasonings from stuffing mix; bring to a boil. Remove from heat. Add stuffing crumbs; mix lightly with fork until moist. Let stand to cool slightly, about 15 minutes; fold in cheese.

2. Wash chickens; pat dry with paper toweling. Rub inside and out with salt. Lightly stuff body and neck cavities with stuffing. Skewer neck skin to body; securely close body cavity; tie legs and wings tightly to body.

3. Place chickens on rotisserie spit and roast 1 hour and 45 minutes, brushing every 15 minutes with Lemon-Herb Butter Baste, until chickens are richly browned and tender.

Lemon-Herb Butter Baste: Melt 3 tablespoons butter or margarine in a small saucepan; add 1 teaspoon grated lemon peel, 2 tablespoons lemon juice, 1 teaspoon Angostura Bitters, and ½ teaspoon basil, crumbled.

SERVING SUGGESTIONS: Whole Wheat and Corn Muffins ■, tossed green salad, and Carrot-Nut Cake ■.

---

*A roasting chicken (4 to 4½ pounds) can be substituted for broiler-fryers. Increase roasting time about 30 minutes. Extra stuffing can be wrapped in aluminum foil and heated on grill.

TO TRUSS POULTRY

Secure neck skin with a metal skewer; push tail into cavity and secure with a metal skewer. Press wings against side of breast and wrap a long piece of cotton twine twice around bird and tie securely; loop a second long piece of twine several times around drumsticks and tie. If poultry is stuffed, be sure to secure opening with small metal skewers and lace closed with twine.

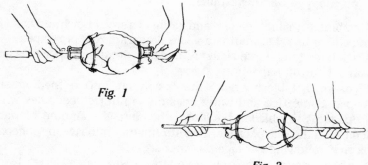

Fig. 1

Fig. 2

POINTS ON ROTISSERIE COOKING

Roasts, chickens, turkeys, and Rock Cornish hens are even more moist and flavorful when cooked over the coals, turning slowly on a rotisserie. In Fig.1 you see how the roast or poultry should balance evenly on the rotisserie rod for even cooking. Fig.2 shows how the holding forks should be inserted securely to prevent the meat from slipping while roasting. Fig.3 illustrates how the gray coals should be piled to the back of the grill with the drip pan directly under the grilling meat or poultry to prevent fat flare-ups that give a burned, rather than a charcoal taste to foods.

Fig. 3

SAVORY CHICKEN LIVERS AND RICE

Makes 4 servings.

¼ cup soy sauce
½ teaspoon ground ginger
1 clove garlic, crushed
¾ pound chicken livers
5 slices bacon
1 cup long-grain rice
½ cup chopped water chestnuts

2 chicken bouillon cubes
Water
¼ cup firmly packed light brown sugar
½ cup chopped green onions, with green tops

1. Combine soy sauce, ginger, and garlic in a small bowl; add chicken livers; stir to mix. Let marinate while preparing rest of recipe.
2. Cook bacon in a large skillet until crisp; drain on paper toweling; crumble. Pour off bacon fat; reserve.
3. Measure 1 tablespoon of the bacon fat into a medium-size saucepan. Sauté rice and water chestnuts until rice becomes white and opaque. Stir chicken bouillon cubes into the amount of water called for on the rice package; then stir mixture into rice in saucepan. Cook rice following package directions.
4. Sprinkle brown sugar onto a square of wax paper. Drain livers, reserving marinade. Roll livers in sugar to coat.
5. Heat 2 tablespoons of the bacon fat in the just-used large skillet; sauté livers until no longer pink, about 5 minutes. Stir in reserved marinade and any sugar remaining on wax paper; heat until piping hot. Spoon rice onto a warm platter; spoon chicken liver mixture over.

SERVING SUGGESTIONS: Broccoli vinaigrette, Baked Acorn Squash Slices ■, and Vanilla Pudding ■.

BIG IS BETTER

When buying turkeys, think big because the prices are lower as the weight goes up. You can cut the whole bird into parts and freeze in meal-size portions. The breast makes an ideal roast; the legs can be roasted or braised for another meal. Freeze the breast or legs for up to 6 months. Or you can roast the whole turkey at once and freeze any leftovers, in meal-size portions, about 3 months.

TURKEY AND CARROT LOAF

Bake at 375° for 1 hour.
Makes 6 servings.

1½ pounds ground turkey	1 teaspoon salt
2¼ cups grated carrots (about 4 medium size)	¼ teaspoon pepper
	1¼ cups dairy sour cream
1 cup chopped parsley	1 chicken bouillon cube
1 small onion, chopped (¼ cup)	¾ cup boiling water
	1 tablespoon all-purpose flour
½ cup packaged bread crumbs	2 tablespoons dry sherry

1. Grease a small, shallow baking pan. Preheat oven to 375°. Combine turkey, 1½ cups of the carrots, ½ cup of the parsley, the onion, bread crumbs, salt, pepper, and 1 cup of the sour cream in a large bowl; mix well.

2. Press one third of the mixture firmly into an 8½ x 4½ x 2½-inch loaf pan. Sprinkle remaining carrots over top. Press half of remaining turkey mixture over carrots; sprinkle with remaining parsley. Top with remaining turkey mixture; press down firmly. Run a metal spatula around sides of pan to loosen. Invert loaf onto prepared baking pan.

3. Bake in a preheated moderate oven (375°) for 1 hour or until golden brown. Transfer loaf to a warm serving platter.

4. Add bouillon cube to boiling water in a cup; stir to dissolve. Sprinkle flour into pan drippings; cook 1 minute. Stir in bouillon mixture. Cook, stirring constantly, until sauce thickens and bubbles. Stir a little of the hot sauce into the remaining ¼ cup sour cream in a small bowl. Return blended mixture to saucepan; stir in sherry. Cook, stirring constantly, just until sauce is hot. Add salt and pepper to taste. Slice turkey loaf; spoon sauce over.

SERVING SUGGESTIONS: Tomato-Orange Soup ■, baked potatoes, buttered string beans, and Mousse de Bananes ■.

COST-PER-SERVING

When you're shopping for meats, poultry, and fish, don't be fooled into thinking that the cheapest price-per-pound is the best value. What really counts is the cost-per-serving. Although a pound of beef round costs more than a pound of spare ribs, the round will provide 4 servings and the ribs only 2.

CALICO BEEF BURGERS

Makes 4 servings.

¾	pound ground chuck	1	egg
1	cup cold cooked potatoes, riced or mashed*	1	tablespoon steak sauce
½	cup shredded carrot	½	teaspoon salt
¼	cup finely chopped green onions	⅛	teaspoon pepper
¼	cup grated Parmesan cheese	4	hamburger buns, split and toasted

1. Combine beef, potato, carrot, onion, cheese, egg, steak sauce, salt, and pepper; mix lightly with a fork and shape into patties.

2. Grill, 4 inches from heat, 6 to 8 minutes per side or until done as you like them. Serve on toasted hamburger buns.

SERVING SUGGESTIONS: Sliced tomatoes on lettuce and Apple Brown Betty.

---

*You may substitute ¾ cup herb-flavored stuffing mix, mixed with 2 tablespoons warm water, for the 1 cup potatoes.

BREADED BURGER CUTLETS WITH SOUR CREAM GRAVY

Bake at 350° for 15 minutes.
Makes 6 servings.

1	pound ground round	1	tablespoon milk
1	small onion, minced (¼ cup)	2	tablespoons butter or margarine
½	teaspoon marjoram, crumbled	2	tablespoons vegetable oil
¼	teaspoon thyme, crumbled		*Gravy:*
¾	teaspoon salt	1	can condensed beef broth
⅛	teaspoon pepper	2	tablespoons all-purpose flour
4	cups soft bread crumbs (8 slices bread)	¼	cup dairy sour cream (at room temperature)
½	cup water		
1	egg		

1. Combine beef, onion, marjoram, thyme, salt, pepper, 1½ cups of the bread crumbs, and the water in a large bowl.

2. Beat egg lightly with milk in a small bowl; spread the remaining 2½ cups crumbs on wax paper. Pinch off about 3 tablepoonfuls of the meat mixture for each cutlet and shape into 2-inch balls. Dip into the egg, then into crumbs, flattening each meatball into an oval cutlet about ⅜ inch thick.

3. Arrange breaded cutlets in a single layer in a shallow baking pan and refrigerate several hours before frying (this is to firm the meat mixture and to help make the breading stick).

4. When ready to cook, remove cutlets from refrigerator. Preheat oven to 350°. Brown the cutlets quickly on both sides in the butter and oil in a large skillet; then arrange in 1 layer in shallow baking pan.

5. Bake, uncovered, in a preheated moderate oven (350°) for 15 minutes.

6. Meanwhile, prepare the Gravy: Combine ⅓ cup of the broth with the 2 tablespoons flour to form a smooth paste. Pour the remaining broth into the skillet and heat and stir 2 to 3 minutes, scraping up browned bits from the bottom of the skillet. Stir in the flour paste and heat, stirring constantly, until thickened and smooth, about 3 minutes. Turn heat to low; stir in the sour cream (do no allow to boil or the gravy may curdle).

7. To serve, arrange the cutlets on a heated platter and pour some of the gravy on top; pass the remaining gravy in a separate bowl.

SERVING SUGGESTIONS: Marinated cucumber salad, whipped potatoes, and fresh grapes.

HOW TO THAW FROZEN MEAT

To thaw frozen ground meat in the refrigerator:
• Remove package from freezer the night before and place in the refrigerator for up to 24 hours. Cook, even if you must then again refreeze in freezer wrap, but *never* refreeze thawed, ground raw meat.

To thaw frozen ground meat in a microwave oven:
• Remove aluminum foil wrapping, if used, and place in a plastic bag or in plastic wrap. Set in a microwave-safe shallow dish.
• Cook in the microwave on low for 3 minutes for each pound of frozen ground meat; turn thawing ground meat over from time to time.
• Remove meat from oven and scrape off all thawed meat and place in a bowl; break up remaining block of frozen ground meat.
• Set microwave on low for 2 to 3 minutes longer, turning and breaking often with a fork.

To get the most from ground meat you buy fresh in your supermarket, here are a few tips:

• Plan to stop at the meat counter of your supermarket just before checking out. Then bring the ground meat home as soon as possible and refrigerate it right away. Once any meat is ground, it becomes more perishable and the longer it is away from refrigeration, the greater the chances of the ground meat spoiling.

• Buy fresh ground meat on the day or the day before you plan to use it; otherwise divide ground meat into patties or serving-size portions and freeze (see below for directions).

• Don't be upset if the inside of your freshly purchased ground meat is darker than the surface. The change in color "bloom," as the butcher calls it, has left the meat because much of the air has ben closed out of the package. Leave the ground meat unwrapped in the refrigerator for a short time and the meat will "bloom" once more.

• To store ground meat overnight, loosen the plastic covering it was packaged in at the supermarket, or remove plastic wrap and re-cover with wax paper. Store in the meat storage drawer or the coldest section of the refrigerator.

• To freeze ground meat, divide ground meat into patties or serving-size portions as soon as you come from the supermarket. Wrap in convenient freezer wrap or freezer-weight plastic wrap, being sure to have a double layer of wrap between patties that will be frozen in the same package for ease of separating later. Label, date, and freeze; plan to use within 1 month of purchase.

• To freeze a large batch of ground meat patties, shape meat into patties and place 1-inch apart on a cookie sheet. Fast-freeze in the coldest part of the freezer. Pack into freezer-weight plastic bags or heavy-duty aluminum foil. Label, date, and return to freezer.

• To cook frozen patties, you can remove the patties from the freezer the night before and thaw in the refrigerator. However, if for some reason your plans change and you don't want to serve the patties the next night, the meat must first be cooked before it can be refrozen. Frozen patties can be cooked but will take a little longer to pan-grill or broil than if using refrigerated ground meat, as indicated by the times given in the recipes. To pan-grill, sprinkle a heavy skillet with salt and heat until pan is very hot; brown frozen patties quickly on both sides; lower heat and cook, turning several times, until meat is done as you like it. To broil, place patties on a rack in a broiler pan and place pan on lower broiling position in broiler; broil 3 to 5 minutes longer than usual on first side, or until surface is browned, then turn and broil until patties are done as you like them.

QUICK BEEF STROGANOFF

Makes 5 servings.

1½ pounds boneless beef rump	¼ cup water
¼ cup (½ stick) margarine	2 beef bouillon cubes
1 medium-size onion, chopped (½ cup)	1 cup dairy sour cream
	1 cup plain yogurt
⅓ cup undrained canned mushroom pieces (½ of a 7-ounce can)	¼ cup all-purpose flour

1. Cut meat diagonally across the grain into ¼-inch-thick strips.
2. Heat 2 tablespoons of the margarine in a large skillet; add half the meat strips; sauté quickly, stirring constantly, until browned on both sides. Remove with a slotted spoon to a plate. Repeat with remaining margarine and meat.
3. Push meat to one side of skillet; add onion. Cook, stirring constantly, until onion is tender. Return first batch of meat to skillet; add undrained mushrooms, water, and bouillon cubes, stirring to dissolve cubes; bring to a boil.
4. Combine sour cream, yogurt, and flour in a small bowl; mix until smooth; stir into a skillet (A whisk works well for this). Bring to a boil; lower heat and simmer for 5 minutes, stirring constantly.

SERVING SUGGESTIONS: Buttered noodles with dill, rye rolls, and poached fruit compote.

MEAT LOAF WITH SHREDDED VEGETABLES

Bake at 350° for 1 hour.
Makes 4 servings.

4	cups packed, shredded cabbage (about a 1-pound head cabbage)	2	eggs
		⅓	cup packaged bread crumbs
		1	teaspoon basil, crumbled
½	cup finely chopped onion (1 medium-size onion)	¼	teaspoon oregano, crumbled
		1	teaspoon salt
3	tablespoons vegetable oil	¼	teaspoon pepper
1	cup packed, shredded carrot (1 medium-size carrot)	¼	cup water
		2	tablespoons white vinegar
1	clove garlic, minced	1	cup packed, shredded potato
½	pound ground round		(1 medium-size potato)

1. Sauté cabbage and onion in oil in a large skillet over medium heat, stirring often, for 5 minutes. Lower heat slightly; continue to sauté until cabbage turns golden brown, about 5 minutes. Add carrot and garlic; sauté until vegetables turn light golden brown, about 5 minutes. Remove from heat; cool to room temperature.

2. Preheat oven to 350°.

3. Combine beef, eggs, bread crumbs, basil, oregano, salt, pepper, water, and vinegar in a large bowl. Add vegetable mixture and shredded potato; mix well. Shape mixture into a loaf about 8 inches long and place in a shallow baking pan. Cover tightly with aluminum foil.

4. Bake in a preheated moderate oven (350°) for 30 minutes. Uncover; bake 30 minutes longer. Let meat loaf rest 15 minutes before slicing.

SERVING SUGGESTIONS: Horseradish cream (for meat loaf), cherry tomatoes, parsleyed potatoes, and Applesauce Cake ■.

EXTEND A MEAT LOAF

Vary your meat loaf mixture by using a variety of extenders. Not only will you lower the cost, but you'll also add interest. Keep your family guessing as to what foods were used: Grated carrots or potatoes, cooked rice, mashed, cooked dried beans, and cooked or raw oatmeal. For even more savings, use the extended meat mixture to stuff vegetables such as cabbage or green peppers.

CHILI CON CARNE

Small cubes of beef cook quickly in this chili.

Makes 4 servings.

¾ pound chuck
(from blade chuck steak)
1 tablespoon vegetable oil
1 medium-size onion, chopped
(½ cup)
¼ cup chopped green pepper
1 large clove garlic, minced

1 tablespoon chili powder
1 cup tomato puree
(from a 29-ounce can)
1 cup water
½ teaspoon salt
½ teaspoon oregano, crumbled
1 can (15 ounces) kidney beans

1. Cut meat into ½-inch cubes. Brown, a few at a time, in oil in a large skillet. Remove cubes with a slotted spoon as they brown. Add onion, green pepper, and garlic; sauté, stirring often, until tender, about 3 minutes. Sprinkle chili powder over mixture; cook and stir 1 minute.
2. Return meat to skillet; add tomatoes, water, salt, and oregano; bring to a boil. Lower heat; cover; simmer 30 minutes, stirring occasionally.
3. Drain beans, reserving about half the liquid. Add beans and reserved liquid to skillet; simmer, uncovered, 15 minutes.

SERVING SUGGESTIONS: Warm cornbread, tossed green salad, and orange custard.

HANDLING GROUND MEAT

Handle ground meat as little as possible to avoid making it too compact and heavy. You'll keep it lighter and juicier if you add a tablespoon or two of cold water or red wine to each pound of meat. If you dip your hands into a bowl of cold water frequently when making meatballs or hamburger patties, the meat won't stick to your hands.

TWO FOR THE PRICE OF ONE

You can often save money by substituting a similar meat for a more expensive type. For instance, you can buy 2 packages of chicken franks for almost the same price as 1 package of beef franks.

PEPPERS 'N' BEEF LIVER

Makes 6 servings

1	pound beef liver	2	large onions, cut into rings
¼	cup all-purpose flour	2	cups water
1	teaspoon salt	2	envelopes or teaspoons
¼	teaspoon pepper		instant beef broth
3	tablespoons vegetable oil	1	tablespoon Worcestershire
2	large peppers, halved,		sauce
	seeded, and cut into large		Peas 'n' Rice (recipe below)
	pieces (one red and		
	one green)		

1. Cut liver into 2-inch pieces; coat with a mixture of flour, salt, and pepper on wax paper.

2. Heat oil in a large skillet; sauté peppers and onion rings until both are soft, but peppers are still bright; remove with slotted spoon; reserve.

3. Cook liver quickly (about 2 minutes), a few pieces at a time, in oil in skillet; remove when done and reserve. Stir in the 2 cups water, instant beef broth, and Worcestershire sauce; bring mixture to bubbling, stirring constantly; return onion rings, peppers, and liver and heat slowly, 2 minutes. Serve with Peas 'n' Rice.

Peas 'n' Rice: Combine 1 cup raw long-grain rice, 2¼ cups water, and 1 teaspoon salt in a medium-size saucepan; bring to a boil; lower heat and cover saucepan. Cook 25 minutes or until rice is tender and water is absorbed; toss with 1 package (10 ounces) frozen peas, cooked, and spoon into a heated serving dish.

SERVING SUGGESTIONS: Tossed green salad and sliced oranges.

STUFF AND "STRETCH"

One of the best ways to "stretch" your meats further is to stuff them with a savory filling. For instance, chicken breasts are great with an herbed rice stuffing; flank steak is zesty with a chili-flavored cornbread stuffing; breast of veal is a gourmet delight with a buttery celery-bread stuffing.

CURRIED LAMB RIBLETS

Broil for 15 minutes.
Makes 4 servings.

2 **pounds breast of lamb**	2 **tablespoons margarine**
1 **small onion**	1 **tablespoon curry powder**
2 **cloves garlic**	½ **cup plain yogurt**
1½ **teaspoons salt**	⅛ **teaspoon pepper**
1 **medium-size onion, chopped**	
(½ cup)	

1. Combine lamb, onion, 1 clove garlic, and 1 teaspoon of the salt in a kettle or Dutch oven; cover; simmer 45 minutes or until tender. remove to a bowl; cool.

2. Mince remaining 1 clove garlic; sauté with chopped onion in margarine in a small skillet until tender, about 3 minutes. Add curry; cook 1 minute longer. Remove from heat; stir in yogurt, remaining ½ teaspoon salt and the pepper. Preheat oven to broil.

3. Cut lamb into 1-rib pieces; place on a rack in a shallow baking pan about 6 inches from the heat. Spread half the curry mixture over the lamb. Broil for 10 minutes. Turn ribs over; brush with remaining curry mixture; broil 5 minutes longer.

SERVING SUGGESTIONS: Hot cooked rice, Beets with Orange Sauce ■, and lemon sherbet.

GRAVY TIPS

• If you do not have bottled gravy browner on hand, just use a little liquid coffee. A few tablespoons will give your gravy an appealing brown color. No one will be the wiser because the coffee taste will not come through.

• Don't throw out leftover gravy! Freeze it in an ice cube tray and then transfer to a container in your freezer. The gravy cubes are convenient to use and can be defrosted quickly when you need to perk up meat.

CREOLE-STYLE HAM AND RICE

A quick and easy skillet meal of ham and rice with tomatoes and green peppers.

Makes 4 servings.

1 package (6 ounces) sliced, cooked ham	1½ cups long-grain rice
2 tablespoons vegetable oil or bacon fat	1 can (1 pound) tomatoes
1 medium-size onion, chopped (½ cup)	1 can (13¾ ounces) chicken broth
1 medium-size green pepper, halved, seeded, and cut into strips	1 bay leaf
	½ teaspoon salt
	½ teaspoon thyme, crumbled
1 clove garlic, minced	4 drops liquid red pepper seasoning

1. Sauté ham slices in oil in a large skillet until lightly browned. Remove ham to a plate. Stir onion, green pepper, garlic, and rice into oil remaining in skillet. Sauté, stirring often, until vegetables are just tender, about 3 minutes.

3. Stir in tomatoes and their liquid, breaking them up with a spoon. Stir in broth, bay leaf, salt, thyme, and red pepper seasoning. Bring to a boil; lower heat; cover. Simmer for 15 minutes. Return ham to skillet. Continue cooking, covered, until rice is tender and liquid is absorbed, about 20 minutes. Remove bay leaf.

SERVING SUGGESTIONS: Lima Beans with Bacon■ and fresh (or canned) apricots.

GINGERY BAKED HAM AND BEANS

Bake at 400° for 1 hour, 30 minutes.
Makes 6 servings.

2 cans (1 pound, 5 ounces each) baked beans	½ teaspoon dry mustard
	½ teaspoon ground ginger
1 cup diced leftover baked ham	1 medium-size onion, thinly sliced
1 envelope onion soup mix	
½ cup molasses	1 lemon, thinly sliced

1. Preheat oven to 400°.
2. Combine beans, ham, soup mix, molasses, dry mustard, and ginger in an 8-cup baking dish. Arrange onion slices evenly on top.
3. Bake, uncovered, in a preheated hot oven (400°) for 1 hour; stir onion slices down into beans; bake 15 minutes longer. Arrange lemon slices on top; bake another 15 minutes.

SERVING SUGGESTIONS: Coleslaw, Boston brown bread, and spiced baked apples.

MEXICALI PORK CHOPS

Bake at 350° for 30 minutes.
Makes 6 servings.

6	thin pork chops (about 1¾ pounds)	1	package (10 ounces) frozen whole kernel corn
1	tablespoon vegetable oil	3	cups boiling water
2	small green peppers	¾	teaspoon salt
1	medium-size onion, chopped (½ cup)	¼	teaspoon pepper
1	clove garlic, minced	2	envelopes instant chicken broth
1½	cups long-grain rice		

1. Preheat oven to 350°. Brown pork chops in oil in a large skillet; remove with a slotted spatula and set aside. Cut a few thin rings from peppers; seed, and coarsely chop remainder.
2. Sauté chopped peppers, onion, and garlic in fat remaining in skillet until tender, about 3 minutes. Combine sautéed vegetables and rice in a large, shallow baking dish; stir in corn. Add boiling water, salt, pepper, and instant chicken broth; stir to mix. Arrange pork chops and pepper rings on top; cover.
3. Bake in a preheated moderate oven (350°) for 30 minutes or until chops and rice are tender.

SERVING SUGGESTIONS: Cornbread, tossed green salad, and Apricot-Yogurt Whip ■.

SAUSAGE AND APPLE SKILLET

Makes 4 servings.

1	package (1 pound) pork sausage links	1	can (6 ounces) apple juice
2	large onions, sliced	1	teaspoon cornstarch
1	can (1 pound, 4 ounces) pie-sliced apples, undrained		

1. Cook sausages in a large skillet, over low heat until lightly browned, about 10 minutes or until no longer pink. Remove sausages to a plate. Pour off all but 2 tablespoons fat from skillet.

2. Sauté onion slices in fat in skillet until tender, about 5 minutes. Stir in apples and sausages. Stir a small amount of apple juice into cornstarch in a cup; blend well. Stir mixture into skillet; stir in remaining apple juice. Cook over low heat, stirring often, for 5 minutes or until sauce is slightly thickened and sausages are heated through.

SERVING SUGGESTIONS: Marinated cucumber salad, buttered noodles, and lemon pound cake.

BRATWURST AND ONIONS IN BEER

Grill sausages 10 minutes.
Makes 8 servings.

8	bratwursts (two 12-ounce packages)	½	teaspoon salt
3	medium-size onions, sliced	1	can (12 ounces) beer
2	tablespoons vegetable oil	8	frankfurter rolls, split and toasted
1	teaspoon caraway seeds, crushed		

1. Brown bratwursts on a grill close to grayed coals, about 10 minutes.

2. While sausages brown, sauté onions in oil in a large saucepan on grill for 2 to 3 minutes; stir in caraway seeds, salt, and beer; and bring to a boil. Add sausages; cover and keep saucepan on side of grill to heat for at least 10 minutes. Serve on toasted frankfurter folls.

SERVING SUGGESTIONS: Dilled Potato and Apple Salad ■ and peach kuchen.

SAUSAGE AND CHICKEN LIVERS EN BROCHETTE

Grill about 6 to 8 minutes.
Makes 4 servings.

½ pound chicken livers, washed and halved

1 package (8 ounces) brown-and-serve sausages, cut in half

3 slices bacon, cut into 1½-inch pieces

1 red apple, quartered, cored, and cut into chunks

1 bunch green onions, cut into 2-inch pieces

2 tablespoons soy sauce

2 tablespoons Worcestershire sauce

1 tablespoon lemon juice

¼ teaspoon thyme, crumbled

1. Alternate pieces of liver, sausage, bacon, apple, and onion on skewers.

2. Combine soy and Worcestershire sauces, lemon juice, and thyme in a small cup.

3. Grill skewers on a grill 5 to 6 inches from grayed coals for 6 to 8 minutes or until cooked through. Turn and brush often with soy sauce mixture.

SERVING SUGGESTIONS: Celery and rice salad and pear cobbler.

COLORFUL KABOBS

You can get away with using a smaller amount of meat in your kabobs if you choose colorful vegetables to alternate with the meat. When your skewers are studded with cubes of green pepper, cherry tomatoes, parboiled carrot chunks, and zucchini slices, the effect will be stunning and attention will be diverted from the fact that only a small amount of meat was used. Brush with a zesty sauce and serve on a bed of tasty rice and everyone will be happy.

BARBECUE SAFETY

• Never use a charcoal grill in your home or garage; indoors, only use equipment especially designed for indoor use.
• Set the grill in an open area on level ground. Check for stability before lighting the fire. Be extra cautious on windy days.

BAVARIAN SKILLET SUPPER

Chicken hot dogs are found right in the meat department, next to the regular frankfurters—they taste the same, but cost a lot less.

Makes 6 servings.

1	package (1 pound) chicken frankfurters	2	tablespoons light brown sugar
2	tablespoons margarine	1	package (10 ounces) frozen lima beans
1	large onion, sliced		
1	clove garlic, minced	½	cup beer or beef broth
1	can (1 pound, 13 ounces) sauerkraut, drained		Parsleyed Potatoes (recipe below)
1	teaspoon caraway seeds		

1. Score each frank, then cut into thirds and brown quickly in margarine in a large skillet; remove with a slotted spoon and reserve. Sauté onion and garlic until soft; stir in drained sauerkraut, caraway seeds, brown sugar, and lima beans and toss to coat well. Place franks on top; pour beer over; cover.

2. Cook over low heat for 30 minutes or until flavors are blended. Arrange Parsleyed Potatoes in a ring around edge of skillet.

Parsleyed Potatoes: Pare and boil 6 medium-size potatoes in salted boiling water in a large saucepan for 25 minutes or until tender when pierced with fork; drain water from pan. Return potatoes in saucepan to burner and toss over low heat for 3 minutes. Roll in ¼ cup chopped parsley.

SERVING SUGGESTIONS: Tomato juice, rye rolls, and sliced fresh fruit.

SPECIAL ROTISSERIE TIPS

• If the electric rotisserie cord on a charcoal grill has an ordinary two-prong plug, place the grill on a non-conductive surface—never on damp concrete or grass. Even when a three-prong plug is provided, extension cords should be the same three-wire type.

FRANKFURTERS MEXICAN STYLE

Makes 8 servings (2 frankfurters per serving).

1	medium-size onion, chopped (½ cup)	2	packages (1 pound each) frankfurters
2	tablespoons vegetable shortening	16	tortillas, frozen or canned Chili Sauce (recipe below)
1	can (1 pound) red kidney beans		Shredded lettuce Shredded Cheddar cheese

1. Sauté onion in shortening in a medium-size skillet on a grill over grayed coals for 5 minutes or just until soft. Add beans and mash with the back of a wooden spoon. Continue cooking, stirring often, until thickened and heated through; keep warm.

2. Score frankfurters; grill 3 to 4 inches from grayed coals until heated through, about 10 minutes.

3. While frankfurters grill, heat tortillas on grill, turning with tongs, about 1 minute on each side.

4. For each taco, spread 1 tablespoon bean mixture on a tortilla, top with frankfurter, Chilli Sauce, lettuce, and cheese; roll up and serve hot.

Chili Sauce: Combine one 8-ounce can tomatoes, ¼ cup chopped onion, 2 to 3 tablespoons chopped green chili (from a 4-ounce can), ½ teaspoon salt, and ¼ teaspoon oregano in a small saucepan; bring to a boil while crushing tomatoes with the back of a spoon. Serve hot or cold.

THE FIRE

• The safest way to start a fire is to spread charcoal over lighted wood shavings or kindling. There are also commercially available products that are quite safe when used as directed—electric starters with the UL Label and "treated" solid starters.

• To freshen a fire, place more charcoal briquets around those already smoldering.

• We don't recommend liquid starters; however, if you prefer them, never use them once the fire is started, even if it appears to be out.

ITALIAN FIESTA SAUSAGES

Grill 20 to 30 minutes.
Makes 8 servings.

1½ pounds Italian-style
   sausages, sweet or hot
   (8 to 10 sausages)
2 medium-size zucchini, split
   lengthwise, then halved
2 small red peppers, quartered
   and seeded

1 small onion, peeled and
   halved
½ cup Italian or oil and vinegar
   salad dressing

1. Alternate sausages, zucchini, and peppers on skewers; thread ½ onion on the end of each skewer; brush generously with salad dressing.
2. Grill about 5 inches from heat over grayed coals, turning skewers often and brushing with dressing, for 20 minutes or until sausages are cooked through.

SERVING SUGGESTIONS: Crisp hard rolls, tomato-lettuce salad, and raisin bar cookies.

GRILLED KNACKWURST WITH FRUIT GLAZE

Grill 10 to 15 minutes.
Makes 8 servings.

6 tablespoons grape jelly
3 tablespoons bottled chili
   sauce
1 tablespoon prepared
   mustard

¼ teaspoon ground cloves
1 pound knackwurst, Polish
   sausage, or frankfurters,
   scored

1. Heat jelly, chili sauce, mustard, and cloves in a small saucepan, stirring occasionally, just until smooth.
2. Grill sausages about 5 inches from grayed coals, brushing often with glaze, just until heated through, 10 to 15 minutes.

SERVING SUGGESTIONS: Cabbage-carrot salad, potato salad, and beer.

8
Fish

F ish is an ideal protein food because it's packed with nutrients, yet it's low in calories and fat. If you've shied away from it because you thought it was too expensive, just look at our recipes. You'll find lots of inexpensive, tasty, and imaginative ways to use fish.

FRESH, FROZEN, OR CANNED FISH

If you live near the sea, you're probably able to buy fresh fish. Fish fillets are usually more expensive than whole fish, but remember there's less work and no waste when you buy them; 1 pound serves 4.

If you're not a coastal dweller, don't forget frozen and canned fish; they're less expensive than fresh fish and available in a multitude of delicious preparations:

- Fish sticks and cakes are pre-breaded, ready to be baked or fried.
- Uncooked fillets come packaged in blocks; cut off as much as you

want, then return the remainder to the freezer before it thaws. Cod, flounder, and haddock are thrifty choices.

● Canned fish, such as sardines, tuna, and salmon, is already cooked; serve it hot or cold.

MEDITERRANEAN FILLETS

Broil for 5 minutes.
Makes 4 servings.

¼	cup vegetable oil	4	fresh, or frozen and thawed, fish fillets (about 1 pound)
2	tablespoons lemon juice		
1	teasoon oregano, crumbled		Salt and pepper

1. Preheat broiler. Cover broiling rack with aluminum foil; pierce foil with a fork in several places. Place rack in a broiler pan or on a jelly roll pan. This will allow for drainage of fat and juices and prevent a flare up in broiler.
2. Combine oil, lemon juice, and oregano; thoroughly coat fish fillets. Transfer fillets to broiling rack. Sprinkle fish with salt and pepper. Broil about 5 minutes or until fish barely flakes.

SERVING SUGGESTIONS: Stuffed Tomatoes, coleslaw, and anise biscotti.

DANISH FISH BAKE

Frozen fish fillets are poached in milk, then topped with buttery crumbs and sour cream.

Bake at 350° for 40 minutes.
Makes 6 servings.

2	packages (1 pound each) frozen cod	2	tablespoons butter or margarine
¼	cup all-purpose flour	2	teaspoons dillweed
2	teaspoons salt	1	cup dairy sour cream
¼	teaspoon pepper	1	lemon, sliced
1	cup milk		Parsley
2	cups coarse fresh bread crumbs (4 slices bread)		

1. Preheat oven to 350°. Cut frozen fillets into serving-size pieces with a sharp knife; coat with a mixture of flour, salt, and pepper. Arrange in a single layer in a 6-cup shallow casserole; pour milk over. Do not cover.

2. Bake in a moderate preheated oven (350°) for 30 minutes.

3. Toast crumbs lightly in butter in a small skillet. Stir dill into sour cream. Remove fish from oven; spoon cream mixture over; top with toasted crumbs.

4. Bake 10 minutes longer or until sour cream is set. Garnish with lemon slices and parsley.

SERVING SUGGESTIONS: Buttered sliced beets, rye rolls, and fruit tarts.

OVEN "FRIED" FISH FILLETS

Bake at 475° for 8 minutes.
Makes 4 servings.

1	pound frozen flounder or sole fillets, thawed	1¼	teaspoons lemon (or lime) juice
2	tablespoons plain low-fat yogurt	¼	cup packaged bread crumbs
1	tablespoon polyunsaturated oil	1	teaspoon seasoned salt
		½	teaspoon pepper
			Paprika (optional)

1. Preheat oven to 475°. Spray a nonstick cookie sheet or shallow baking pan liberally with cooking spray (or wipe with vegetable oil).

2. Combine yogurt, oil, and juice in a shallow dish; mix well. Sprinkle bread crumbs on wax paper.

3. Dip fillets in the yogurt mixture, then press into the crumbs, lightly coating both sides.

4. Arrange fish in a single layer on the cookie sheet. Sprinkle with salt, pepper, and paprika, if using.

5. Bake fish, uncovered, in a preheated very hot oven (475°) for 8 minutes (or longer, depending on thickness of the fillets). Do not turn fillets. Fish is done when coating is golden and fish flakes easily. Remove fish with a spatula.

SERVING SUGGESTIONS: Sliced tomatoes, Stir-Fried Broccoli ■, and sliced peaches.

LINGUINE AND CLAM SAUCE

Makes 4 servings.

1	package (8 ounces) linguine or thin spaghetti	2	cans (7 ounces each) chopped clams
¼	cup olive or vegetable oil	1	teaspoon salt
¼	cup (½ stick) butter or magarine	¼	teaspoon freshly ground pepper
1	large onion, chopped (1 cup)	½	cup grated Parmesan cheese
2	cloves garlic, minced	¼	cup chopped parsley

1. Bring 3 quarts of water to a boil in a large, covered kettle. Cook pasta following package directions; drain and return pasta to kettle.
2. While pasta cooks, heat oil and butter in a medium-size saucepan; sauté onion and garlic until soft; add clams and liquid, salt, and pepper. Heat slowly, just until hot.
3. Add clam sauce, Parmesan cheese, and parsley to pasta in kettle. Toss over *very low heat* for 2 minutes or until well blended.

SERVING SUGGESTIONS: Herbed string beans, warm Italian bread, fresh fruit, and almond macaroons.

SPAGHETTI WITH CLAM SAUCE

Makes 4 servings

1	package (1 pound) spaghetti	½	cup light cream (optional)
⅓	cup olive or vegetable oil	1	tablespoon butter or margarine
1	clove garlic, halved		Freshly grated Parmesan cheese
1	can (7 ounces) minced clams		
1	tablespoon chopped parsley	1	egg (optional)
	Freshly ground pepper		
½	teaspoon oregano, crumbled		

1. Bring 4 to 6 quarts of salted water to a boil in a large, covered kettle.
2. Heat oil in a medium-size saucepan and sauté garlic, mashing into oil until golden and fragrant; remove garlic and discard.

3. Drain liquid from clams into saucepan; add parsley, pepper, and oregano; heat until bubbling; allow to bubble until liquid is reduced.
4. When spaghetti water starts to boil, add a few tablespoons oil and spaghetti; cook following package directions; drain, return to kettle.
5. Add clams and cream to saucepan; simmer until sauce thickens slightly.
6. Toss spaghetti with butter, Parmesan cheese, and raw egg until well coated; add clam-cream sauce and toss until well coated; pour into heated a serving dish.

SERVING SUGGESTIONS: Breadstick Bundles ∎, fried zucchini slices, and Elegant and Easy Peach Dessert ∎.

SEAFOOD PILAF

Bake at 350° for 40 minutes.
Makes 6 servings.

½ cup frozen chopped onion	2½ cups water
1 tablespoon olive or vegetable oil	1 package (1 pound) frozen flounder or haddock fillets
1 package (6 ounces) curried rice mix	1 package (9 ounces) frozen cut green beans

1. Preheat oven to 350°. Sauté onion in oil until soft in a large flame-proof casserole or ovenproof skillet; stir in rice and contents of the seasoning packet. Cook over low heat, stirring constantly, just until rice is golden.
2. Stir in water; bring to a boil.
3. Cut fish into 1-inch cubes with sharp knife; stir into rice along with green beans; bring to a boil; cover.
4. Bake in a preheated moderate oven (350°) for 40 minutes or until rice is tender and liquid is absorbed.

SERVING SUGGESTIONS: Tangy Cucumber Salad ∎, Whole Wheat and Corn Muffins ∎, and Apricot-Glazed Peach Cake ∎.

SURFSIDE CASSEROLE

Bake at 375° for 20 minutes.
Makes 6 servings.

1 package (1 pound) frozen pollock fish fillets	2 teaspoons prepared mustard
¼ cup (½ stick) butter or margarine	1 package (9 ounces) frozen French green beans with toasted almonds
1 teaspoon salt	3 cups *cooked* macaroni
1½ cups milk	4 slices Swiss cheese, cut into triangles
⅓ cup all-purpose flour	(from an 8-ounce package)
½ cup cold water	

1. Cut fillets into 1-inch pieces with a sharp knife. Sauté fish with butter and salt for 15 minutes in a large skillet. Remove from pan with a slotted spoon and reserve. Preheat oven to 375°.

2. Add milk to liquid in pan and bring to a boil. Combine flour and water in a cup to make a paste; blend into milk and cook, stirring constantly, until sauce thickens. Stir in mustard, frozen beans, macaroni, and fish. Pour into a 12-cup shallow casserole.

3. Bake in a preheated moderate oven (375°) for 15 minutes or until bubbly hot; remove from oven; arrange cheese on top; return to oven, just until cheese melts.

SERVING SUGGESTIONS: Tossed green salad, buttered broccoli, and spiced stewed plums.

THAWING FROZEN FISH

Don't thaw frozen fish at room temperature because your fish will develop a soggy texture and you risk flavor deterioration. The most effective way to thaw fish is in the refrigerator, wrapped, just until the portions can be separated easily. Drain the thawed fish, blot dry with paper toweling, and use immediately.

TUNA SUPPER BAKE

Bake at 350° for 30 minutes.
Makes 4 servings.

2 packages (10 ounces each) frozen chopped spinach, cooked and drained
1 can (7 ounces) tuna, drained and flaked
2 hard-cooked eggs, shelled and chopped
1 teaspoon mixed Italian herbs, crumbled
1 can condensed Cheddar cheese soup
2 medium-size tomatoes, sliced
1 cup fresh white bread crumbs (2 slices bread)
2 tablespoons melted butter or margarine

1. Spread spinach in the bottom of a 6-cup shallow casserole. Combine tuna, chopped eggs, and mixed Italian herbs in a small bowl; add half of the canned soup and mix. Preheat oven to 350°.
2. Arrange halved tomato slices on spinach in a ring and spoon tuna-egg mixture inside ring; top with dollops of remaining canned soup. Toss bread crumbs with melted butter and sprinkle on top.
3. Bake in a preheated moderate oven (350°) for 30 minutes or until casserole is bubbly hot and crumbs are golden.

SERVING SUGGESTIONS: Tossed green salad, Herb-Onion Rolls ■, and Carrot-Nut Cake ■.

CHOOSING CANNED TUNA

Tuna is one of the most popular types of canned fish. It's available packed in water or oil, as either solid-pack (the fanciest and most expensive), chunk-style, or flaked. Don't pay more than you have to buying a fancier type than you need. For many recipes, such as sandwich spreads and dips, flaked tuna (the least expensive) will work just fine. The oil drained from tuna can be used in a tossed salad.

TUNA PIZZA

A pizza that's sure to please the entire family, including the children.

Bake at 450° for 25 minutes.
Makes 6 servings.

Cornmeal
1 frozen pizza pie shell
(14 inches)
Or: ⅓ canister (18.7
ounces) pizza crust mix
1 medium-size onion, chopped
(½ cup)
1 tablespoon vegetable oil
2 cans (8 ounces each)
tomato sauce
1½ teaspoons oregano,
crumbled
¼ teaspoon salt

¼ teaspoon pepper
1 can (7 ounces) oil-packed
tuna, undrained
1 can (3¼ ounces) pitted black
olives, drained and sliced
(½ cup)
1 medium-size green pepper,
halved, seeded, and cut into
strips
4 ounces thinly sliced
mozzarella cheese
¼ cup grated Parmesan cheese

1. Grease a 14-inch pizza pan; sprinkle with cornmeal. Preheat oven to 450°.
2. Place frozen pizza shell on prepared pan. Or prepare dough from pizza crust mix following package directions; place on pan.
3. Bake shell in a preheated very hot oven (450°) for 10 minutes; remove on pan to a wire rack.
4. Sauté the chopped onion in oil in a medium-size saucepan until tender, about 3 minutes. Stir in tomato sauce, oregano, salt, and pepper. Cook, stirring constantly, until mixture is thick, about 5 minutes. Cool slightly.
5. Spread the tomato mixture over the partially baked crust. Arrange the tuna, some of the olives, and the green pepper strips over the sauce. Place the mozzarella slices in the center of the pie; garnish with the remaining olives; sprinkle with Parmesan cheese.
6. Bake in a preheated very hot oven (450°) for 15 minutes or until crust is browned and topping is piping hot.

SERVING SUGGESTIONS: Tossed green salad and watermelon (or other seasonal fruit).

TUNA-RICE CROQUETTES

Makes 6 servings.

1 medium-size onion, chopped (½ cup)	¼ teaspoon pepper
2 tablespoons butter or margarine	1 can (7 ounces) tuna, drained and flaked
3 tablespoons all-purpose flour	2 cups *cooked* rice
½ cup milk	2 teaspoons lemon juice
2 teaspoons salt	2 tablespoons water
1 teaspoon dry mustard	1 egg, slightly beaten
	1½ cups dry bread crumbs
	Oil for frying

1. Sauté onion in butter until soft in a medium-size saucepan. Blend in flour and cook, stirring constantly, until mixture bubbles for 1 minute.

2. Add milk, salt, dry mustard, and pepper. Cook, stirring constantly, until sauce bubbles for 3 minutes; remove from heat. Add tuna, rice, and lemon juice. Chill at least 2 hours.

3. Form mixture into 12 patties. Mix water and egg in a pie plate with a fork. Dip tuna patties into egg mixture. Roll in crumbs on wax paper. Chill for 15 minutes to dry.

4. Heat a 1-inch depth of oil to 375° on a deep-fat frying thermometer in a large skillet. (A 1-inch square of white bread will brown in 50 seconds.) Fry tuna patties until a delicate brown on each side.* Drain on paper towels. Serve with a sharp mustard sauce or tartar sauce if you wish.

SERVING SUGGESTIONS: Spinach, Chick-pea, and Mushroom Salad ■ and fresh fruit salad.

---

*To oven-fry croquettes, place on a 15 x 10 x 1-inch baking pan. Drizzle with 3 tablespoons melted butter or margarine and bake in a very hot oven (450°) for 15 minutes or until brown.

SALMON SUPREME

Bake at 400° for 15 minutes.
Makes 6 servings.

1 can (7 ounces) salmon	Few drops liquid red pepper
3 tablespoons butter or	seasoning
margarine	2 packages (10 ounces each)
3 tablespoons all-purpose	frozen spinach, cooked and
flour	drained
1 teaspoon salt	1 cup shredded Cheddar
1 teaspoon dry mustard	cheese (4 ounces)
1½ cups milk	

1. Drain salmon, reserving liquid. Flake fish into a small bowl, discarding any small bones and skin.

2. Melt butter in a medium-size saucepan. Blend in flour, salt, and dry mustard; stir in milk, salmon liquid, and red pepper seasoning. Cook, stirring constantly, until sauce thickens and bubbles for 3 minutes. Fold in flaked salmon.

3. Spoon cooked spinach into 6 individual casseroles. Fill with salmon mixture; top with shredded cheese. (Casseroles can be covered and refrigerated at this point if you wish.)

4. Preheat oven to 400°. Bake in a preheated hot oven (400°) for 15 minutes or until bubbly hot.

SERVING SUGGESTIONS: Marinated sliced tomatoes, buttered noodles, and lemon pound cake.

9

Vegetables

As you can see from the growing number of greengrocers and the ever-expanding size of the vegetable section of your supermarket, vegetables have become increasingly popular. If you haven't been a vegetable fan, let this chapter tempt you with Eggplant Parmesan, Stir-Fried Broccoli, and Sour Cream Potato Pancakes. And learn how to salvage limp vegetables, what to do with celery leaves, and how to use potato skins as a tasty hors d'oeuvre.

VEGETABLE TECHNIQUES

● To preserve the nutrients and flavor of vegetables, steam rather than boil them, just until vegetables are crisp-tender. (Cut large vegetables, such as beets, into small pieces first.) The inexpensive fan-shaped steamers that fit any pot, are ideal for this purpose.
● To bring out the bright color in raw vegetables, such as carrots, string beans, or broccoli, use a quick-blanch method: Drop vegetables into a large pot of boiling water for 10 to 20 seconds. Drain off water and immediately plunge vegetables into a bowl of ice water. Drain and

pat dry. These colorful, crisp vegetables can then be used in salads or for crudités. Or reheat them in a skillet with seasonings and butter and oil.

● Many vegetables are a great nutritional buy—especially the dark green leafy or deep yellow type, which are rich in vitamin A and minerals. Some of these vegetables, such as broccoli, spinach, and green peppers, offer generous amounts of vitamin C as well. For a change of pace, try other vegetables rich in vitamin A and C—kale and collard, mustard, and turnip greens.

● If your fresh vegetables have gone limp, use them to flavor soups, stuffings, and stews. Or cook soft vegetables and turn them into a puree—minted pureed carrots or spinach puree with nutmeg—delicious!

● Enliven leftover cooked vegetables by marinating them for a salad.

● Add crunch and color to sandwiches by tucking in some slices of raw vegetables; try radishes, zucchini, green pepper, or cucumbers.

● To save the most money, comparison-shop among the frozen, canned, and fresh varieties of vegetables. The best buy changes according to the season of the year. The best guide is to buy whatever form is cheapest per serving. When buying frozen vegetables, remember that the least expensive are those in poly bags. Shake out only the amount of vegetables needed.

BAKED ACORN SQUASH SLICES

Bake at 400° for 50 minutes.
Makes 4 servings.

1	acorn squash (about 2 pounds)	3	tablespoons butter or margarine, melted
½	cup orange juice	1	teaspoon salt
¼	cup firmly packed light brown sugar		

1. Preheat oven to 400°. Cut squash into ¾-inch-thick crosswise slices; remove seeds. Arrange slices in a shallow baking dish.

2. Combine orange juice, sugar, butter, and salt in a cup; blend well. Pour over squash slices.

3. Bake in a preheated hot oven (400°) for 50 minutes or until tender.

EGGPLANT PARMESAN

Bake at 375° for 40 minutes.
Makes 6 servings.

1	large eggplant (about 1½ pounds) Salt
2	eggs
1	tablespoon water
½	cup all-purpose flour
⅓	cup vegetable oil
2	cups shredded mozzarella cheese (8 ounces)
½	cup grated Parmesan cheese Marinara Sauce (recipe below)

1. Cut unpeeled eggplant lengthwise into ¼-inch slices; sprinkle lightly with salt. Let stand 1 hour; squeeze to extract liquid.
2. Preheat oven to 375°. Beat eggs with water in a shallow dish until frothy. Dip eggplant first in flour, then in egg mixture.
3. Sauté eggplant in 2 tablespoons of the oil in a large skillet until lightly browned on both sides; drain on paper toweling. Repeat with remaining eggplant and oil until all slices are browned.
4. Spoon ½ cup Marinara Sauce over bottom of a 13x9x2-inch baking dish. Sprinkle mozzarella cheese evenly over slices; sprinkle with 2 tablespoons of the Parmesan cheese. Spoon a little Marinara Sauce on each slice. Roll up eggplant from narrow ends, jelly roll fashion.
5. Place eggplant rolls in sauce, seam side down. Spoon remaining sauce over top; sprinkle with remaining Parmesan cheese.
6. Bake in a preheated moderate oven (375°) for 40 minutes.

Marinara Sauce: Sauté 1 large chopped onion in 1 tablespoon vegetable oil until tender. Add 1 can (2 pounds, 3 ounces) tomatoes, ½ teaspoon crumbled basil, and ¼ teaspoon *each* salt and pepper. Bring to a boil; stir to break up tomatoes. Lower heat; simmer, uncovered, about 30 minutes or until sauce is reduced to about 2¼ cups.

Discover the versatility of a grapefruit knife and use it to hollow out vegetables such as eggplant, tomatoes, zucchini, or yellow squash. Then stuff vegetables with a savory, but inexpensive rice or kasha mixture.

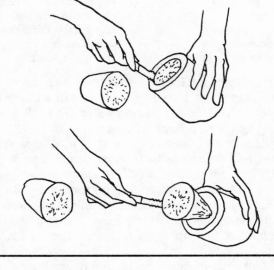

BEETS WITH ORANGE SAUCE

Makes 4 servings.

2	**large oranges**	**Dash ground nutmeg**
1	**tablespoon cornstarch**	**Dash pepper**
2	**to 3 large beets, cooked, drained, skinned, and sliced**	

1. Grate 1 teaspoon orange rind; reserve. Squeeze 1 cup juice.

2. Combine orange juice with cornstarch in a medium-size saucepan. Cook, stirring constantly, until mixture thickens and bubbles. Add beets, nutmeg, pepper, and reserved orange rind. Heat until piping hot.

STIR-FRIED BROCCOLI

To make this dish company fare, add 4 ounces of
sliced fresh mushrooms.

Makes 4 servings.

1 bunch broccoli	**½ clove garlic, minced**
2 teaspoons vegetable oil	**⅛ teaspoon ground ginger**
2 teaspoons margarine	
1 medium-size onion, chopped (½ cup)	

1. Trim broccoli; split stems; cut into 2-inch lengths. Break off flowerets; split if large.

2. Heat oil and margarine in a large skillet. Add garlic and gently sauté. Add broccoli and onion; sprinkle with ginger. Stir-fry over medium heat until broccoli is just tender. Add a small amount of water to keep from sticking if necessary.

CUTTING VEGETABLES

A sharp chef's knife works best to slice broccoli, cauliflower, carrots, celery, and other vegetables into very thin slices for stir-fry dishes.

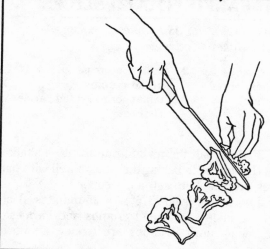

SOUR CREAM POTATO PANCAKES (Latkes)

Sour cream makes these pancakes extra light and tangy.

Makes about 2½ dozen pancakes.

2 pounds Idaho potatoes (about 3 large)	½ cup *sifted* all-purpose flour
2 eggs	¼ teaspoon baking powder
1 small onion, grated (¼ cup)	1 teaspoon salt
1 cup (8 ounces) dairy sour cream	¼ teaspoon white pepper
	Vegetable oil for frying
	Cranapple sauce

1. Pare potatoes; shred coarsely into a large bowl of cold water. Drain, then rinse in cold running water. Squeeze firmly in clean linen toweling to remove as much water as possible.
2. Beat eggs in a large bowl until frothy. Add potatoes, onion, sour cream, flour, baking powder, salt, and pepper; stir.
3. Heat a ¼-inch depth of oil in a large skillet. Drop potato mixture by tablespoonsful into hot oil (add more oil as needed); flatten with pancake turner to make an even thickness. Brown on one side (about 5 to 6 minutes); turn and brown other side. Drain on paper toweling. Serve warm with cranapple sauce.

BUTTERED BAKED POTATO SLICES

Bake at 375° for 35 minutes.
Makes 4 servings.

½ cup (1 stick) butter, melted	2 tablespoons packaged bread crumbs
4 small Idaho potatoes, pared and sliced ½ inch thick	2 tablespoons grated Parmesan cheese
1 teaspoon salt	
¼ teaspoon pepper	

1. Preheat oven to 375°. Pour half the melted butter into a shallow baking dish; place sliced potatoes in baking dish; baste well with part of the remaining butter; sprinkle with salt and pepper.
2. Bake in a preheated moderate oven (375°) for 25 minutes. Baste with remaining butter. Sprinkle with bread crumbs and Parmesan cheese and continue baking until potatoes are tender, about 10 minutes.

POTATO POINTERS

• Potatoes are one of the least expensive vegetables and offer many nutrients. They provide vitamin C, thiamine, niacin, and iron.

• Potatoes combine well with many other foods and can stretch the servings of higher-priced ingredients.

• To prevent loss of nutrients, use as little water as possible when cooking potatoes. Try steaming—it's an excellent way to preserve nutrients.

• When peeling potatoes before cooking, keep the peelings as thin as possible to prevent the loss of nutrients right under the skin.

• Keep peeled potatoes snow white by placing them in a bowl of cold water as soon as they are peeled. (Add a little lemon juice or some ascorbic acid powder to the water before adding the potatoes.)

• Ideally, potatoes should be stored in a cool (45° to 50°), dry, dark place that is well ventilated; they'll keep for several weeks. At room temperature, potatoes should not be kept beyond a week because they will start to sprout and shrivel. Potatoes should not be refrigerated because temperatures below 40° cause the starch in the potato to turn to sugar and the potatoes develop a sweet taste.

• For tasty hashed potatoes, cut boiled potatoes into chunks and brown in bacon drippings.

• Slice cooked potatoes and pan-fry with onion and green pepper slices to make a filling for a main-dish omelet.

• Grate cooked potatoes and use as an extender in ground meat mixtures or as a stuffing for poultry, tomatoes, or green peppers.

• Before baking potatoes, scrub the skins well so that you can use them later for a tasty snack. Store skins in a container in the freezer. When you have collected as many as needed, cut into strips and bake in a preheated hot oven (425°) for about 30 minutes or until crisp. Season as desired and serve as a unique hors d'oeuvre or snack.

• For an elegant treat, prepare Pommes de Terre. It's easily done by making vertical cuts, at ¼-inch intervals, halfway through plain boiled potatoes. Brush with butter and sprinkle with grated cheese or desired seasonings. Bake in a preheated moderate oven (350°) until crisp and golden.

CHEESE-STUFFED POTATOES

Bake at 350° for 20 minutes.
Makes 4 servings.

8 new potatoes (2 inches in diameter)	**⅓** cup shredded Cheddar cheese
½ teaspoon salt	**1** egg
Water	**⅛** teaspoon salt
1½ tablespoons butter or margarine	**⅛** teaspoon pepper

1. Scrub potatoes and place in a large saucepan. Add the ½ teaspoon salt and water to cover; simmer 15 minutes or until just tender. Drain well and let stand until cool enough to handle. Preheat oven to 350°.
2. Cut potatoes in half. Scoop out centers, using a melon-ball scoop or a small spoon, leaving a ¼- to ⅜-inch shell. Mash potato centers with butter until smooth; stir in cheese, egg, salt, and pepper. Spoon or pipe mashed potato filling back into potato shells, mounding high; place on a cookie sheet.
3. Bake in a preheated moderate oven (350°) for 20 minutes or until lightly browned.

GLAZED SWEET POTATOES WITH PRUNES

Bake at 350° for 10 minutes.
Makes 6 servings.

¼ cup (½ stick) butter or margarine	**8** pitted prunes
⅓ cup sugar	**2** cans (17 ounces each) sweet potatoes
¼ cup light corn syrup	

1. Preheat oven to 350°. Combine butter, sugar, and corn syrup in a small saucepan. Cook over medium heat, stirring, until well blended.
2. Place prunes and sweet potatoes in a baking dish. Pour butter mixture over potatoes.
3. Bake in a preheated moderate oven (350°) for 10 minutes.

AU GRATIN BAKED POTATOES

Delicious, nutritious, and relatively inexpensive—that's the story behind
Au Gratin Baked Potatoes. Each spud is stuffed with a mixture of
ham, eggs, and cheese, and makes a filling meal.

Bake at 425° for 55 minutes.
Makes 4 servings.

4	**large baking potatoes**	**1**	**hard-cooked egg, chopped**
	(2 pounds)	**2**	**tablespoons chopped parsley**
	Vegetable oil	**¼**	**teaspoon pepper**
1	**cup diced cooked ham**	**⅓**	**cup low-fat milk**
½	**cup shredded Swiss cheese**		
	(2 ounces)		

1. Preheat oven to 425°. Scrub potatoes; rub skins lightly with oil.
2. Bake in a preheated hot oven (425°) for 45 minutes or until tender.
Remove potatoes from oven; leave oven on. Cut a thin lengthwise slice
from top of each potato; carefully scoop out insides leaving shells
intact.
3. Place pulp in a medium-size bowl; mash with a fork. Gently mix in
ham, 6 tablespoons of the cheese, egg, parsley, pepper, and milk;
spoon mixture into potato shells.* Sprinkle tops with remaining 2
tablespoons of the cheese. Place in a shallow baking pan.
4. Bake in a hot oven (425°) 10 minutes longer or until piping hot.

SERVING SUGGESTIONS: Broccoli spears, tomato wedges, and frozen
fruit yogurt.

---

*Any extra potato-ham mixture can be baked in a small baking dish with the
stuffed potatoes.

BUY VEGETABLES IN SEASON AND SAVE $

VEGETABLES	JAN-FEB	MAR-APR
Beans		
Broccoli	✸	✸
Brussels Sprouts	✸	
Corn		
Cucumber		
Eggplant		
Peas	✸	✸
Peppers		
Spinach	✸	✸
Summer Squash		
Sweet Potato		
Tomato		
Winter Squash		

STRING BEANS WITH WATER CHESTNUTS

Makes 6 servings.

1½ pounds fresh string beans, trimmed
2 tablespoons vegetable oil
2 slices gingerroot, about ¼ inch thick
2 cloves garlic, halved
1 cup sliced celery

1 can (8 ounces) water chestnuts, drained and halved
½ teaspoon salt
⅛ to ¼ teaspoon red pepper flakes
¼ cup water

1. Slice beans in half lengthwise.

2. Heat oil in a large, deep skillet; add ginger and garlic; stir-fry 1 minute. Add celery and water chestnuts; stir-fry for 2 to 3 minutes or until crisp-tender. Remove celery and water chestnuts to a small bowl. Leave ginger and garlic in skillet.

3. Add beans, salt, pepper flakes, and water to skillet. Cover; steam 15 minutes, or until crisp-tender. Discard ginger and garlic. Add celery and water chestnuts. Heat 1 minute. Spoon into a serving dish.

MAY-JUNE	JULY-AUG	SEPT-OCT	NOV-DEC
●	●		
		●	●
		●	●
●	●	●	
●	●		
	●	●	
●	●		
●	●	●	
●	●	●	
		●	●
●	●		
		●	●

TRIMMING STRING BEANS

The fastest way to trim string beans is by the handful. Using a sharp chef's knife, trim the ends off a bunch of beans. Then cut on the diagonal into pieces.

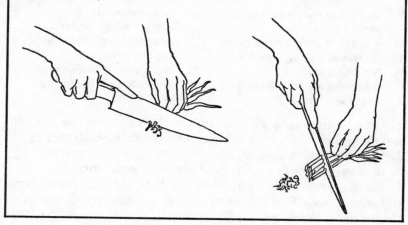

STIR-FRIED CORN AND PEPPERS

This colorful vegetable melange complements broiled fish
or roasted meats.

Makes 6 servings.

1 medium-size red pepper, halved, seeded, and cut into strips	1 clove garlic, crushed
	¼ cup vegetable oil
	4 ears cooked corn
1 medium-size green pepper, halved, seeded, and cut into strips	1 teaspoon basil, crumbled
	1 teaspoon thyme, crumbled
2 medium-size zucchini, thinly sliced	½ teaspoon salt
	¼ teaspoon pepper

1. Sauté red pepper, green pepper, zucchini, and garlic in oil in a large skillet just until tender, about 5 minutes.
2. Cut corn kernels from cobs. Add to mixture in skillet with basil, thyme, salt, and pepper. Cook, stirring, until heated.

FRESH CORN FRITTERS

Fresh sweet corn, cut from the cob, is blended into a light batter and pan-fried. Delicious drizzled with maple syrup and served with baked ham for a hearty breakfast.

Makes 6 servings (about 2 dozen fritters).

3 to 4 large ears sweet corn, shucked	2 tablespoons milk
	¼ cup (½ stick) butter or margarine, melted and slightly cooled
⅔ cup *sifted* all-purpose flour	
1 teaspoon baking powder	
½ teaspoon salt	¼ cup sliced green onions
¼ teaspoon ground nutmeg	Vegetable oil for frying
2 eggs, separated	

1. Cut corn from cobs with a sharp knife into a bowl. Press out pulp and milky liquid with back of knife. (You should have about 2 cups.)
2. Sift flour, baking powder, salt, and nutmeg onto wax paper.
3. Beat egg whites in a small bowl until soft peaks form.
4. Beat egg yolks with milk in a large bowl; stir in melted butter, corn, and green onions. Fold in flour mixture; fold in beaten whites until no streaks of white remain.

5. Heat a ½-inch depth of oil in a large, deep skillet until a small amount of batter cooks quickly at the edges.

6. Gently add slightly rounded tablespoons of batter to the hot oil; cook, turning once, 3 to 4 minutes or until golden on both sides. Remove with slotted spoon; drain on paper toweling. Keep hot until all are cooked.

HERBED CARROTS

Makes 4 servings.

1 pound carrots, thinly sliced	**¼ teaspoon pepper**
3 tablespoons butter or margarine	**2 tablespoons chopped parsley**
⅓ cup water	**2 tablespoons snipped dill**
½ teaspoon salt	**Or: 1 teaspoon dillweed**
	2 teaspoons lemon juice

1. Combine carrots, butter, water, salt, and pepper in a medium-size saucepan. Bring to a boil; lower heat; cover. Simmer until carrots are crisp-tender, about 15 minutes.

2. Uncover; continue to cook to evaporate any liquid. Sprinkle with parsley, dill, and lemon juice.

VERSATILE CARROTS

Carrots have many virtues: They're inexpensive, attractive, available all year, and loaded with vitamin A and other nutrients. In addition, they can be used in hundreds of ways. They're wonderful raw or cooked and can be sliced, shredded, grated, diced, or julienned. Use carrots for soups, stews, salads, snacks, sandwich spreads, relish trays, and even desserts—such as puddings and the ever-popular carrot cake. Unless appearance is important, such as carrots for a salad plate, don't peel them. Simply scrub the carrots and enjoy the fact that you have preserved all the nutrients right under the skin.

THE GOOD COOK'S GUIDE
TO VEGETABLES

Use the chart below for your best vegetable sources
of a variety of very important vitamins and minerals.

Vitamin A	B Complex Vitamins	Protein
Carrots	Dry Kidney Beans	Broccoli
Corn	Dry Lima Beans	Brussels Sprouts
Cucumbers	Dry Navy Beans	Collard Greens
Lettuce	Dry Split Peas	Corn
Okra	Dry Soybeans	Dried Beans
Peas	Dry White Beans	Kale
Pumpkin	Lentils	Lentils
Soybeans	Peas	Lima Beans
String Beans		Peas
Turnip Greens	**Potassium**	Soybeans
Winter Squash	Broccoli	
Zucchini	Cabbage	**Calcium**
	Carrots	Collard Greens
Vitamin C	Celery	Dry Kidney Beans
Brussels Sprouts	Kale	Dry Lima Beans
Cabbage	Kohlrabi	Dry Split Peas
Cauliflower	Leeks	Dry White Beans
Parsnips	Lentils	Kale
Potatoes, white	Lima Beans	Mustard Greens
Sauerkraut	Mustard Greens	Soybeans
	Parsnips	Turnip Greens
Vitamins A & C	Potatoes, white	Watercress
Beets	Radishes	
Broccoli	Sweet Potatoes	**Magnesium**
Collard Greens	Tomatoes	Black-eyed Peas
Green Peppers	Yams	Collard Greens
Kale		Dry Kidney Beans
Mustard Greens	**Iron**	Dry Lima Beans
Spinach	Beet Greens	Dry Split Peas
Sweet Potatoes	Dry Split Peas	Dry White Beans
Tomatoes	Dry Lima Beans	Lima Beans
Turnip	Lentils	Okra
Yellow Squash	Soybeans	Peanuts
	Spinach	Spinach

HERBED SPINACH RING

Bake at 350° for 20 minutes.
Makes 8 servings.

2   **packages (10 ounces each) frozen chopped spinach**
    Or: frozen chopped broccoli
2   **cups herb seasoned stuffing mix**
¾   **cup (1½ sticks) butter or margarine, melted**
½   **cup grated Parmesan cheese**
½   **cup chopped celery**
1   **medium-size onion, chopped (½ cup)**

1   **tablespoon garlic salt**
½   **teaspoon thyme, crumbled**
    Or: 1½ teaspoons chopped fresh thyme
½   **teaspoon pepper**
    Dash liquid red pepper seasoning
6   **eggs, beaten**

1. Grease a 6½ cup ring mold. Preheat oven to 350°.

2. Cook spinach following package directions; drain well.

3. Combine spinach, stuffing mix, butter, Parmesan cheese, celery, onion, garlic salt, thyme, pepper, liquid red pepper seasoning, and eggs in a large bowl. Spoon into ring mold, spreading evenly.

4. Bake in a preheated moderate oven (350°) for 20 minutes or until spinach pulls away from side of mold and center springs back when lightly pressed with fingertip.

5. Carefully pour off excess accumulated liquid. Run a knife carefully around edges. Unmold onto a serving plate.

SERVING SUGGESTIONS: Steamed yellow squash and steamed or sautéed mushrooms.

USE IT ALL

If you've been enjoying just the ribs from a bunch of celery, try using the leaves also. Celery leaves add a wonderful flavor to soups and stews and can even be used to garnish platters of food. The ribs of celery can be used for salads, vegetable dishes, snacks, and as an ingredient that adds crunch to so many dishes. For best quality, store celery in a plastic bag in the refrigerator and use within a week.

LIMA BEANS WITH BACON

Makes 4 servings.

4 slices bacon	⅛ teaspoon pepper
1 package (10 ounces) frozen lima beans	⅛ teaspoon rosemary, crumbled
½ cup water	2 tablespoons chopped parsley
¼ teaspoon salt	

1. Cook bacon in a medium-size skillet until crisp; drain on paper toweling; crumble; reserve.

2. Add lima beans, water, salt, pepper, and rosemary to fat remaining in pan. Bring to a boil; lower heat slightly; cover. Cook until beans are tender, about 8 minutes.

3. Uncover; cook beans over high heat, shaking pan frequently, until almost all the liquid has evaporated. Sprinkle with reserved bacon and parsley.

OVEN "FRIED" ZUCCHINI

It's hard to believe that these crisp, golden spears of zucchini are only 55 calories per serving. The secret is oven "frying," with a minimum of oil.

Bake at 475° for 7 minutes.
Makes 4 servings.

3 tablespoons packaged herb-seasoned bread crumbs	2 medium-size unpeeled zucchini or yellow squash
1 tablespoon grated Parmesan cheese	2 teaspoons vegetable oil
¼ teaspoon onion salt	2 tablespoons water
⅛ teaspoon pepper	

1. Preheat oven to 475°. Spray a nonstick cookie sheet liberally with cooking spray (or wipe lightly with vegetable oil). Combine bread crumbs, Parmesan, salt, and pepper on a sheet of wax paper.

2. Quarter the zucchini lengthwise, then slice each spear in half (or thirds) to make shorter spears. Put them in a plastic bag. Add the oil and water. Close the bag and shake so squash spears are lightly coated with oil.

3. Roll each spear in crumb mixture until lightly coated. Arrange spears in a single layer on prepared cookie sheet.

4. Bake, uncovered, in a preheated very hot oven (475°) for 7 minutes or until spears are browned and tender-crunchy.

STUFFED TOMATOES

Bake at 400° for 5 minutes.
Makes 4 stuffed tomatoes.

4	medium-size tomatoes	¼	cup grated Parmesan cheese
¼	cup olive or vegetable oil	1	teaspoon basil, crumbled
1	clove garlic, crushed		Or: 1 tablespoon chopped
4	cups fresh bread crumbs		fresh basil
	(about 8 slices bread)	1	teaspoon salt
¼	cup finely chopped parsley	⅛	teaspoon pepper

1. Grease an 8 x 8 x 2-inch baking dish. Preheat oven to 400°.
2. Cut off tops of tomatoes. Scoop out seeds and pulp; reserve pulp. Chop tomato tops and pulp to measure about ½ cup. Turn tomatoes upside down to drain.
3. Heat the oil in a medium-size skillet. Sauté chopped tomato and garlic until tomato softens, about 2 minutes. Remove from heat. Stir in bread crumbs, parsley, 2 tablespoons of the Parmesan cheese, basil, salt, and pepper.
4. Place tomatoes, right side up, in prepared dish. Fill each with stuffing. Sprinkle with remaining 2 tablespoons grated Parmesan; moisten tops with oil.
5. Bake in a preheated hot oven (400°) for 5 minutes or until tops are lightly toasted.

STUFFED GREEN PEPPERS

Green peppers can be stuffed with many tasty, yet inexpensive mixtures such as rich, kasha, or other vegetables. To make serving green peppers a breeze, place each one in a greased custard cup. The cup will give the green pepper support and prevent it from sagging. The same technique can be used for stuffed tomatoes and onions.

10
Sandwiches

Delight your family with unusual sandwiches such as Cheese and Bean Burritos or a "dressed-up" favorite—Chicago Steakhouse Burger. Or treat them to ethnic fare like Texas Chicken Flautas with Salsa. They're all delicious and easy on your budget. Learn the best way to freeze sandwiches—and which fillings to use and which to avoid. Discover why sandwiches can save money and how to keep your total lunch fresh for 3 or more hours without refrigeration.

Sandwiches provide a great opportunity to use up leftovers. You can use diced leftover meat, poultry, or fish as the basis of delicious fillings. Add some chopped fresh or leftover cooked vegetables for crunch and color, an appropriate binder (mayonnaise or salad dressing), and some seasonings. Presto! You've created an original sandwich.

Stretch expensive protein ingredients by using more vegetables, fruits, and whole grain breads in your sandwiches. You'll save money and cut calories, too. For instance, you can get away with less ham if you add juicy pineapple slices; and less cheese if you include green pepper and onion slices. For added interest, embellish sandwiches with vegetable and fruit garnishes. Use whole grain breads as much as possible—they're more filling and nutritious.

THE BASIC BURGER

"Travel" all around the country with one of America's favorite foods. Prepare the Basic Hamburger Mix and then choose your area of travel—sunny Florida, with its colorful avocado, grapefruit, and red pepper filling, or Oregon, with its unusual pear, cucumber, and cheese combination. There are 5 delicious combinations. Try them all.

BASIC HAMBURGER MIX

1½   pounds ground chuck
¼   cup grated onion
1   tablespoon Worcestershire sauce
1½   teaspoons salt
¼   teaspoon pepper

Combine ground beef lightly with onion, Worcestershire, salt, and pepper. Divide into 6 equal portions; shape lightly into 1-inch thick patties.

Select cooking method:

Open grill: Grill on oiled grill rack 4 inches from coals for 4 minutes; turn; cook to desired degree of doneness.

Broil: Broil 3 inches from heat on oiled rack for 4 minutes; turn; cook to desired degree of doneness.

Pan-Fry: Brown hamburgers in 1 to 2 tablespoons butter or margarine in a large, heavy skillet for 4 minutes; turn; cook to desired degree of doneness.

FLORIDA CITRUS BURGER

Makes 6 servings.

¼ cup guava (or other) jelly
1 recipe Basic Hamburger Mix
  (page 198), but omit
  Worcestershire sauce
  Lettuce leaves
6 slices egg bread (challah),
  toasted and buttered

1 small ripe avocado, peeled,
  pitted, and thinly sliced*
1 small grapefruit, pared
  and sectioned
¼ cup diced red pepper
  Guava jelly for garnish

1. Combine ¼ cup guava jelly with Basic Hamburger Mix. Shape and cook, following method of your choice.
2. For each burger, place a lettuce leaf on bread slice; top with 3 to 4 slices avocado, hamburger, grapefruit sections, some red pepper, and dollop of jelly. Serve remaining avocado on side.

---

*Coat avocado slices with grapefruit juice to prevent darkening.

BIG APPLE BURGER

There's only one Big Apple: New York City.

Makes 6 servings.

1 recipe Basic Hamburger Mix
  (see page 198)
1 package (6 ounces) sliced
  Cheddar cheese rounds
6 poppy seed-onion rolls, split,
  toasted, and buttered
  Lettuce leaves

1 large tomato, cut into 6 slices
1 medium-size red onion,
  thinly sliced
1 medium-size apple,
  quartered, cored, and
  thinly sliced*

1. Shape and cook Basic Hamburger Mix following method of your choice.
2. For each burger, lay cheese slice on top of patty. On bottom half of roll, layer lettuce leaf, tomato slice, onion slice, cheese-topped burger, and 3 to 4 slices apple. Cover with top half of roll.

---

*Coat apple with lemon juice to prevent darkening.

OREGON BURGER

Makes 6 servings.

¼ cup Roquefort or blue
cheese, crumbled
1 recipe Basic Hamburger Mix
(see page 198), but omit
Worcestershire sauce
Romaine lettuce leaves
6 English muffins, split,
toasted, and buttered
1 medium-size ripe pear,
halved, cored, and
thinly sliced

½ small cucumber, thinly sliced
6 tablepoons bottled blue
cheese salad dressing
2 tablespoons Roquefort or
blue cheese, crumbled
1 tablespoon chopped red
pepper

1. Combine the ¼ cup Roquefort with Basic Hamburger Mix. Shape and cook hamburgers following method of your choice.

2. For each burger, place romaine leaf on bottom half of English muffin; top with 3 pear slices, hamburger, some cucumber slices, 1 tablespoon of the blue cheese salad dressing, a sprinkling of Roquefort cheese, and some chopped red pepper. Cover with top muffin half. Serve with ripe olives, if you wish.

CALIFORNIA BEACH BURGER

Makes 6 servings.

1 recipe Basic Hamburger Mix
(see page 198)
Spinach leaves
6 sesame seed hamburger
buns, split, toasted
and buttered
1 container (1 pint)
alfalfa sprouts

2 large navel oranges, pared
and cut into 12 slices
6 tablespoons plain yogurt
1 tablespoon dry-roasted
sunflower nuts
Carrot curls (optional)

1. Shape and cook Basic Hamburger Mix following method of your choice.

2. For each burger, place spinach on bottom half of roll; top with sprouts, burger, 2 orange slices, 1 tablespoon of yogurt, sprinkling of sunflower nuts. Cover with top half of roll. Add carrot curls if you wish.

CHICAGO STEAKHOUSE BURGER

Makes 6 servings.

½ pound small mushrooms, sliced
3 tablespoons butter or margarine
2 teaspoons Dijon-style mustard
2 tablespoons bottled steak sauce
1½ teaspoons grated lemon rind
1 tablespoon finely chopped parsley

1 recipe Basic Hamburger Mix (see page 198), but omit Worcestershire sauce
Romaine lettuce leaves
6 hard round rolls, split, toasted, and buttered
1 large tomato, cut into 6 slices
2 tablespoons snipped chives
6 green onions, cut into fans (optional)

1. Sauté mushrooms in butter in a skillet until lightly browned and liquid has evaporated. Add mustard; keep warm.
2. Combine steak sauce, lemon rind, and parsley with Basic Hamburger Mix. Shape and cook, following method of your choice.
3. For each burger, place romaine leaf on bottom half of roll; top with burger, tomato slice, mushrooms, and garnish with chives. Cover with top half of roll. Garnish with green onion brushes if you wish.

HAM, TURKEY, CHEESE TRIO

Make up the savory lettuce topping and keep sandwich ingredients in refrigerator. Let everyone make their own.

Makes 6 servings.

½	cup mayonnaise or salad dressing	6	slices turkey roll (6 ounces)
2	tablespoons sweet pickle relish	3	slices Swiss cheese (from an 8-ounce package)
2	teaspoons Dijon-style mustard	3	slices caraway Muenster cheese (from an 8-ounce package)
¼	teaspoon salt		
¼	teaspoon pepper	1	package (8 ounces) poppy seed dinner rolls (12 rolls)
2	cups shredded iceberg lettuce		
6	slices boiled ham (from an 8-ounce package)		

1. Combine mayonnaise, relish, mustard, salt, and pepper in a small bowl; mix well. Add lettuce; toss to coat.
2. Cut meats and cheeses in half, then into triangles.
3. On bottoms of 6 of the rolls, divide ham and caraway Muenster; on remaining bottoms divide turkey roll and Swiss cheese; top all 12 with 1 tablespoon lettuce mixture; press top of rolls down gently. Serve 1 ham and Muenster sandwich and 1 turkey and Swiss to each person.

HAM AND AVOCADO PITA-WICHES

Makes 8 sandwiches.

2	cups cubed cooked ham	⅓	cup mayonnise
1	large avocado, diced	8	small pita bread
2	tablespoons chopped onion		

1. Combine ham, avocado, onion, pepper, and mayonnaise in a medium-size bowl.
2. Cut breads along edges to make pockets; spoon filling into each.

SALAD BOWL SANDWICH

Tuck this Italian-style tuna salad into pita pockets.

Makes 6 servings.

1 can (7 ounces) tuna, drained and flaked	1 package (8 ounces) mozzarella cheese, diced
1 cup cherry tomatoes, halved	½ cup bottled oil and vinegar dressing
1 medium-size green pepper, halved, seeded, and diced	2 teaspoons basil, crumbled
¼ cup diced red onion	6 whole wheat or white pita bread
¼ cup sliced pitted black olives	

1. Combine tuna, cherry tomatoes, green pepper, red onion, olives, mozzarella cheese, oil and vinegar dressing, and basil in a large bowl; toss to mix. (Turn into an insulated bowl with tight-fitting cover for toting.)

2. To serve, open pocket of each pita bread with a small knife; tuck tuna filling into pita bread pockets.

LUNCH BOX TIPS

• Keep moist ingredients (lettuce, tomato, pickle slices) separate and add to sandwich just before eating.

• Wrap sandwiches individually (in moisture-proof wrap) to prevent transfer of flavors and for ease in eating.

• If sandwich will be exposed to warm temperatures, keep it fresh by placing it in an insulated lunch box or an insulated paper or plastic disposable bag. (Either buy them or save them from frozen food purchases.) In a pinch, insulate a sandwich by wrapping it in several layers of newspaper. A good technique is to place a small can of frozen juice in a lunch box. It will thaw in about 3 hours and meanwhile help to keep your sandwich cold.

MEATBALL HERO SANDWICHES

Makes 9 servings.
Bake at 325° for 10 minutes.

9 individual hero rolls
1½ pounds ground beef
1 egg, slightly beaten
1 tablespoon instant minced onion
1½ teaspoons salt
¼ teaspoon pepper
¼ cup milk
2 tablespoons vegetable oil

1 green pepper, sliced
1 red pepper, sliced
1 medium-size onion, sliced
1 tablespoon all-purpose flour
¾ cup bottled chili sauce
½ cup water
1½ teaspoons light brown sugar
½ teaspoon dry mustard

1. Cut a thin slice from the top of each roll; scoop out. Crumble enough insides to make 1¼ cups; reserve. Cover rolls to keep them from drying out.

2. Combine beef, egg, onion, salt, pepper, milk, and the reserved crumbs in a large bowl; mix well; shape into 2-inch balls (makes about 27).

3. Brown, a few at a time, in 1 tablespoon of oil in a large skillet; remove to a large bowl.

4. Add remaining oil; sauté peppers and onion until tender. Remove to bowl.

5. Stir flour into fat remaining in skillet and heat just until bubbly. Stir in chili sauce and water. Cook, stirring constantly, until sauce thickens and bubbles. Stir in brown sugar and dry mustard.

6. Add meatball-pepper mixture; cover; simmer for 20 minutes.

7. Preheat oven to 325°. Heat rolls in a preheated slow oven (325°) for 10 minutes. Spoon in meatballs and sauce.

DRESS UP A SANDWICH

Make a sandwich look special with attractive garnishes. Try pickle fans, carrot curls, green onion "brushes," cherry tomatoes, radish roses, celery sticks with leaves, or scored cucumber slices.

CHICKEN-CHEESE SANDWICHES

Makes about 2½ cups.

2 cups chopped cooked chicken	2 tablespoons chopped parsley
1 cup diced Cheddar cheese (4 ounces)	1 teaspoon lemon juice
	½ teaspoon salt
⅓ cup mayonnaise	⅛ teaspoon pepper
2 tablespoons chopped onion	12 slices whole wheat bread

1. Combine chicken and cheese in a medium-size bowl. Combine mayonnaise, onion, parsley, lemon juice, salt, and pepper in a small bowl; stir into chicken-cheese mixture; blend well. Cover; refrigerate until well blended.

2. To serve, spread filling evenly over 6 slices of bread; top with remaining bread slices.

CHICKEN 'N' EGG SANDWICH

Chicken wing meat is combined with hard-cooked eggs for great sandwiches.

Makes 4 sandwiches.

4 cooked chicken wings (leftover from 2 roasting chickens)	¼ cup mayonnaise
	¼ teaspoon salt
	Dash peppeer
2 hard-cooked eggs, chopped	½ teaspoon curry powder (optional)
¼ cup chopped celery	

1. Remove skin from chicken wings; discard. Remove meat from bones; chop finely. Combine with eggs, celery, mayonnaise, salt, pepper, and curry powder, if using, in a medium-size bowl; mix well. Cover and refrigerate until serving time.

2. To serve, spread filling evenly over 4 slices of bread; top with remaining bread slices.

CHEESE AND BEAN BURRITOS

A burrito is sometimes called the Mexican sandwich. The flour tortilla, thinner and softer than the familiar corn tortilla, is stuffed or rolled with a filling, then eaten out of hand.

Bake at 350° for 25 minutes.
Makes 12 burritos.

1 **small onion, chopped (¼ cup)**	1 **cup shredded Monterey Jack cheese (4 ounces)**
2 **tablespoons vegetable oil**	**Flour Tortillas**
1 **can (1 pound) refried beans**	**(recipe below)**
1 **can (4 ounces) green chili peppers, seeded and chopped**	**Shredded romaine lettuce (optional)**
1 **cup shredded Cheddar cheese (4 ounces)**	**Tomato wedges (optional)**

1. Sauté onion in oil in a medium-size saucepan until tender, about 3 minutes. Stir in refried beans and green chili peppers; heat thoroughly. Combine Cheddar and Monterey Jack cheeses on wax paper. Preheat oven to 350°.

2. Heat 1 tortilla on a large griddle or in a very large skillet over medium-low heat until soft and pliable. Spread about 2 tablespoons of the bean filling and 2 tablespoons cheese mixture in center of tortilla. Work quickly so the tortilla does not get crisp. Fold the 2 sides in toward the center over the filling; bring bottom over the folds and then flip over so you have a rectangular package. Repeat with remaining tortillas.

3. Place burritos in a shallow casserole just large enough to hold the 12 burritos. Reheat in a moderate oven (350°) for 25 minutes. Serve with shredded lettuce and tomato wedges or Salsa (page 209) if you wish.

Flour Tortillas: Combine 3 cups *sifted* all-purpose flour, 1½ teaspoons salt, and 1 teaspoon baking powder in a large bowl. Cut in ¼ cup lard (not shortening) with a pastry blender or fork until crumbly. Add ¾ cup very warm (110° to 115°) water, mixing lightly with a fork until dough is thoroughly moistened and just begins to cling together. Dough should feel moist, but not sticky. (If necessary, add additional water, 1 tablespoon at a time.) Gather dough with hands and knead 1 minute in the bowl. Cover and let rest for 30 minutes. Cut dough into 12 pieces; shape into balls. Keep dough covered to prevent drying out. Roll each piece into a 9-inch paper-thin circle between two lightly floured pieces of wax paper, lifting and turning wax paper from tortilla to prevent sticking. Stack tortillas between layers of wax paper. Heat a large griddle or skillet until hot. Cook 1 tortilla at a time, pressing with a large pancake turner as dough begins to blister and bubble during baking. Cook just until tortilla is dry, and blisters are browned; flip to bake a few seconds on the other side. Keep in a plastic bag while making others. These can be made ahead and frozen. Reheat on griddle until soft and pliable.

FREEZING SANDWICHES

If sandwich-making time is like a madhouse, resolve to get organized and make up a whole batch of sandwiches to store in your freezer. Here are some tips:

• Line up all ingredients production-line-style. Work quickly with chilled, fresh ingredients.

• Spread bread with butter or margarine; this prevents filling from soaking into bread. (Mayonnaise or salad dressing separates when frozen.)

• Use filling ingredients that freeze well: Cooked poultry, meat, or fish, peanut butter, hard cheese, dried fruits, cream cheese, cheese spreads, hard-cooked egg yolks, or cooked dried beans.

• Assemble sandwiches, using *thin* slices of meat, poultry, or fish. Or, make a tasty filling of ingredients such as dried fruit or beans.

• Some filling ingredients that do not freeze well are: cottage cheese, hard-cooked egg whites, cooked bacon, jams or jellies, raw vegetables, and raw fruits.

• Wrap sandwiches in moisture-proof wrap. Label and date sandwiches.

• Place sandwiches together in a large container in the freezer so you can find them easily. Use them within 1 month.

• Pack sandwiches in a lunch box while they are still frozen. Although they'll thaw in about an hour at room temperature, they'll stay fresh for 3 to 4 hours.

"SLOPPY JOES"

This is an ideal recipe for anyone watching their sodium intake. However, it's so flavorful that everyone will enjoy it. The recipe illustrates the use of tomato paste or puree when tomato is needed. Most tomato pastes and purees are packed without salt, so it is not necessary to buy a dietetic brand. Substitute the paste or puree for canned tomatoes or sauce, and thus lower the sodium content of the dish. Of course, if fresh tomatoes are available they are always great to use.

Makes 8 servings.

1½	pounds ground round	½	to ¾ teaspoon cayenne
1	large onion, chopped (1 cup)		pepper
½	teaspoon minced garlic	1	can (6 ounces) low-sodium
¼	teaspoon ground cumin*		tomato paste
½	teaspoon oregano, crumbled	1	cup water
½	teaspoon fennel seed, crushed*	8	hamburger buns, heated

1. Cook meat in a large skillet until no longer pink; skim off any fat. Add onion and garlic; cook, stirring often, until onion is tender, about 3 minutes. Stir in cumin, oregano, fennel, cayenne, and tomato paste. Add enough of the water to make a thick sauce. Simmer, stirring occasionally, 15 minutes.
2. Serve on split, heated hamburger buns.

---

*If you do not have cumin, you can use chili powder, but also omit oregano and cayenne. Chili powder is a mixture of these plus salt. Add more of the spices if you like the meat hotter. Using a regular hamburger bun furnishes 150 mg of sodium, so if you want to reduce that, you could make your own or use low-sodium bread.

TEXAS CHICKEN FLAUTAS WITH SALSA

Makes 6 servings.

1 medium-size onion, chopped (½ cup)	2¼ cups chopped or shredded cooked chicken
1 clove garlic, minced	1 can (4 ounces) chopped green chilies
2 tablespoons vegetable shortening or lard	Vegetable oil for frying
1 tablespoon cornstarch	12 canned, refrigerated, or thawed, frozen corn tortillas
1¼ teaspoons salt	Salsa (recipe below)
¼ teaspoon pepper	Lettuce (optional)
¼ cup chicken broth	

1. Sauté onion and garlic in shortening in a large saucepan until tender, about 3 minutes. Stir in cornstarch, salt, and pepper; mix well. Stir in broth, chicken, and chilies. Cook, stirring constantly, until very thick and bubbly.

2. Heat a ¼-inch depth of oil in a large skillet. Dip tortillas into hot oil for a few seconds to soften them; drain on paper toweling. Spoon a heaping tablespoon of filling in center of each tortilla; roll up.

3. Sauté flautas, a few at a time, in the hot oil in the skillet, turning often, until crisp, about 2 minutes. Keep flautas warm until all are cooked. Serve with Salsa. Garnish with lettuce, if you wish.

Salsa: Chop 2 medium-size ripe tomatoes, 1 medium-size onion, and 1 medium-size green pepper, halved and seeded. Combine with ¼ cup chopped parsley, 1 clove garlic, minced, ½ teaspoon salt, ⅛ teaspoon pepper, and ⅛ teaspoon ground cumin in a small bowl; mix well. Refrigerate 1 hour or until cold.

SERVING SUGGESTIONS: Orange sherbet with chocolate cookies.

11

Quick and Easy Money Savers

When a hectic schedule dictates quick and easy meals, rely on recipes such as Chicken Rosemary, Blender Banana Cake, and No-Fuss Chocolate Chewy Squares.

Turn to this chapter also for fast techniques—the marvels of microwaves, stir-fry cooking, and pressure-pot cooking. Discover how appliances can save time and make meal preparation easy.

MICROWAVE MAGIC

Microwave cooking seems like magic because food is cooked by electro-magnetic waves, rather than by direct heat. Microwaves pass right through dishes of glass, ceramic, plastic, or paper and penetrate the food. The food molecules are then set into motion and the food cooks quickly.

The advantages of microwaving are numerous and save time and money:
- There's less energy usage—savings may be up to 75%; you spend

less clean-up time—some foods can be cooked on paper plates or towels. Also, the oven interior stays cool and is easy to wipe out.
● The bright colors of vegetables and fruits are preserved.
● It can be used to reheat leftovers so they taste great—no dried-out foods with a "reheated" taste.

There are disadvantages of microwave cooking, too, though. Foods often don't brown properly. Formerly a big problem, this can be overcome by special browning cookware, ovens with variable power, or browning units. And cheaper cuts of meat don't get tender enough, because tenderizing those meats requires a long cooking time.

Tips and Techniques
● Overcome lack of browning in older units by brushing meats, etc., with a deep-colored sauce, or sprinkle with spices such as paprika.
● Add color and crispness to microwave-cooked foods, such as crumb-topped casseroles, by slipping them under the broiler briefly before serving.
● Avoid metal cookware, because it deflects microwave energy and may damage the oven. The exception is the new browning cookware designed especially for microwave ovens.
● Invest in cookware that allows you to freeze, microwave-cook, and serve in the same dish.
● Know the limitations of your microwave oven. Don't expect it to cook a large amount of food in a flash or tenderize a tough piece of meat.

FOODS THAT DON'T MICROWAVE WELL

• Eggs in the shell can burst.
• Pancakes don't get crisp when micro-cooked.
• Canning requires too high a temperature.
• Hot fat for deep-fat frying could cause burns.
• Extra-large turkeys (over 25 pounds) or a dozen potatoes or large casseroles (over 12-cup size) are best cooked in conventional ovens.
• Dried peas and beans, and other low-moisture foods, should be prepared by conventional methods. Then, they may be reheated or added to casseroles in the microwave oven.

MICRO-COOKING'S TOP 21

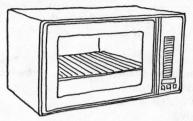

Here is a list of outstanding ways to let your microwave serve you:
• Potatoes bake in about 5 minutes.
• Eggs scramble to the fluffiest ever.
• Vegetables stay crisp and bright in color.
• Fish steams in its natural juices.
• Bacon browns flat on paper towels.

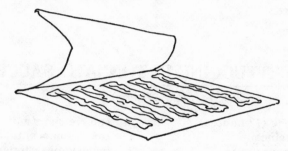

• Meats defrost at 8 minutes to the pound.
• One person's meal reheats on the dinner plate.
• Meats reheat with no "leftover" flavor.
• Butter, margarine, or chocolate melt perfectly in their wrappers or in a glass measuring cup.
• Frozen entrées heat up in minutes.
• Rice or pasta reheat without overcooking.
• Custards bake to smooth perfection.
• Beef roasts in 11 minutes to the pound.
• Appetizers heat on a serving tray in seconds.
• Casseroles reheat with freshly-made taste.
• Meat loaves are ready to serve in 20 minutes.
• Hamburgers can be cooked in their rolls.
• Pancakes, tacos, and crêpes heat in seconds.
• Whole chickens cook in 20 minutes.
• Fudgy brownies cook in 6 minutes.
• Sausages cook with no greasy spatters.

HERBED PARSLEY-GARLIC TOAST

Broil for 5 minutes.
Makes 4 servings.

2 cloves garlic, minced	4 French rolls, halved
5 tablespoons minced parsley	lengthwise
½ teaspoon basil, crumbled	
¼ cup (½ stick) unsalted butter	
or margarine	

1. Preheat broiler. Sauté garlic and parsley in butter in a small skillet for 2 minutes. Spread mixture on rolls.
2. Broil in a preheated broiler about 5 inches from heat, until butter mixture is bubbly.

FETTUCCINE IN TONNATO SAUCE

Makes 4 servings.

1 package (12 ounces) fettuccine	½ cup cream or milk
½ cup mayonnaise	1 can (7 ounces) tuna
1 can (2 ounces) flat anchovies, drained	2 tablespoons chopped parsley
1 clove garlic	1 tablespoon finely slivered lemon rind
2 tablespoons lemon juice	Grated Parmesan cheese

1. Bring 3 quarts of water to a boil in a large, covered kettle. Add salt. Cook fettuccine in boiling salted water following package directions; drain.
2. Combine mayonnaise, anchovies, garlic, lemon juice, and cream in the container of an electric blender; whirl until smooth. Break tuna up with a fork in a small bowl. Pour sauce over tuna.
3. Combine hot fettuccine and sauce in a heated serving bowl; toss to mix well. Sprinkle parsley and lemon rind over. Serve with Parmesan cheese.

SERVING SUGGESTIONS: Sesame breadsticks, stir-fried peppers and onions, and spiced stewed plums.

TORTILLA BAKE

These flavors may be borrowed from South of the Border, but the dish fits into any busy life-style.

Bake at 350° for 30 minutes.
Makes 6 servings.

5	corn tortillas (6-inch diameter), cut into quarters	2	cups milk
6	ounces chorizo or pork sausage (about 3)	¼	teaspoon salt
1	small onion, chopped (¼ cup)	4	ounces sharp Cheddar cheese, shredded (1 cup)
3	eggs	1	can (8 ounces) whole kernel corn, drained
		¼	cup seeded, chopped, canned green chilies

1. Preheat oven to 350°. Grease 1½-quart shallow baking dish. Line quartered tortillas on bottom and sides of dish.

2. Remove casing from chorizos. Brown chorizo with the onion in a small skillet; pour off fat.

3. Beat eggs in a medium-size bowl. Add milk, salt, cheese, corn, and chilies. Stir in cooked, drained chorizo. Spoon egg mixture into tortilla-lined dish.

4. Bake in a moderate oven (350°) for 30 minutes or until firm in center.

SERVING SUGGESTIONS: Fried tomato slices, hot cooked rice, avocado-grapefruit salad, and lemon or lime sherbet.

FAST COOKERY

Finely divide, chop, shred, or julienne your meats, poultry, fish, and vegetables for super-quick cooking. Make use of variety meats, such as kidneys and liver, and fish. They cook in less time than most other meats and poultry. Stock up with fully cooked meats—like ham and smoked or brown-and-serve sausages. They need only be reheated before serving. Always keep pasta and the makings for sauces on hand. This kind of meal takes less than 30 minutes to prepare.

FOOD PROCESSOR BASICS

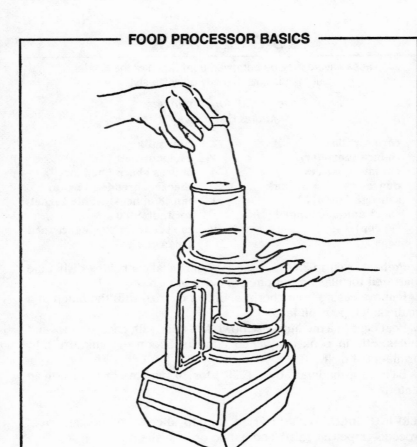

A food processor can save time and money in many ways. Here are some ideas:

• Process several different ingredients, in quick succession, and save clean-up time. Process dry foods first, wet or sticky foods last.

• Puree cooked vegetables for a soup, baby food, or very ripe fruits for a sauce. Whirl cooked meat for a sandwich spread.

• Use up bits of cheese; whirl with sour cream or cottage cheese until smooth. Enjoy as a dip or add a little lemon juice and use as a salad dressing.

• Chop or slice raw meats. For ease in processing, freeze the meat first for 30 minutes.

• Chop ingredients, such as nuts, onions, or parsley, in quantity and store in containers in the refrigerator or freezer.

CRUNCHY CHICKEN CASSEROLE

A fast and fantastic way to use leftover chicken or turkey.

Bake at 450° for 20 minutes.
Makes 6 servings.

2 cups chopped celery	½ cup shredded sharp or mild
2 cups chopped cooked	Cheddar cheese (2 ounces)
chicken or turkey	2 teaspoons lemon juice
1 cup mayonnaise	1 teaspoon salt
½ cup chopped walnuts	¼ teaspoon pepper
(optional)	½ cup crushed potato chips

1. Butter a 1½-quart casserole. Preheat oven to 450°. Combine celery, chicken, mayonnaise, walnuts (if using), cheese, lemon juice, salt, and pepper in a large bowl; mix well.
2. Turn into prepared casserole. Sprinkle with crushed chips.
3. Bake in a preheated hot oven (450°) for 20 minutes.

SERVING SUGGESTIONS: Warm crusty rolls, tossed green salad, and lemon Bavarian.

EASY SIDE DISHES

For a quick-cooking vegetable, broil tomato halves sprinkled with herbs, seasonings, and Parmesan cheese. Boil or bake twice as many potatoes as you need for a meal. Refrigerate leftovers and use within 2 or 3 days for potato salad, hash browns, fried potato skins, or scalloped potatoes. Or dice and add to a frozen stew or casseroles.

FREEZE IT

When preparing casseroles, make 2—one for now, the other to freeze for later. Remember: Thawing and reheating are quicker with smaller portions. (Leave out the potatoes when freezing!) Freeze leftover rice in serving-size portions. To reheat: Defrost at room temperature and steam, covered, until thoroughly heated.

CREAMY SHELLS WITH BROCCOLI AND HAM

Makes 6 servings.

1 package (1 pound) medium-size macaroni shells	1 clove garlic, crushed
½ pound cooked ham	½ cup (1 stick) butter or margarine
1 package (10 ounces) frozen broccoli spears, thawed	1 cup (½ pint) heavy cream
	1 cup grated Parmesan cheese

1. Bring 4 to 5 quarts of water to a boil in a large, covered kettle. Add salt. Cook macaroni shells in boiling salted water following package directions.

2. Slice ham into slivers; cut broccoli into ½-inch pieces.

3. Sauté garlic, ham, and broccoli in butter in a large skillet until broccoli is crisp-tender, about 5 minutes.

4. Stir in heavy cream. Cook over medium heat for 3 minutes. Stir in cheese. Lower heat; cook, stirring frequently, until cheese is melted.

5. Drain macaroni shells; toss with sauce.

SERVING SUGGESTIONS: Garlic bread, tomatoes vinaigrette, and pear halves topped with lemon yogurt.

SPEEDY SLICING

If you've ever been faced with slicing a block of cheese or potatoes for chips, you know how frustrating and time-consuming this chore can be. Furthermore, you've probably cut uneven slices.

To get around these problems, use a slicing machine. In addition to time, you'll save money because you can cut meats and other costly foods into wafer-thin slices.

HUNGARIAN BEEF AND NOODLES

Makes 4 servings.

1	pound ground chuck	1	tablespoon tomato paste
1	small onion, chopped	1	cup dairy sour cream
	(¼ cup)	¾	pound fine noodles, cooked
¼	cup beef broth		and drained
2	teaspoons prepared mustard		

1. Cook meat in large skillet, breaking it up with a spoon as it cooks, until no longer pink. Stir in onion; cook until tender, about 3 minutes.
2. Blend in broth, mustard, and tomato paste. Bring to a boil; lower heat; cover; simmer 5 minutes.
3. Stir in sour cream very slowly to prevent curdling. Heat gently, but do not allow to boil. Serve over hot cooked noodles.

SERVING SUGGESTIONS: Poppy seed rolls, steamed cabbage, and fresh apple cake.

POTATO FANS

Bake at 550° for 15 minutes.
Makes 4 servings.

2	large oval-shaped baking	Vegetable oil
	potatoes (about 1 pound)	Salt and pepper

1. Preheat oven to extremely hot (550°). (The oven need not reach that temperature before potatoes are put in.)
2. Cut potatoes into thin crosswise slices, keeping the slices in place as you cut. Divide slices into 4 groups.
3. Grease a cookie sheet with vegetable oil; fan out each portion of slices to form 4 semi-circles of overlapping potato slices on cookie sheet. Gently brush exposed surfaces of potatoes with oil; sprinkle with salt and pepper.
4. Bake in a preheated extremely hot oven (550°) for 10 minutes. Gently brush potato fans with more oil; return to oven for 5 minutes more or until potatoes are tender. Remove potato fans to a serving dish with an extra-wide spatula or pancake turner.

CHICKEN AND RICE SKILLET MEAL

The next time you roast 2 chickens, save the livers, gizzards, necks, and ½ cup of gravy to use in this bonus recipe.

Makes 4 servings.

1	large onion, chopped (1 cup)	2	chicken bouillon cubes
1	clove garlic, minced	½	cup gravy
1	tablespoon vegetable oil		(from roast chickens)
	Livers, gizzards, and necks	½	cup chopped parsley
	from 2 chickens	2	tablespoons chopped green
3	cups water		onions with green tops
1	small bay leaf		Salt
1	cup long-grain rice		Pepper

1. Sauté onion and garlic in oil in a large skillet until tender, about 3 minutes. Finely chop livers and gizzards; add to skillet with necks.* Sauté until lightly browned, stirring constantly. Pour in 1 cup of the water; add bay leaf. Bring to a boil; lower heat; cover; simmer for 20 minutes.

2. Add rice, the remaining 2 cups water, and bouillon cubes; bring to a boil; stirring to dissolve cubes. Lower heat; cover; simmer 20 minutes longer. Mix in gravy, parsley, and green onions; taste; season with salt and pepper.

SERVING SUGGESTIONS: Buttered herbed carrots, celery and tomato salad, and chocolate pudding.

---

*Remove meat from necks and stir into mixture in skillet if you wish.

"RELAX" SPINACH

Strange as it may sound, you'll have a much easier time with sandy vegetables, such as spinach, broccoli, or certain varieties of lettuce, if you "relax" them first. Simply place the vegetables in salted warm water until they've loosened up a bit and released the sand. Then lift the vegetables out of the water and rinse in a colander under cold running water.

RAISIN GRANOLA

An easy-to-make, delicious, nutritious snack for any time at all.

Bake at 300° for 30 minutes.
Makes 3 cups.

1½ cups quick-cooking oats	¼ cup water
¼ cup firmly packed brown sugar	¼ teaspoon ground cinnamon
	⅛ teaspoon salt
¼ cup vegetable oil	½ cup raisins

1. Preheat oven to 300°. Pour oats into a large shallow baking pan. Combine brown sugar, oil, water, cinnamon, and salt; stir into oats to mix well. Spread mixture evenly into pan.
2. Bake in a preheated slow oven (300°) for 30 minutes or until lightly toasted. (Stir every 10 minutes.) Remove from oven; stir in raisins. Cool; store in a tightly covered container.

PRESSURE COOKING

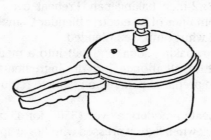

• You can prepare a wide variety of foods with a pressure cooker in a fraction of the time it would take with conventional range-top cooking. Plus, it saves energy because foods cook more quickly. It's especially ideal for dense or large vegetables, such as carrots, beets, yams, and potatoes, and for stews, soups, and some meats.

• A pressure cooker also reduces mineral and water-soluble vitamin loss in vegetables and fruits because you are not using a large amount of water, which tends to "flood" out the nutrients.

GINGERED GRAPEFRUIT

Makes 4 servings.

2 large pink grapefruit
2 tablespoons raisins

2 tablespoons slivered candied
   ginger

1. Halve and section the grapefruit.
2. Combine raisins and ginger in a cup; sprinkle over grapefruit.

BLENDER BANANA CAKE

Bake at 350° for 45 minutes.
Makes 9 servings.

3 fully ripe bananas
1 cup vegetable oil
2 eggs
1½ cups *sifted* all-purpose flour

1 cup sugar
1 teaspoon baking soda
½ teaspoon salt

1. Grease a 9 x 9 x 2-inch baking pan. Preheat oven to 350°. Whirl bananas in the container of an electric blender to make 1 cup puree. Add oil and eggs; whirl until well blended.
2. Sift flour, sugar, baking soda, and salt into a medium-size bowl. Pour banana mixture, all at once, into dry ingredients. Mix just until blended. Pour into prepared pan; rap on table to remove any large air bubbles.
3. Bake in a preheated moderate oven (350°) for 45 minutes or until center springs back when lightly pressed with fingertip. Cool on a wire rack; serve right from pan.

NO-FUSS CHOCOLATE CHEWY SQUARES

This is a simplified version of the famous Magic Cookie Bars, with fewer ingredients and no layering, that can be prepared in 5 minutes.

Bake at 350° for 25 minutes.
Makes about 16 squares.

1½ cups finely crushed graham cracker crumbs
1 can (14 ounces) sweetened condensed milk

1 package (6 ounces) semisweet chocolate pieces
½ cup chopped walnuts
½ teaspoon salt

1. Grease a 9 x 9 x 2-inch baking pan. Preheat oven to 350°. Combine all ingredients in a large bowl. Mix until well blended. Spread evenly in prepared pan.

2. Bake in a preheated moderate oven (350°) for 25 minutes. Cool in pan on a wire rack. Cut into squares.

INSTANT SNACKS ON HAND

- Miniature raisin bagels with whipped cream cheese
- Raisins, dried fruits, nuts, sunflower seeds
- Apple wedges spread with peanut butter
- Tiny rounds of cheese and whole grain crackers
- Kabobs of crunchy vegetables or fruit
- Homemade puddings or custard
- Celery strips spread with softened cheese spread
- Popcorn
- Mixed fresh fruit salad
- Oatmeal-raisin cookies
- Yogurt and fruit
- Vegetable or fruit juices
- Frozen orange juice pops
- Hard-cooked eggs

BAKED STREUSEL PEARS

Bake at 350° for 10 minutes.
Makes 6 servings.

½ cup flaked coconut
⅓ cup firmly packed light
    brown sugar
¼ cup chopped walnuts

3   tablespoons butter or
    margarine
1   can (29 ounces) pear halves,
    drained

1. Combine coconut, sugar, walnuts, and butter in small saucepan. Heat, stirring until well blended.
2. Arrange pear halves in a shallow baking pan. Spoon topping over each.
3. Bake in a preheated moderate oven (350°) for 10 minutes. Serve warm or at room temperature.

GLAZED PEARS

Broil for 5 minutes.
Makes 4 servings.

2   large ripe pears
2   teaspoons firmly packed
    dark brown sugar
1   tablespoon butter or
    margarine

2   tablespoons brandy or
    orange juice (optional)
1   orange, thinly sliced
    (for garnish)

1. Preheat broiler. Halve and core pears. Arrange in a baking pan, cut side up; sprinkle with sugar; dot with butter.
2. Broil with tops 5 inches from heat for 3 to 5 minutes or until glazed. (Watch carefully!) Pour a little brandy or orange juice, if using, over each half just before serving. Garnish with orange slices.

12

Make-Ahead Meals

M aking foods in advance is a technique often used by busy homemakers. How else would it be possible to dash off to the office or a day of shopping and still have a delicious dinner ready in a flash? Fortunately the flavor of many dishes improves when they are made in advance. The recipes have a variety that is guaranteed to suit any taste and all occasions—from Country Picnic Loaf to zesty Brazilian Black Beans with Rice and Tomato Salsa.

HOW TO FREEZE BREADS, CAKES, COOKIES, AND ROLLS

Freezing Yeast Breads and Rolls:
● Bake yeast breads and cool completely before freezing; slice for quicker thawing, then wrap in aluminum foil, following directions for drugstore wrap; freeze up to 12 months. Thaw in original wrappings for 3 hours at room temperature or place frozen sliced bread in the toaster.

- Overwrap bakery bread if it is to be stored more than 3 months.
- Bake rolls before freezing and cool completely, then wrap in aluminum foil in serving-size packages, following directions for drugstore wrap. Freeze up to 9 months. Place frozen packages in moderate oven (350°) and heat for 20 minutes, or thaw for 2 hours in original package at room temperature.

Freezing Quick Breads and Muffins:
- Bake and cool completely before freezing, then wrap in aluminum foil in serving-size packages, following directions for drugstore wrap. Freeze up to 2 months. Thaw in original wrapping for 3 hours at room temperature, or place frozen package in a moderate oven (350°) and heat until warm.

Freezing Cakes:
- Unfrosted cakes freeze best—as long as 4 months. Wrap in aluminum foil, following directions for drugstore wrap. Freeze up to 4 months. Thaw at room temperature for 1 hour.
- Frosted cakes should be frozen on a piece of cardboard or cookie sheet until firm. Wrap in aluminum foil, plastic wrap, or very large plastic bags. Freeze up to 3 months. Thaw at room temperature for 2 hours.

Freezing Cookies:
- Both dough and baked cookies can be frozen and stored for 9-12 months.
- Baked cookies should be frozen in a strong box lined with plastic wrap or aluminum foil; separate each layer with more wrap or foil; thaw cookies at room temperature for 10 minutes.
- Cookie dough may be frozen in aluminum foil or plastic wrap.
- Drop cookie dough should be thawed just until soft enough to use.
- Refrigerator cookie rolls should be thawed just enough to slice.
- Rolled cookies can be frozen already shaped; place, still frozen, onto cookie sheets.
- Freeze bar cookie dough in pan in which it is to be baked; cover with plastic wrap, then foil.

The Drugstore Wrap:
This is the best way to wrap and seal packages of baked goods for freezing. It is essential that the seal be tight so that the air won't get into the food and cause freezer-burn. Start by placing the item to be wrapped in the center of a piece of heavy-duty aluminum foil that is large enough to go around the food and allow for folding at the top and sides. Bring the two long sides up and over the food and fold them over about 1 inch (Fig. 1). Make a crease the entire length; make one more tight fold to bring the wrapping down to the level of the food surface. Press out the air toward the ends (Fig. 2). Fold the ends up and over, pressing out air and shaping to the contour of the food (Fig. 3).

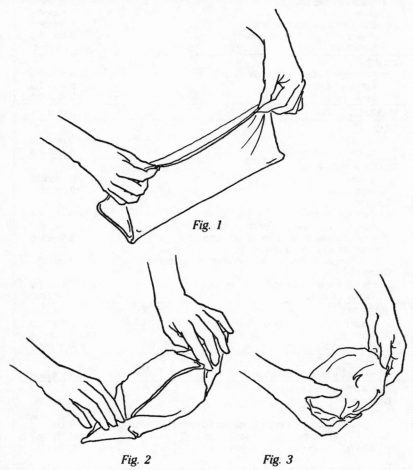

Fig. 1

Fig. 2   *Fig. 3*

RECOMENDED FREEZER-STORAGE TIMES

FOOD	MAXIMUM STORAGE TIME
APPETIZERS (Canapés, hors d'oeuvres)	½ to 1 month
BREADS	
Quick	
Baked muffins, biscuits, and simple quick breads	2 to 3 months
Rich, fruit, nut, or spicy quick breads	1 to 2 months
Unbaked dough	Up to 1 month
Yeast	
Baked bread and rolls	3 months
Danish pastry	3 months
Doughnuts, cake or yeast	3 months
Half-baked ("brown 'n' serve")	2 to 3 months
Unbaked	Up to 1 month
CAKES	
Any type butter cake, frosted or unfrosted	4 to 6 months
Angel or chiffon	2 months
Fruit	12 months
CANDIES	12 months
COOKIES	
Baked	6 to 8 months
Unbaked refrigerator	6 months
DAIRY PRODUCTS	
Butter	6 months
Margarine	12 months
Cheese	
Cottage, uncreamed	2 to 3 months
Natural Cheddar (all forms) and natural Swiss	1½ months
Cream cheese, for use as an ingredient	2 months
Process cheese products (identified on the label.	
If not so designated, the cheese is natural.)	4 months
Cream	
Heavy cream and half and half	2 months
Whipped cream	1 month
DESSERTS	
Cream puffs or éclairs	1 to 2 months
Fruit	2 to 4 months
Steamed Puddings	6 months
EGGS	
Whole, yolks or whites separated	12 months
FISH AND SHELLFISH	
Cooked	3 months
Raw	
Lean (bass. cod, perch, pike sunfish etc.)	6 to 8 months
Oily (Catfish, herring, salmon, mackerel)	2 to 3 months
Shrimp	9 to 12 months

FOOD	MAXIMUM STORAGE TIME
MEATS (RAW)	
Beef	
Steaks, roasts	8 to 12 months
Ground	2 to 4 months
Stew meats	2 to 4 months
Lamb	
Roasts	6 to 9 months
Chops	3 to 4 months
Pork	
Cured (bacon, ham)	Up to 2 months
Roasts	4 to 8 months
Chops	3 to 4 months
Sausage	1 to 3 months
MEAT (COOKED)	
Casseroles, pies, prepared dinners	2 to 3 months
Gravy, broth, sauces, and steaks	2 to 3 months
Loaves	2 to 3 months
MEAT (PROCESSED)	
Frankfurters	Up to 3 months
Bologna and luncheon meats	Not recommended
POULTRY (RAW)	
Chicken	
Cut up	9 months
Whole	12 months
Livers	1 month
Duck (Whole)	6 months
Turkey	
Cut up	6 to 9 months
Whole	12 months
POULTRY (COOKED)	
Casseroles, pies, prepared dinners	6 months
Without gravy or broth	1 month
Fried	4 months
Stuffing	1 month
Whole, unstuffed*	6 months
PASTRIES	
Pastry dough	
Unbaked	1½ to 2 months
Baked	6 to 8 months
Pies	
Unbaked	2 to 4 months
Baked	6 to 8 months
Chiffon	Up to 2 months
SANDWICHES	
Meat, poultry, cheese, jelly, or jam	1 to 2 months
SOUPS	
Including concentrated and stock	1 to 3 months
VEGETABLES (Most)	8 to 12 months depending on original quality

*Do not freeze home-stuffed poultry, because of the danger of bacterial contamination.

ORIENTAL CHICKEN SALAD

Makes 4 servings

2½ cups shredded cooked
    chicken
⅔ cup chopped radishes
¼ cup chopped green onions
3 tablespoons soy sauce

2 tablespoons honey
1 tablespoon vegetable oil
1 teaspoon vinegar
½ teaspoon ground ginger
4 cups shredded lettuce

1. Combine chicken, radishes, and green onions in a medium-size mixing bowl. Blend soy sauce, honey, oil, vinegar, and ginger in a cup; pour over chicken mixture; toss to coat evenly. Cover bowl with plastic wrap. Refrigerate at least 3 hours before serving.

2. Remove chicken mixture from refrigerator 20 to 30 minutes before serving. Toss well again.

3. Place lettuce on a serving platter; spoon chicken mixture in center, mounding slightly; drizzle over liquid remaining in bowl; toss again.

SERVING SUGGESTIONS: Piping hot crescent rolls, shredded carrot salad, and gingered pineapple.

RICE SALAD PRIMAVERA

Prepare several hours or a day ahead to allow flavors to blend.

Makes 12 servings.

1 cup long-grain rice
1 bunch broccoli
    (about 1 pound)
½ pound snow peas or sugar
    snap peas
½ pound mushrooms, thinly
    sliced
1 pint cherry tomatoes, halved
1 red pepper, halved, seeded,
    and cut into ¼-inch strips

1 green pepper, halved,
    seeded, and cut into
    ¼-inch strips
4 green onions, thinly sliced
1 cup olive or vegetable oil
2 tablespoons lemon juice
2 tablespoons tarragon vinegar
2 cloves garlic, finely chopped
1 teaspoon dry mustard
¾ teaspoon tarragon, crumbled
½ teaspoon salt
½ teaspoon pepper

1. Cook rice, following label directions. Cool to room temperature.

2. Wash and trim broccoli. Cut into bite-size pieces. Cook broccoli in a large saucepan of boiling salted water until crisp-tender; drain. Snip off the tips and remove the strings from snow peas.

3. Combine rice, broccoli, snow peas, mushrooms, cherry tomatoes, red and green pepper strips, and green onions in a large salad bowl; toss to mix lightly.

4. Combine oil, lemon juice, vinegar, garlic, mustard, tarragon, salt, and pepper in a screw-top jar. Cover; shake well. Pour over rice mixture; toss until thoroughly coated. Refrigerate until serving time.

SERVING SUGGESTIONS: Cheese Soufflé ■, dinner rolls, and Gingercake with Hot Lemon Drizzle ■.

FREEZE-AHEAD MEALS

How to Pack It
To prevent deterioration you must wrap food properly—
• Use plastic freezer wrap, durable plastic bags (heat-sealed bags give best results), aluminum foil, or rigid plastic or glass containers made especially for freezing.
• To shorten reheating time, freeze food in individual food containers, or boilable bags (when not baking).
• In a 24-hour period, never freeze more than 3 pounds of food per cubic foot or freezer capacity. Package foods in meal-size portions for easy use. (Small quantities freeze and thaw much faster than large ones).
• Label all packages with contents and date.
• Be sure to keep an inventory.

From Freezer to Table
To reheat frozen foods, you can first defrost them, or cook straight from the freezer—
• Defrosting: Thawing in the refrigerator is always safer than at room temperature. But if you must defrost at room temperature, cook the food while still cool.
• Defrosting time in refrigerator: At 40 degrees, allow 6 hours per pound.
• Defrosting at room temperature: Allow 3 hours per pound.
• Straight from the freezer: When you haven't time to defrost, or if you're heating up frozen vegetables or unbaked pies, you can cook food still frozen.
• If oven-heating, use freezer-to-oven ware, and allow 50% more baking time. Top-of-the-stove heating will require only a little more time than the recipe calls for.

COUNTRY PICNIC LOAF

A handsome make-ahead with rounds of yellow and white egg centered in the pork and ham mixture—ideal for picnicking in the park or lunching at the beach.

Bake at 350° for 2 hours.
Makes 12 servings.

2	pounds boneless shoulder or leg of pork, cut into ¼-inch cubes	½	teaspoon marjoram, crumbled
1	pound fully cooked ham, cut into ¼-inch cubes	1½	teaspoons salt
1	medium-size onion, finely chopped (½ cup)	¼	teaspoon pepper
		¼	teaspoon ground nutmeg
2	small cloves garlic, finely chopped	1½	packages piecrust mix
		6	hard-cooked eggs, shelled
3	tablespoons chopped parsley	1	egg, beaten
1	teaspoon thyme, crumbled	1	envelope unflavored gelatin
		1	can (13¾ ounces) chicken broth

1. Combine pork, ham, onion, garlic, parlsey, thyme, marjoram, salt, pepper, and nutmeg in a large bowl; blend well. Cover; reserve.

2. Prepare piecrust mix following package directions. Roll out two thirds of the pastry on a floured surface to 15-inch circle; fit into an 8- or 9-inch springform pan, pressing pastry against side and bottom of pan with pastry extending about ¼ inch above edge.

3. Spread about half of the pork mixture over bottom of pastry-lined pan. Arrange hard-cooked eggs in a circle in pan with pointed ends toward center. Cover eggs with remaining pork mixture. Preheat oven to 350°.

4. Roll out remaining pastry to a 10- or 11-inch circle; cut out a round hole in center for steam vent. Adjust pastry over filling; trim excess pastry. Press edges together to seal well and pinch to form a sharp fluted edge. Roll out trimmings; cut into leaf shapes. Arrange leaf shapes on top of loaf. Brush with beaten egg.

5. Bake in a preheated moderate oven (350°) for 2 hours or until golden brown. Place pan on a wire rack; cool 30 minutes.

6. Sprinkle gelatin over ½ cup of chicken broth in a small saucepan to soften, about 5 minutes. Cook over low heat, stirring often, until gelatin is dissolved and mixture is clear. Add remaining broth. Slowly spoon gelatin mixture through hole in center of pie. Let cool at least 2 hours longer, then refrigerate overnight.

7. To serve, loosen around edge with small knife; remove side of pan. Place pie on serving plate or cutting board; cut into wedges for serving.

SERVING SUGGESTIONS: Autumn Barley Loaf ■, cherry tomatoes, lettuce wedges with dressing, dill pickles, and assorted fresh fruit.

ZESTY PICADILLO

A spicy stew that can be quickly reheated for dinner.

Makes 6 servings.

1 large onion, sliced	½ cup pimiento-stuffed green
2 cloves garlic, finely chopped	olives or pitted black olives,
2 tablespoons vegetable oil	quartered
1½ pounds ground chuck	½ teaspoon chili powder
1 can (8 ounces) tomato sauce	½ teaspoon ground cumin
¼ cup dry white or red wine	¼ teaspoon ground cinnamon
Or: beef or chicken broth	1¼ teaspoons salt
1 large tomato, peeled and	¼ teaspoon pepper
chopped	2 green peppers, halved,
½ cup seedless raisins, plumped	seeded, and cut in strips
in warm water and drained	Hot cooked rice

1. Sauté onion and garlic in oil in a large skillet, for 5 minutes or until soft but not browned. Stir in beef, breaking up with a wooden spoon. Cook for 5 minutes, stirring frequently, until meat is no longer pink. Drain well.

2. Add tomato sauce, wine, chopped tomato, raisins, olives, chili powder, cumin, cinnamon, salt, and pepper to meat mixture. Bring to a boil; lower heat; simmer for 15 minutes.

3. Add green pepper to the meat mixture; cover; cook 1 more minute.

4. Cool; cover skillet; refrigerate.

5. About 30 minutes before serving, remove from refrigerator. Skim and discard any fat. Simmer for 10 to 15 minutes or until heated through. Serve over hot rice.

SERVING SUGGESTIONS: Tossed green salad and Apricot-Glazed Peach Cake ■.

VEGETABLE AND TOFU STEW

This stew is even better the second day after it is prepared.

Makes 6 servings.

2	large green peppers, halved, seeded, and cut into 2 x ¼-inch pieces (about 2 cups)	1	can (14½ ounces) sliced baby tomatoes
½	pound mushrooms, sliced (2 cups)	½	pound zucchini, thinly sliced
		1½	teaspoons basil, crumbled
		1½	teaspoons dillweed
¾	cup chopped onion	1	can (15 ounces) black-eyed peas, rinsed and drained
2	cloves garlic, minced		
3	tablespoons olive or vegetable oil	1	pound soybean curd or tofu, preferably firm-style, drained and cut into ½-inch cubes
2	tablespoons all-purpose flour		
2	cups water	½	cup grated Parmesan cheese

1. Sauté green pepper, mushrooms, onions, and garlic in oil in a large skillet until tender, but not brown.

2. Stir in flour until well combined. Remove skillet from heat; stir in water, tomatoes, zucchini, basil, and dill. Return to heat; cook, stirring constantly, until zucchini is almost tender.

3. Add peas and tofu; heat thoroughly, stirring very gently, so tofu does not break up. Sprinkle with Parmesan cheese just before serving.

SERVING SUGGESTIONS: Wheat Germ Bread ■, fresh spinach and tomato salad with mustard vinaigrette dressing, and sliced fresh peaches (or other seasonal fruit).

SUMMERTIME EATING: KEEP IT HEALTHY

When the weather gets hot, take extra precautions to keep outdoor eating healthy. To guard against food going bad, wrap it in aluminum foil and pack in a thermal container. (Ice substitutes will help keep cold foods chilled.) Today's containers are so pretty. You can use them to serve food as well as transport it, but be sure to choose containers with tight-fitting lids. Remember: If you're picnicking, don't put the food out until you're ready to eat. This way you will keep it free from bugs and heat.

BRAZILIAN BLACK BEANS WITH RICE AND TOMATO SALSA

This is a hearty vegetarian version of the traditional Brazilian Feijoada. The bean mixture improves if it is made 1 or 2 days before serving.

Makes 6 servings.

½ pound dried black beans (about 1¼ cups)
4 cups water
1 teaspoon salt
1 medium-size onion, peeled and studded with 4 whole cloves
1 clove garlic, peeled
½ teaspoon thyme, crumbled
½ teaspoon oregano, crumbled
1 large onion, chopped (1 cup)

1 large green pepper, halved, seeded, and diced
1 small clove garlic, minced
2 tablespoons vegetables oil
2 medium-size tomatoes, skinned and chopped (1 cup)
3 cups *cooked* brown or white rice
Tomato Salsa (recipe below)
Oranges slices
Dairy sour cream

1. Bring beans and water to a boil in a kettle or Dutch oven. Lower heat; simmer for 2 minutes. Remove from heat; cover; let stand 1 hour. Add salt, clove-studded onion, and peeled garlic; simmer for 1 hour or until beans are almost tender. Add thyme and oregano and cook for 30 minutes or until beans are tender.

2. Sauté onion, pepper, and garlic in oil in a large skillet until tender but not brown. Add beans with liquid and chopped tomatoes. Cook, stirring occasionally, until tomatoes are soft. Remove 1 cup bean mixture and mash with a fork. Return to skillet and cook a few minutes longer or until sauce thickens slightly. (May be prepared ahead to this point. Reheat, stirring occasionally.)

3. Spoon rice onto a warm serving platter. Top with black bean mixture and Tomato Salsa. Garnish with orange slices; serve with sour cream.

Tomato Salsa: Mix 1 can (14½ ounces) sliced baby tomatoes (drained), ¾ cup chopped red onion, 1 tablespoon red wine vinegar, 1 teaspoon vegetable oil, ½ teaspoon salt, 1 small clove garlic, minced, and a few dashes liquid red pepper seasoning in a bowl until combined.

SERVING SUGGESTIONS: Cornbread ■, tossed green salad, and lime sherbet.

CHILI PIE CASSEROLE

This version of a popular casserole can be prepared way ahead.

Bake at 375° for 45 minutes.
Makes 8 servings.

Cornbread (recipe below)
¾ pound ground chuck
1 medium-size onion, chopped (½ cup)
2 teaspoons salt
1 tablespoon plus 1 teaspoon chili powder
1 can (6 ounces) tomato paste
2 cups water
4 ounces Cheddar cheese, shredded (1 cup)
4 eggs, slightly beaten
3 cups milk

1. Make cornbread. Butter a 11 x 7½ x 1¾-inch baking pan. Remove cooled cornbread from pan; carefully split crosswise to make 2 thin layers. Cut bottom layer into nine 2½-inch squares. Cut each square to make 2 triangles. Crumble remaining layer and place in bottom of prepared baking pan.

2. Sauté meat and onion in a heavy skillet for 5 minutes. Stir in 1 teaspoon of the salt, the chili powder, tomato paste, and water. Cook, uncovered, stirring occasionally, 15 minutes. Spread over cornbread in pan. Sprinkle with ½ cup of the cheese.

3. Arrange cornbread triangles on top. Combine eggs with milk and remaining 1 teaspoon of salt. Pour over cornbread. Sprinkle with remaining ½ cup cheese. Cover and chill at least 1 hour or overnight. When ready to bake, preheat oven to 375°.

4. Bake uncovered in a preheated moderate oven (375°) for 45 minutes or until puffed and golden.* Remove a to wire rack. Let stand 10 minutes before serving.

Cornbread: Grease an 8 x 8 x 2-inch baking pan. Preheat oven to 425°. Combine 1 cup cornmeal, 1 cup *sifted* all-purpose flour, 4 teaspoons baking powder, and ½ teaspoon salt in a large bowl. Stir in 1 cup milk, 1 egg, and ¼ cup vegetable shortening. Beat until fairly smooth, 1 minute. Pour into prepared pan. Bake in a preheated oven (425°) 20 minutes or until center springs back when lightly pressed with fingertip; cool in pan on a wire rack.

SERVING SUGGESTIONS: Tomato-green pepper salad and fresh fruit salad.

---

*Cover tips of cornbread with aluminum foil if they are browning too rapidly.

SPINACH-CHEESE STRATA

The flavor of this convenient dish is similar to a spinach quiche.

Bake at 375° for 45 minutes.
Makes 6 servings.

1 loaf day-old French bread	1 teaspoon dillweed
1 large onion, chopped (1 cup)	1 teaspoon salt
2 tablespoons butter or	Dash pepper
margarine	6 ounces shredded Swiss
¾ cup cooked, chopped spinach	cheese (1½ cups)
(8 cups fresh)	3 eggs
Or: 1 package (10 ounces)	2½ cups milk
frozen chopped spinach,	
thawed	

1. Butter a shallow 6-cup baking dish. Cut bread into thin slices; line bottom of baking dish with half of the slices.

2. Sauté onion in butter in a large skillet for 5 minutes. Squeeze spinach dry and add to pan with dill, ¼ teaspoon of the salt, and the pepper. Stir just to combine.

3. Spread spinach over bread in pan; sprinkle with 1 cup of the cheese. Arrange remaining half loaf of the bread overlapping on top.

4. Beat eggs in a medium-size bowl; stir in milk and remaining ¾ teaspoon salt. Pour over bread. Sprinkle with remaining ½ cup cheese. Cover and chill at least 1 hour or overnight. When ready to bake, preheat oven to 375°.

5. Bake uncovered in a preheated moderate oven (375°) for 45 minutes or until puffed and golden. If bread is browning too quickly, cover with aluminum foil. Remove to a wire rack. Let stand 10 minutes before serving.

SERVING SUGGESTIONS: Giant Whole Wheat Twists ■, Carrot Salad in Lemon and Mustard Dressing ■, and butterscotch pudding.

CHILI BEEF-RICE LOAF

Sprightly and spicy with chili peppers, layered with rice and cheese.
Tastes great cold, too!

Bake at 350° for 50 minutes.
Makes enough for 2 meals (6 servings each).

1 can (13¾ ounces) chicken broth	***Meat Layer:***
	1½ pounds ground chuck or round
¼ cup water	
½ teaspoon salt	½ pound bulk sausage
1 cup long-grain rice	1½ cups fresh whole wheat bread crumbs (3 slices)
1 package (10 ounces) leaf spinach	
	2 eggs
¼ pound Monterey Jack cheese, shredded (1 cup)	1 medium-size onion, grated
	¼ cup chopped parsley
1 egg	1 teaspoon salt
1 can (4 ounces) chilies, chopped	¼ teaspoon pepper
	⅔ cup cold water
	Chopped tomatoes (optional)
	Sliced green onions (optional)

1. Bring chicken broth, water, and salt to a boil in a medium-size saucepan; stir in rice. Cover; simmer for 15 minutes or until tender. Fluff with a fork; remove from heat. Cool slightly.

2. Cook spinach following package directions. Drain well; squeeze dry. Roughly chop spinach. Preheat oven to 350°.

3. Combine rice, spinach, cheese, egg, and ¼ cup of the chilies in a medium-size bowl. Reserve remaining chilies.

4. Combine beef, sausage, bread crumbs, eggs, onion, parsley, salt, pepper, and water in a large bowl; mix just until well blended.

5. Grease two 8½ x 4½ x 2¼-inch loaf pans; line bottom and ends with a double-thick strip of aluminum foil leaving a 1-inch overhang; grease foil.

6. Press one quarter of meat mixture into each prepared pan; smooth ½ of rice mixture over each; then top with remaining meat mixture.

7. Bake both loaves in a preheated moderate oven (350°) for 50 minutes or until firm, pouring off any accumulated fat. Cool in pans for 10 minutes; loosen from sides; lift up ends of foil and set loaf to be served on a heated board; slide out foil. Serve with reserved chilies, chopped tomato, and sliced green onions, if you wish.

8. Cool, wrap, label, and freeze second meat loaf.

9. To reheat: Remove loaf from freezer to refrigerator in the morning. Unwrap; transfer to a shallow baking pan. Preheat oven to 350°. Bake, loosely covered, in a preheated moderate oven (350°) for 1 hour or until heated through.

SERVING SUGGESTIONS: Marinated vegetables in lettuce cups and fruit-topped sherbet.

"TV DINNERS"

Recycle your leftovers and use them for "TV dinners." Buy divided aluminum foil trays from a variety store and use them for holding the leftovers. Wrap, label, and freeze. Store for one of those hectic days and you'll have dinner ready in a flash.

IF THE POWER FAILS

- A fully-packed freezer will stay frozen for 48 hours if the door is not opened.
- After 36 hours, locate a freezer locker or some dry ice in case power is off longer than 48 hours.
- Order dry ice sliced, and keep in cardboard containers—never in direct contact with foods.
- If foods are firm and have ice crystals, they may be refrozen.
- If foods are no longer frozen solid, but still cool, cook and serve immediately.
- Never use warm food—it could be harmful.

SUPER MACARONI AND CHEESE

Macaroni twists and vegetables in a creamy smooth
double cheese sauce.

Bake at 350° for 40 minutes.
Makes 4 servings for dinner plus 4 servings to freeze.

1 package (1 pound) elbow twists	1 teaspoon salt
½ cup sliced green onions	¼ teaspoon pepper
½ cup diced celery	2½ cups milk
½ cup chopped carrots	1 package (8 ounces) cream cheese, at room temperature, cut into cubes
¼ cup (½ stick) butter or margarine	1 package (10 ounces) sharp Cheddar cheese, shredded
¼ cup all- purpose flour	
1 teaspoon dry mustard	

1. Cook macaroni following package directions until tender but still firm to the bite. Drain; turn into a large bowl.

2. Sauté green onions, celery, and carrot in butter in a large saucepan until crisp-tender, about 3 minutes. Add flour, dry mustard, salt, and pepper; toss to coat vegetables; cook for 1 minute. Stir in milk and continue to cook, stirring constantly until thickened and bubbly. Stir in cream cheese until melted. Add Cheddar cheese; stir until melted. Pour over macaroni; mix thoroughly.

3. Lightly butter an 8-cup baking dish. Spoon half the macaroni mixture into a prepared baking dish. Bake in a preheated moderate oven (350°) for 40 minutes or until browned and bubbly. Serve immediately.

4. Divide remaining macaroni mixture into four 4½ x 1¼-inch individual aluminum foil tart pans. Cover securely with foil; label, date, and freeze. Recommended freezer storage: 4 weeks.

5. To reheat: Remove from freezer. Preheat oven to 425°. Place tart pans on a cookie sheet. Bake, covered in a preheated hot oven (425°) for 30 minutes. Remove foil and continue to bake an additional 10 minutes or until lightly browned and bubbly.

SERVING SUGGESTIONS: Warm Italian bread, string beans vinaigrette, and Carrot-Nut Cake ■.

MACARONI AND CHEESE PIES

Bake at 375° for 30 minutes.
Makes 8 servings.

½ cup fine dry bread crumbs, or as needed

1½ pounds ground round or chuck

1 medium-size onion, chopped (½ cup)

1 clove garlic, finely chopped

1½ teaspoons salt

½ teaspoon oregano, crumbled

1 jar (15½ ounces) spaghetti sauce

1 package (8 ounces) elbow macaroni

½ cup (1 stick) butter or margarine

¼ cup all-purpose flour

½ teaspoon salt

2 cups milk

2 eggs

1 cup grated Parmesan cheese (about 3 ounces)

1. Preheat oven to 375°. Line eight 4-inch tart pans with aluminum foil; grease foil thoroughly. Sprinkle with some of the bread crumbs.

2. Sauté beef, onion, garlic, 1½ teaspoons salt, and the oregano in a large skillet, using a wooden spoon to break beef into small pieces, until beef is well browned. Drain off any excess fat. Stir in spaghetti sauce. Cook until mixture is thick enough to hold its shape. Cool.

3. Cook macaroni following package directions. Drain. Combine with butter, flour, ½ teaspoon salt, milk, and eggs, in a large bowl; blend well. Stir in cheese.

4. Spoon half of the macaroni mixture into prepared pans, dividing evenly. Spoon cooled meat mixture over macaroni, dividing evenly. Fill each pan with remaining macaroni, covering meat completely. Sprinkle each with fine dry bread crumbs.

5. Bake in a preheated moderate oven (375°) for 30 minutes. Lift foil with pie out of pan; serve hot. Or, cool pies on a wire rack. Rewrap pies completely in foil; freeze.

6. To reheat: Unwrap pies and place in a preheated moderate oven (350°); bake until heated through, about 45 minutes.

SERVING SUGGESTIONS: Tossed green salad, fried zucchini spears, and lemon pound cake.

WHAT NOT TO FREEZE

You can freeze most foods, but some suffer at freezer temperatures. For example:
• Canned beans become watery and soft
• Cooked egg white gets rubbery
• Salad dressings or mayonnaise (unless in very small amounts in a mixture) separate
• Milk sauces curdle
• Fresh salad ingredients wilt
• Processed meats (such as cold cuts) have high salt content that speeds rancidity
• Cooked white potatoes become mealy
• Home-stuffed whole poultry (still on carcass) has a danger of contamination due to slow freezing
• Gelatin-based dishes "weep" upon thawing
• Cream pie fillings become watery and lumpy

ALL-AMERICAN PASTA AND CHEESE

Almost any pasta or cheese you have on hand can be used
for this casserole.

Bake at 350° for 30 minutes.
Makes 4 servings*

1½ cups rigati, ziti, or elbow macaroni	3 tablespoons all-purpose flour
¼ cup (½ stick) margarine	Nonfat dry milk powder
1 cup fresh bread crumbs (2 slices bread)	2 tablespoons prepared mustard
1 large zucchini, sliced	1 teaspoon Worcestershire sauce
1 small onion, chopped (¼ cup)	6 ounces American cheese
	1 large tomato

1. Cook pasta in salted boiling water following package directions.
2. While pasta cooks, melt margarine in a medium-size saucepan; toss 1 tablespoon with bread crumbs in a small bowl and reserve.
3. Sauté zucchini slices in margarine in saucepan for 2 minutes; remove with a slotted spoon and reserve. Sauté onion until soft in margarine; stir in flour and cook 1 minute; add enough dry milk to equal 2 cups of prepared milk, and 2½ cups of the boiling pasta

cooking water. Cook, stirring constantly, 3 minutes; stir in mustard and Worcestershire sauce. Preheat oven to 350°.

4. Shred 1 cup of the cheese (about 4 ounces) and stir into saucepan until melted; drain pasta and return to kettle; pour sauce over and blend well; pour into 8-cup shallow casserole.

5. Cut tomato into wedges; make a pretty pattern on pasta of sautéed zucchini slices, tomato wedges, and buttered crumbs; cut remaining cheese into thin slices; place on top of casserole.

6. Bake in a preheated moderate oven (350°) for 30 minutes or until crumbs are golden and casserole is bubbling hot.

SERVING SUGGESTIONS: Broccoli vinaigrette, breadsticks, and orange-grapefruit salad.

---

*This recipe can easily be doubled, with half spooned into an 8-cup oven-proof casserole lined with heavy-duty aluminum foil. (Do *not* include tomato wedges in freezer dish.) Seal, label, date, and freeze. When solid, remove foil package from casserole. To serve, peel foil from frozen pasta, place in original casserole. To reheat: Bake in a preheated moderate oven (350°) for 55 minutes.

MORE ON FREEZING

- Cool hot foods rapidly by placing in ice water or in the refrigerator.
- To free baking dishes for other uses while storing frozen food, line dish with aluminum foil, leaving enough extra foil to wrap over top of food; freeze (preferably overnight). When frozen solid, lift contents from dish and wrap. Label with date and contents; return to freezer. To reheat: Peel off foil, return to baking dish and bake.
- Always check that your freezer temperature is about 0°F or below to ensure good freezing quality.
- If your family eats in shifts, you might package some single servings for easy defrosting and cooking later.
- Rotate frozen foods so that the most recent foods aren't always up front.
- Freeze soups and rich sauces in ice cube trays, then remove cubes and store in plastic bags.
- Always fill pie shells with cool or cold filling before freezing.
- Divide your freezer into sections for meats, poultry, desserts, etc., to make searching for what you need easier.

PORK CHOPS VALENCIA

Look for the family-size package of pork chops to make this succulent dish.

Bake at 350° for 40 minutes.
Makes enough for 2 meals (6 servings each).

½   cup chopped celery
4   tablespoons butter or
    margarine
1¼ cups water
1   package (6 ounces)
    cornbread stuffing mix
¼   cup chopped parsley
1   navel orange, cut into
    6 wedges and thinly sliced
1   tablespoon vegetable oil, or
    more as needed
3½ to 4 pounds thin loin pork
    chops (16 to 20)

1   teaspoon salt
½   teaspoon pepper
1   can (6 ounces) orange juice
    concentrate
1¼ cups water
¾   cup chili sauce
2   teaspoons Worcestershire
    sauce
    Celery leaves (optional)
    Parsley sprigs (optional)
    Orange slices (optional)

1. Sauté celery in butter in a large saucepan for 5 minutes; add water, stuffing mix and seasoning packet, parsley, and about ⅔ of the sliced orange. Toss lightly with a fork; cover; let stand while browning chops. Preheat oven to 350°.

2. Heat oil in a large skillet; brown pork chops on both sides over high heat; remove as they brown. Sprinkle with salt and pepper.

3. When all chops are browned, add orange juice concentrate, water, chili sauce, and Worcestershire sauce to skillet; stir to loosen any brown bits. Remove from heat; add remaining sliced orange.

4. Arrange pork chops in two 12 x 8 x 1½-inch baking dishes (one lined with foil), overlapping slightly, with a rounded tablespoon of stuffing between each. Spoon sauce around pork chops.

5. Bake both dishes, uncovered, in a preheated moderate oven (350°), brushing meat with sauce several times, for 40 minutes or until tender. If serving unlined dish right away, garnish the chops with celery leaves, parsley sprigs, and orange slices if you wish.

6. Cool, wrap, label, and freeze second dish.

7. To reheat: Remove second dish from freezer to refrigerator in the morning. Preheat oven to 350°. Bake, covered, in a preheated moderate oven (350°) for 50 minutes or until heated through.

SERVING SUGGESTIONS: Hot cooked rice, sautéed green peppers, and raisin-stuffed baked apples.

LEMON-DILL MEATBALLS
WITH ARTICHOKES

Delicate nuggets of turkey flavored with lemon and dill, sauced with lemon, capers, and artichoke hearts, is truly company fare.

Make 4 servings for dinner plus 4 servings to freeze.

4 slices white bread	3¾ cups water
¼ cup milk	½ cup (1 stick) butter or
2 pounds raw ground turkey	margarine
or chicken	½ cup all-purpose flour
¼ cup grated onion	¼ cup lemon juice
2 eggs	2 tablespoons drained capers
1 tablespoon chopped fresh	2 cans (16 ounces each)
dill	artichoke hearts, drained
Or: 1 teaspoon dillweed	and cut in half
1 tablespoon grated lemon rind	Lemon wedges (optional)
1 teaspoon salt	Parsley sprigs (optional)
¼ teaspoon pepper	
1 can (10¾ ounces) condensed	
chicken broth	

1. Soak bread in milk in a large bowl; crumble or mash with fork. Add turkey, onion, eggs, dill, lemon rind, salt, and pepper; mix thoroughly. Chill in refrigerator for 1 hour.

2. Moisten palms of hands. Shape meat mixture into 32 walnut-size meatballs (about 2 level tablespoonsful).

3. Combine chicken broth and water in a large skillet; bring to a boil. Add meatballs in a single layer. (You may have to do this twice). Lower heat; cover. Simmer for 15 minutes. Remove meatballs with a slotted spoon to a shallow dish; cover loosely with wax paper to prevent drying.

4. Strain poaching liquid through a cheesecloth-lined strainer into a 4-cup glass measure. (You should have 4 cups liquid.) Add water, if necessary.

5. Melt butter in same skillet; stir in flour and cook until bubbly, 1 minute. Stir in poaching liquid and continue to cook until thickened and bubbly. Stir in lemon juice and capers. Return meatballs; add artichokes; heat thoroughly.

6. Spoon half the meatballs, artichokes and sauce into a shallow serving casserole. Garnish with lemon wedges and parsley if you wish. Serve immediately.

7. To freeze the remaining portions, spoon 4 meatballs, a few artichoke halves, and some sauce (about ⅓ cup each) into individual boilable bags; heat-seal. Label, date, and freeze. Recommended freezer storage: 2 months.

8. To reheat: Bring water to a boil in a medium-size saucepan. Place boilable bag into water, boil 15 minutes. Remove bag from water; cut off top of bag with scissors; slide mixture into a serving casserole or individual serving dishes.

SERVING SUGGESTIONS: Small dinner rolls, hot cooked rice, buttered carrots, and orange pound cake.

NUTMEG LEAVES

Bake at 350° for 8 minutes.
Makes 8 dozen cookies.

1½ cups *sifted* all-purpose flour	½ cup sugar
1 teaspoon baking powder	1½ tablespoons milk
½ teaspoon baking soda	1 teaspoon vanilla
½ teaspoon ground nutmeg	4 squares (1 ounce each)
½ cup (1 stick) butter or	semisweet chocolate, melted
margarine, softened	½ cup chopped pistachio nuts
1 egg	

1. Sift flour, baking powder, baking soda, and nutmeg onto wax paper.
2. Beat butter, egg, and sugar in a large bowl with an electric mixer until fluffy, about 3 minutes. Stir in milk and vanilla. Stir in flour mixture until blended and smooth. Chill several hours or overnight.
3. Preheat oven to 350°.
4. Roll out a quarter of the dough on a lightly floured surface to a ¼-inch thickness. Cut out dough with a small floured leaf-shape cookie cutter. Reroll scraps of dough and cut out as many leaves as you can. Arrange on an ungreased cookie sheet, 1 inch apart. Repeat with remaining dough.
5. Bake in a preheated moderate oven (350°) for 8 minutes or until cookies are set and lightly browned. Cool on wire racks. Decorate with the melted chocolate and chopped pistachios.

CARROT-PINEAPPLE UPSIDE-DOWN CAKES

These can be baked ahead, frozen, and then thawed
at room temperature.

Bake at 350° for 30 minutes.
Makes 10 servings.

¼ cup (½ stick) butter or margarine, melted
½ cup firmly packed light brown sugar
1 can (20 ounces) pineapple slices in pineapple juice, drained and juice reserved
20 pecan halves
2 cups finely shredded carrots (about 4 medium-size carrots)

2 cups *sifted* all-purpose flour
1¼ cups sugar
1¼ teaspoons baking soda
1 teaspoon salt
1 teaspoon ground cinnamon
1 teaspoon ground nutmeg
½ teaspoon ground cloves
½ cup vegetable oil
3 eggs
1 teaspoon vanilla

1. Preheat oven to 350°.

2. Pour melted butter into ten 4-inch tart pans, dividing evenly. Sprinkle brown sugar evenly over butter in each pan. Place 1 drained pineapple slice in each pan. Place 2 pecan halves in center of each slice. Set aside.

3. Bring ⅓ cup reserved pineapple juice in small saucepan to a boil. Pour over carrots in large mixing bowl; let stand 5 minutes. Add flour, sugar, baking soda, salt, cinnamon, nutmeg, and cloves; beat with an electric mixer until well blended.

4. Add oil, eggs, and vanilla; beat 2 minutes longer. Pour batter evenly over pineapple slice in each pan.

5. Bake in a preheated moderate oven (350°) for 30 minutes or until center springs back when lightly pressed with fingertip.

6. Invert pans onto a wire rack; leave pans in place for 2 minutes. Carefully lift off pans; cool cakes completely. Serve. To freeze, wrap each tightly in aluminum foil; then freeze. To serve, unwrap cakes; thaw at room temperature for 30 to 45 minutes.

13

Entertaining on a Budget

You don't have to smash your budget when you entertain. You can learn to entertain with ingenuity—rather than with bundles of cash. Here are dozens of pointers to help you plan and execute a perfect party on a meager budget.

In this chapter you'll find recipes for almost every occasion: Hors d'oeuvres and appetizers for cocktail parties, elegant entrées for sit-down dinners, and informal fare for treating the kids next door. And you can toast the most special occasions with sparkling punches—Tangerine-Apricot Champagne Punch or Creamy Pineapple-Coconut Punch.

Here is a checklist to take the worry out of entertaining:

• Plan the entire party menu before you do anything else, and use it as a blueprint from which to shop, prepare food, assemble utensils and serving pieces, and set up table decorations.

• Prepare a countdown list of cooking times, oven temperatures, serving directions and so on, and tape it to the refrigerator or other prominent place for easy reference during the party.

• Don't crowd a small freezer by stockpiling homemade ice. It may be worth the added expense to buy ice right before the party and not sacrifice storage space or to simply keep ice in a picnic cooler.

• Don't assume paper is cheaper; sometimes the cost of renting dishes, glassware, and the like is about the same as—or even less than—buying paper. If you don't own enough place settings in one pattern, mix several different ones for an eclectic, personal look.

• Avoid last-minute confusion by setting out all serving dishes ahead of time and tagging them with the name of the dish they will contain.

• Don't over-extend yourself by cooking every course of the menu. If a local caterer or deli is known for great fried chicken or spaghetti sauce, plan a menu around one of these purchased main dishes and add the simpler homemade dishes yourself.

• Plan your regular weekly food shopping to include family food along with the party food. Remember, when refrigerator and kitchen space will be needed for party preparations, it may not be the week to stock up on extra orange juice, coffee, or bulky staples.

• Prepare the bar and set the table the night before. The best way to remember everything you need is to sit down with a pencil and paper and mentally act out the serving and eating of the meal from start to finish.

• Clear counters of all non-essentials like the toaster, coffeepot, cookie jar, and such. This will give you valuable extra work space.

• Be inventive about seating. Picnic benches, wicker love seats, or stools can all be arranged around a dining table or used to augment seating at a buffet. If you entertain often, invest in cheap, comfortable folding or stacking chairs for reliable extra seating. Tag sale finds can be scrubbed, stripped, or spray-painted and fitted with ribbon-tied seat cushions.

• If you plan to use sterling silver, it can be polished far in advance and wrapped in airtight plastic bags to prevent tarnishing.

• Instead of piling coats on a bed, hang them on an improvised clothing rack made from a sturdy clothesline or broomstick hung between pipes in the laundry room.

• Always start the evening with an empty dishwasher into which used dishes can disappear between courses. If scraping dishes between courses isn't your style, hide the dishes in a soap-and-water-filled tub placed beneath the sink.

• Make sure you have enough coat hangers and ash trays to accommodate a crowd.

• Plan your advance work by thinking through the parts of the menu in terms of how far ahead things may be made. Most cookies lose nothing if they are baked ahead, frozen, and served straight from the freezer. On the other hand highly seasoned garlic or oniony sauces or dressings should usually be made closer to party time since their flavors intensify on standing.

• Don't send "Regrets Only" invitations. That will only lead to worry about who's really coming and who simply forgot to call in.

• Dress for the kitchen as well as the party. Unless you've planned a totally self-service meal, don't wear impractical, fancy outfits to your own party.

• Between dinner and dessert, sneak into the living room to clear away used pre-dinner plates, glasses, and ashtrays. Bring a tray to get it all on one trip.

• If space is limited, plan a moveable feast. Try hors d'oeuvres in the living room, dinner in the dining room, with as few extra plates per person as possible, and dessert and coffee served buffet-style from the kitchen.

• To make the party more fun, plan a menu that you enjoy cooking and eating, and invite the people you really like to be with.

CRUDITÉS WITH AÏOLI

Makes about 1½ cups dip.

3   egg yolks
3   cloves garlic
1   tablespoon Dijon-style
    mustard
1 . tablespoon lemon juice
¼   teaspoon pepper
1¼ cups vegetable oil

1   tablespoon water
1   tablespoon drained capers
Chilled crudités: zucchini
sticks, carrot slices, celery
chunks, cauliflower and
broccoli flowerets

1. Combine egg yolks, garlic, mustard, lemon juice, and pepper in the container of an electric blender; whirl until smooth and thickened.
2. Remove center of blender cover. With blender running, pour in oil in a slow, steady steam. Add water; blend well. Remove to a medium-size bowl. Stir in capers. Refrigerate.
3. Served with chilled crudités.

MINIATURE SAUSAGE-CRÊPE QUICHES

A lively sausage and cheese mixture is baked in a
make-ahead crêpe shell.

Bake at 425° for 5 minutes, then at 350° for 15 minutes.
Makes about 48 miniature quiches.

Crêpe Batter:
3   eggs
¼   teaspoon salt
2   cups *sifted* all-purpose flour
2   cups milk
¼   cup (½ stick) butter or
    margarine, melted

Sausage Filling:
2   cups shredded zucchini
    (about 2 medium-size or
    ½ pound)
2   tablespoons butter or
    margarine

5   sweet Italian sausages
    (5 ounces)
½   cup shredded Swiss cheese
    (2 ounces)
2   eggs, slightly beaten
½   cup milk
¼   cup cup light cream or
    half and half
2   tablespoons grated Parmesan
    cheese
¼   teaspoon salt
⅛   teaspoon white pepper

1. **For crepês:** Beat eggs with salt in a small bowl until foamy. Gradually add flour alternately with milk; beat until smooth. Beat in melted butter; cover; refrigerate 1 hour or more.
2. Make crêpes in a lightly buttered 6- to 7-inch skillet, using 1 tablespoon batter for each crêpe. Cook 1 side of crêpe until golden brown; turn and lightly cook underside. Keep crêpes warm between sheets of wax paper. (Crêpes may be stacked with plastic wrap or aluminum foil, overwrapped with freezer weight plastic wrap and frozen for up to 2 weeks.)
3. Preheat oven to hot 425°. **For filling:** Sauté zucchini in 1 tablespoon of the butter in a large skillet until tender, about 5 minutes. Remove casing from sausages. Cook sausage in remaining 1 tablespoon butter over low heat in same skillet, breaking up with a spoon, until no longer pink or raw. Drain on paper toweling. Add sausage, Swiss cheese, eggs, milk, cream, Parmesan, salt, and pepper to zucchini; mix well. Grease well 1¾-inch miniature muffin pan cups.
4. Press crêpes, browned side out, into prepared muffin pan. Spoon sausage filling into crêpe-lined cups.
5. Bake in a preheated hot oven (425°) for 5 minutes. Lower heat to modeate (350°) and bake an additional 15 minutes or until tops of quiches are lightly golden. Remove to a heated serving dish; serve warm.

CHILLED TOMATO SOUP

Makes 12 first-course servings.

2 cans condensed tomato soup	1 teaspoon salt
2 pints light cream	½ teaspoon pepper
2 teaspoons lemon juice	½ cup chopped green onions
2 teaspoons prepared horseradish	(plus extra for garnish)
Few drops liquid red pepper seasoning	1 cup small curd cottage cheese (plus extra for garnish)
	Dairy sour cream (optional)

1. Combine soup, cream, lemon juice, horseradish, red pepper seasoning, salt, and pepper in a large bowl; beat until well blended.
2. Stir in onions and cottage cheese. Refrigerate until thoroughly chilled. Serve in chilled bowls or cups, topped with dollops of sour cream or additional cottage cheese, and a sprinkling of chopped green onions, if you wish.

BEEF AND CABBAGE PASTIES

Beef, onions, and shredded cabbage make a moist filling for this variation of Cornish pasties. Serve hot with soup, or chill and pack for a picnic.

Bake at 400° for 50 minutes.
Makes 6 servings.

Pastry*:
3   cups *sifted* all-purpose flour
½   teaspoon salt
½   cup (1 stick) chilled unsalted butter or margarine, cut into thin slices
½   cup vegetable shortening
7   to 8 tablespoons ice water

Filling:
5   cups packed shredded cabbage (about a 1½-pound head cabbage)
3   tablespoons vegetable oil
½   pound lean boneless chuck, cut into ¼-inch pieces

1   large onion, finely chopped (1 cup)
1   clove garlic, minced
2   teaspoons Worcestershire sauce
½   teaspoon salt
¼   teaspoon pepper

Glaze:
1   egg yolk
½   teaspoon water
    Pickle fans (optional)
    Black olives (optional)
    Parsley sprigs (optional)

1. Prepare pastry: Combine flour and salt in a medium-size bowl. Cut in butter and shortening with pastry blender or fingertips until mixture resembles coarse meal. Sprinkle water over mixture, 1 tablespoon at a time, mixing lightly with a fork, just until pastry holds together and leaves side of bowl clean. Gather dough together in a ball; wrap in wax paper; refrigerate at least 1 hour.

2. Prepare filling: Sauté cabbage in oil in a large skillet over medium heat, stirring often, until golden brown and tender, about 15 minutes (you should have about 2 cups). Transfer to a medium-size bowl; cool to room temperature.

3. Add beef, onion, garlic, Worcestershire sauce, salt, and pepper to cabbage; mix well.

4. Preheat oven to 400°.

5. Assemble pasties: Divide dough into 6 equal pieces. Roll out each piece on a lightly floured surface to an 8-inch circle. Place ⅔ cup of the filling in center of each; shape filling into an oval mound, leaving

---

*1½ packages (11 ounces each) piecrust mix may be substituted for the pastry ingredients. Prepare following package directions.

a 1-inch margin at either end of filling. Moisten edges of pastry with water. Bring sides of pastry up over filling; pinch pastry together over filling ot make 1-inch seam down center of pastry. Fold seam in half; pinch together securely. Flute or crimp with fork to make decorative edge. Place pasties in a large shallow baking pan.

6. Beat egg yolk and water in a small cup; brush over pasties. Make a small steam vent on each side of seams.

7. Bake in a preheated hot oven (400°) for 50 minutes or until pastry is golden brown and filling is tender when pierced through steam vents with wooden pick. Cool in a baking pan for 5 minutes. Arrange on a serving platter; garnish with pickle fans, black olives, and parsley if you wish.

SERVING SUGGESTIONS: Tomato-Orange Soup ■, Tangy Cucumber Salad ■, and Rice Pudding ■.

RENTING PARTY EQUIPMENT

• Planning a barbecue, party, or home wedding? There's no need to buy all the necessary equipment, especially if you use it only once in a while. It's more economical to rent.

• First, decide on the menu and from that make a list of the equipment you will need to prepare and serve the food. Then, visit a rental center where you'll find everything you need—grills, rotisseries, tables, chairs, china, even beverage fountains! Your rental center will also have table linens, skirting, and other accessories for a successful party.

• Reserve early to assure the quantity and types of equipment you need. Read the rental contract thoroughly so you are familiar with any damage charges. Return the rental equipment clean to avoid additional cleaning charges.

RUSSIAN PIROSHKI

Makes 8 servings.

Russian Piroshki Filling:

1 small onion, finely chopped (¼ cup)
½ cup finely shredded cabbage
3 tablespoons butter or margarine
½ pound ground round
2 hard-cooked eggs, shelled and chopped
¼ cup chopped dill
Or: 2 tablespoons dillweed
¼ cup dairy sour cream or ¼ cup small curd cottage cheese
½ teaspoon salt
Vegetable oil for frying
Sour cream (optional)

Wrapper:

1 package (14 ounces) spring or egg roll wrappers
Or: 1 package piecrust mix*

1. Sauté onion and cabbage in butter in a medium-size skillet until onion is tender, about 3 minutes. Add beef; cook, breaking up with a spoon, until no longer pink. Remove from heat; cool slightly.

2. Stir in eggs, dill, sour cream, and salt; mix well. (Makes about 2 cups filling.)

3. Divide filling evenly among 8 spring roll wrappers. Fold bottom of wrapper over filling; fold in both sides, then fold down top, completely enclosing filling.

4. Pour enough oil into a large saucepan to make a 2-inch depth. Heat to 375° on a deep-fat frying thermometer. Deep-fry rolls, turning often, until golden brown. Drain on paper toweling. Serve with a dollop of sour cream, if you wish.

---

*For piecrust mix, roll out pastry; cut out 4-inch rounds. Fill and fry as above.

MINI BISCUITS

Bake at 450° for 12 minutes.
Makes about 60 biscuits.

2 cups *sifted* all-purpose flour
3 teaspoons baking powder
1 teaspoon salt
1 teaspoon dry mustard
¼ cup vegetable shortening
¾ cup milk

1. Preheat oven to 450°. Sift flour, baking powder, salt, and dry mustard into a medium-size bowl. Cut in shortening with a pastry blender until mixture resembles coarse cornmeal.

2. Make a well in center of dry ingredients; add milk. Stir just enough to mix dough. *Do not overmix.*

3. Knead dough gently about 10 times on a lightly floured board. Using a floured rolling pin, roll dough into a 10 x 6-inch rectangle. Cut into 1-inch squares. Place on an ungreased cookie sheet, 1 inch apart.

4. Bake in a preheated hot oven (450°) for 12 minutes or until lightly browned.

CORN QUICHE

Great as an appetizer or luncheon main dish.

Bake crust at 425° for 5 minutes; bake quiche at 425° for 10 minutes, then at 350° for 30 minutes.
Makes 8 servings.

½ **package piecrust mix**	1⅓ **cups corn kernels**
4 **eggs**	**(from 2 large ears)**
1 **cup heavy cream**	¾ **cup shredded Swiss cheese**
1¼ **teaspoons salt**	**(3 ounces)**
¼ **teaspoon pepper**	**Chopped chives or parsley**
1 **small onion, finely chopped**	**(optional)**
(¼ cup)	**Bacon, crumbled (optional)**

1. Preheat oven to 425°. Prepare piecrust mix following package directions for a 9-inch pastry shell with a high fluted edge.

2. Bake in preheated hot oven (425°) for 5 minutes.

3. Combine eggs, heavy cream, salt, pepper, onion, and corn in a medium-size bowl; beat until well blended. Stir in cheese. Turn into partially baked shell.

4. Bake in a preheated hot oven (425°) for 10 minutes. Lower oven temperature to moderate (350°).

5. Continue baking for 30 minutes or until custard mixture is almost set in center. (Do not overbake.) Sprinkle with chopped chives, parsley, or crumbled cooked bacon if you wish.

SERVING SUGGESTIONS: Cucumber and Tomato Vinaigrette ■, sesame breadsticks, and Hearty Bread Pudding ■.

BEANS NIÇOISE

A tangy bean salad that would serve equally well as a summer luncheon dish. Another make-ahead dish that can also be toted to a picnic or family get-together.

Makes 12 servings.

¾ pound fresh string beans
1 cup vegetable oil
2 tablespoons red wine vinegar
2 tablespoons lemon juice
2 cloves garlic, finely chopped
1 teaspoon dry mustard
½ teaspoon salt
¼ teaspoon pepper
2 cans (20 ounces each) cannellini beans, drained
2 cans (6½ ounces each) chunk white tuna, drained and broken into chunks
1 can (2 ounces) flat anchovies, drained
3 hard-cooked eggs, shelled and quartered
3 ripe tomatoes, cut into wedges
1 medium-size red onion, thinly sliced
1 can (5.7 ounces) pitted ripe olives, drained

1. Trim ends of string beans. Cook in a large pot of boiling salted water just until crisp tender. Drain; rinse under cold water; drain again.

2. Combine oil, vinegar, lemon juice, garlic, basil, dry mustard, salt, and pepper in a screw-top jar. Cover; shake well to mix. Pour about ¼ cup over drained string beans in a salad bowl. Let stand 30 minutes.

3. Combine string beans, cannellini beans, tuna, anchovies, egg, tomatoes, onion, and olives in a medium-size bowl; toss to mix. Pour remaining dressing over all. Chill.

SERVING SUGGESTIONS: Crudités with Aïoli ■, Mini Biscuits ■, Spinach and Carrot Salad ■, and Nutmeg Leaves ■.

SPINACH AND CARROT SALAD

Makes 12 servings.

2 pounds fresh spinach	2 tablespoons sugar
2 heads Belgian endive	2 to 3 teaspoons dry mustard
2 large carrots, pared and diagonally sliced	1 teaspoon salt
⅓ cup olive or vegetable oil	¼ teaspoon pepper
⅓ cup tarragon or cider vinegar	1 cup dairy sour cream

1. Wash spinach; remove and discard stems. Dry thoroughly and break into bite-size pieces into a salad bowl. Reserve and refrigerate 8 endive leaves for garnish; cut remaining endive into ½-inch slices.
2. Combine spinach, endive, and carrot slices in the salad bowl; toss lightly to mix. Refrigerate.
3. Combine oil, vinegar, sugar, dry mustard, salt, and pepper in a screw-top jar. Cover; shake well. Gradually stir in sour cream until well blended. To serve, pour dressing over salad; toss gently to mix. Garnish with the reserved endive leaves.

TOMATO COLESLAW

Makes 12 servings.

1 small head green cabbage (about 1½ pounds)	4 large ripe tomatoes
4 carrots, pared and grated	1 cup mayonnaise
2 medium-size green peppers, halved, seeded, and diced	3 tablespoons white vinegar
	2 teaspoons sugar
1 small onion, chopped (¼ cup)	1 teaspoon celery seed
	1 teaspoon salt
	¼ teaspoon pepper

1. Trim and core cabbage; shred. Combine in a large bowl with carrots, green peppers, and onion.
2. Dice 2 of the tomatoes; add to cabbage. Combine mayonnaise, vinegar, sugar, celery seed, salt, and pepper in a small bowl; blend well. Pour over vegetables; toss. Cover; refrigerate several hours.
3. To serve, slice remaining 2 tomatoes; place around outer edge of bowl.

LIMA BEAN COLESLAW

Makes 12 servings.

4	cups shredded cabbage (½ medium-size head)	⅓	cup tarragon vinegar
		2	tablespoons sugar
2	packages (10 ounces each) frozen lima beans, thawed	1	tablespoon caraway seeds
		1	teaspoon salt
2	red Delicious apples, sliced	1	cup dairy sour cream
⅓	cup olive or vegetable oil		

1. Combine cabbage, beans, and apple slices in a salad bowl; toss lightly.

2. Combine oil, vinegar, sugar, caraway seeds, salt, and sour cream in a small bowl, blending well. Pour over vegetables; toss lightly. Chill until serving time.

USE YOUR IMAGINATION

• Tall glass pitchers make elegant servers for cold soups, such as gazpacho or vichyssoise.

• Large stemmed wineglasses hold toppings such as garlic-flavored croutons, slivers of freshly snipped chives, or chopped fresh tomatoes; serve on a lacy wicker tray.

• Try an assortment of copper molds as containers for crudités in a rustic setting. Choose molds of different heights and line with crushed ice. Arrange celery, carrot and cucumber sticks at back of molds, then fill in front with flowerettes of cauliflower and broccoli, slices of zucchini and mushroom quarters.

• Choose handmade pottery mugs to hold assortments of dips.

• Soup tureens shouldn't be put away in the warm weather. They are unusual choices as punch bowls. Since they are often oval in shape, try freezing the water for the ice block in an oval-shaped pâté mold, slip into the tureen, then fill with your favorite punch ingredients. Garnish the tureen tray with leaves and flowers that complement the tureen's colors.

• Large platters which are usually kept at the top of the highest shelf to hold the holiday bird, make a new and exciting way to present hearty, main-dish salads. Line the platter well with leaf, Boston, or romaine lettuce leaves, and arrange a colorful assortment of vegetables, meats or seafood, and cheese in a decorative pattern. Serve the dressing separately in a gravy boat, then each guest can choose his own portion of salad ingredients and dressing.

• ZIPPY FRANKS: Melt a 10-ounce jar of currant jelly with ½ cup mustard and 1 tablespoon horseradish; add 1 pound frankfurters, cut into 1-inch pieces; heat and serve.

• BEAN DIP: Combine 1 can refried beans, 1 can (4 ounces) chopped, drained green chilies, and ½ cup sour cream. Serve with corn chips.

• BAGNA CAUDA: Heat 1 stick butter, ¼ cup olive oil, a few cloves crushed garlic, 1 can chopped, drained anchovies. Serve with raw vegetable dippers.

• CHEESE SPREAD: Combine 1 cup shredded sharp Cheddar cheese, ½ cup margarine, 1 tablespoon sherry, and 1 tablespoon chutney. Serve with crisp crackers.

• TUNA-WALNUT SPREAD: Combine 1 can (6 ounces) drained tuna, a 3-ounce package cream cheese, lemon juice, chopped onion, chopped walnuts, and pickle relish. Serve with crisp crackers.

• PEPPERED PEAS: Heat 1 can chick-peas; drain well; toss with plenty of black pepper. Serve in place of popcorn or nuts.

• SARDINE TEASER: Arrange boneless, skinless sardines in a small, shallow dish; surround with chopped onions, lemon wedges, crisp crackers.

• CELERY BOATS: Fill with herb-flavored or wine-flavored cheese; cut into 2-inch fingers.

• BITE-SIZE SANDWICHES: Spread assorted crackers with liver pâté, meat or fish pastes; garnish with olives, pimientos, or chopped nuts.

• SALAMI CORNUCOPIAS: Spread salami slices with chive cream cheese; stack; cut into wedges; spear with wooden picks.

POTATO SALAD ROULADE

Makes 8 servings

2   pounds boiled Idaho
    potatoes, pared
½   cup chopped celery
⅓   cup mayonnaise
3   hard-cooked eggs, shelled
    and chopped
2   tablespoons chopped onion
1   teaspoon salt
½   teaspoon paprika
1   cup small curd cottage
    cheese (or low-fat or dry),
    well drained

2   tablespoons mayonnaise
2   tablespoons chopped green
    pepper
2   tablespoons diced pimiento
½   cup chopped parsley
    (optional)
    Hard-cooked egg slices
    (optional)

1. Mash potatoes in a large bowl. Mix in celery, the ⅓ cup mayonnaise, eggs, onion, salt, and paprika. Chill, until firm.
2. Combine cottage cheese, the 2 tablespoons mayonnaise, green pepper, and pimiento in a small bowl.
3. Line a 15 x 10 x 1-inch jelly roll pan with wax paper. Spread potato mixture evenly in pan. Spread cottage cheese mixture over top, leaving a 1-inch border. Roll up from short side, jelly roll fashion. Chill.
4. To serve, sprinkle with parsley. Garnish with hard-cooked egg slices if you wish.

REUBEN POTATO SALAD

Bake at 350° for 8 minutes.
Makes 12 servings.

6   large potatoes
6   slices bacon
1   large onion, chopped (1 cup)
½   teaspoon salt
¼   teaspoon pepper
2   packages (1 pound each)
    sauerkraut

1   bottle (8 ounces) creamy
    Russian dressing
4   slices sandwich-size Swiss
    cheese, cut into lengthwise
    strips
¼   cup chopped parsley
    (optional)

1. Cook potatoes in boiling salted water just until tender. Drain. Peel and cut into ¼-inch-thick slices.

2. Cook bacon in a medium-size skillet until crisp. Drain on paper toweling. Sauté onion in bacon drippings remaining in skillet just until tender, about 3 minutes. Grease a shallow 6-cup baking dish. Preheat oven to 350°.

3. Combine potatoes, salt, pepper, sauerkraut, and salad dressing in prepared baking dish. Crumble bacon over potatoes. Top with cheese strips in lattice design.

4. Bake in a preheated moderate oven (350°) for 8 minutes or just until cheese melts. Sprinkle with parsley if you wish.

SERVING SUGGESTIONS: Cracked Wheat, Corn, and Sesame Loaf ■, Tomato Coleslaw ■, and Oatmeal-Raisin Cookies ■.

COMPANY CHICKEN SALAD

This colorful salad is a great way to use up leftover chicken.

Makes 6 servings.

¾ cup dry white wine	½ cup chopped green pepper
½ cup olive or vegetable oil	½ cup chopped red pepper
¼ cup cider vinegar	1 small head Boston lettuce, separated into leaves
1 small onion, minced (¼ cup)	
1 clove garlic, minced	3 hard-cooked eggs, shelled and sliced
¼ teaspoon tarragon, crumbled	
1 teaspoon salt	2 medium-size ripe tomatoes
¼ teaspoon pepper	Parsley sprigs
4 cups diced cooked chicken (3 to 4 whole cooked chicken breasts)	

1. Combine wine, oil, vinegar, onion, garlic, tarragon, salt, and pepper in a large bowl. Add chicken and green and red pepper; toss to coat. Cover; chill.

2. To serve, drain mixture well. Line a salad bowl with Boston lettuce leaves; spoon salad into bowl. Garnish with hard-cooked egg slices, tomatoes, and parsley.

SERVING SUGGESTIONS: Cold rice salad, string beans vinaigrette, and Cottage Cheese Pound Cake ■.

CUBAN CHICKEN TACOS

Bake at 350° for 20 minutes.
Makes 6 servings.

Cuban Chicken Filling:
1 medium-size green pepper, halved, seeded, and finely chopped
3 green onions, finely chopped
2 tablespoons vegetable oil
¼ cup tomato sauce
½ teaspoon salt
¼ teaspoon pepper
1 bay leaf
1 cup water
2 cups finely chopped cooked chicken
½ cup frozen peas
½ cup finely chopped pitted green olives
¼ cup dry white wine
¼ cup raisins
1 container (2 ounces) pimiento, drained and finely chopped
Salsa (see page 209), (optional)
Chopped lettuce (optional)

Wrapper:
1 package (4½ ounces) taco shells

1. Sauté green pepper and onions in oil in a large skillet until tender, about 3 minutes. Add tomato sauce, salt, pepper, bay leaf, water, chicken, peas, olives, wine, raisins, and pimientos; blend well. Bring to a boil; lower heat. Simmer, uncovered, stirring occasionally, for 20 minutes; remove bay leaf. (Makes about 3½ cups filling.)

2. Preheat oven to 350°. Put tacos on a cookie sheet or in a shallow baking pan. Spoon filling into tacos.

3. Bake in a preheated moderate oven (350°) for 20 minutes or until piping hot. Serve with Salsa and chopped lettuce, if you wish.

SERVING SUGGESTIONS: Spinach, Chick-pea and Mushroom Salad ■, and fresh fruit compote.

ENTERTAINING AT A HAPPY PRICE
26 ways to do it

You can entertain graciously while on a budget and no one but you will ever know how little money your dazzling party cost. Here are cost-cutting tips to show you how.

• Serve omelets for brunch or for an after-theater supper. Let guests choose from an assortment of sweet and savory fillings—like chicken in sherry-cream sauce with toasted almonds and peas; strawberry jam and sour cream; and shredded Cheddar with sliced, cooked sausage and sautéed apples. Serve with hot homemade biscuits, softly whipped butter, and 1 or 2 vegetable or fruit salads.

• Buy meats for stews and casseroles in large, uncut pieces, rather than buying cubed stew meat; whole chickens cost less than parts.

• Give a sausage and mustard tasting party. Choose from sweet and hot Italian Sausage, Polish kielbasa, German bockwurst, or Knockwurst and All-American frankfurters. Serve complementary mustards, a hearty baked bean casserole, and lots of beer.

• Divide the cost—and labor—of entertaining by hosting a co-op party.

• Invite guests for a dessert smorgasbord. Balance 1 or 2 elegant desserts (Frozen Grand Marnier Mousse ■ or Orange Chiffon Cake ■) with butter cookies (Nutmeg Leaves ■), and a fruit dessert (Fresh Fruit Salad with Sour Cream Dressing ■).

• Concentrate on ethnic cuisines that don't emphasize costly meat and seafood. A hearty Italian risotto, colorful Chinese stir-fry, or Mexican bean casserole uses very little, if any, meat—and tastes great.

• Choose from Nature's bounty by season, when produce is most plentiful and least expensive. Strawberries in January or asparagus in October are bound to be pricey.

• Don't eliminate luxury items—just make the most of them. A quarter pound of smoked salmon serves 4 if you add it to a dill-flavored cream sauce for pasta. One pound of crisp asparagus adds elegance to a spring crudité selection.

• Use up what you've got. Waste is a wicked budget eater. If you bought 5 chickens, make pâté from the livers. A sauce prepared with egg yolks leaves you egg whites for making meringues.

• Serve bowls of chili with all the trimmings—chopped onion, chopped tomato and green pepper, crushed taco chips, and cubed Monterey Jack cheese. Mexican beer, orange and avocado salads, and flan with cinnamon butter cookies complete the meal.

• Give a beer-tasting party. Include 6 to 10 domestic and imported varieties. Freeze wet glasses or mugs to keep beer chilled. Pass hearty nibbles such as Beef and Cabbage Pasties ■, Miniature Sausage-Crepe Quiches ■, or Pizza with the "Works." ■

• Serve poultry. Many elegant recipes use chicken or turkey. Your guests will enjoy Chicken Normandy Style ■ as much as Beef Wellington ■.

- Give a breakfast party—even if it's noon. Traditional early morning fare, such as pancakes, eggs, and muffins, is good any time. Try Apple Griddles Cakes ■, Sweet Breakfast Squares ■, Cinnamon Muffins ■, and Cheese 'N' Ham Puff ■.

- Soufflés and quiches are always impressive, yet they are neither difficult nor expensive to prepare.

- Replace veal with chicken or turkey in classic recipes.

- Borrow additional chairs, serving pieces, and appliances for big parties instead of buying or renting them.

- Choose local flowers instead of exotic varieties; they're just as festive. Arrange them yourself and save even more.

- Buy good, inexpensive wines for cooking and drinking at party time; wines specifically for cooking cost more per ounce.

- Prepare your own cold cut and cheese platters. Buy a total of ¼ pound per person. Bulk purchases are great if you've got a slicing machine; otherwise buy items pre-sliced. Arrange meats and cheeses on platters, tuck in garnishs, cover with plastic wrap and chill.

- If you're serving turkey, baste it yourself instead of buying the more costly self-basting birds.

- Plan a pasta buffet: Serve 2 to 3 kinds of pasta, a meat sauce (we like sausage and cubed pepper in spicy tomato sauce), a cream sauce (ham and cheese with caraway), and a vegetable sauce (zucchini and onion in herbed garlic butter). Pass grated cheese, chopped green onions, and toasted bread crumbs for toppings.

- Tenderize chuck steak and use instead of sirloin; tenderized shoulder lamb chops replace loin chops.

- Give a grown-up ice cream buffet: Scoop ice cream onto jelly roll pans (3 quarts serve 8 amply), cover with plastic wrap; freeze at least 2 hours, or until very firm; place in a large metal bowl; return to freezer. Stir creme de cacao into your favorite hot fudge sauce, toasted chopped pecans into butterscotch sauce and a generous splash of Grand Marnier into strawberry sauce. Chopped salted peanuts, toasted coconut, and lightly whipped cream top off the gala affair.

- Shop discount beer and soda distributors for big savings.

- When buying large amounts of beer, soda, wine, or liquor, ask the store manager if there are special case prices.

- Buy store brands and private label liquors; it's a good idea to sample each one before you buy in quantity.

TURKEY CRÊPES WITH CHEESE SAUCE

Bake at 375° for 15 minutes.
Makes 6 servings.

½ cup long-grain rice
3 tablespoons butter or
  margarine
2 tablespoons all-purpose flour
½ teaspoon salt
¼ teaspoon pepper
1 cup water
5 tablespoons nonfat dry
  milk powder
1 cup shredded Swiss cheese
  (4 ounces)

1 small onion, chopped
  (¼ cup)
¾ pound ground turkey
½ cup thawed frozen peas
¼ teaspoon rosemary,
  crumbled
¼ teaspoon thyme, crumbled
¼ teaspoon dry mustard
  Crêpes (recipe below)

1. Prepare crêpes. Cook rice, following label directions; reserve. Preheat oven to 375°.

2. Melt 2 tablespoons of the butter in a small saucepan. Blend in flour, ¼ teaspoon of the salt, and the pepper; cook for 1 minute. Stir water into dry milk in a small bowl until blended; stir into saucepan. Cook, stirring constantly, until mixture thickens and bubbles. Remove from heat; add cheese, stirring until melted; reserve.

3. Sauté onion in remaining 1 tablespoon butter in a large skillet until tender. Add turkey, stirring constantly, until turkey is no longer pink. Stir in cooked rice, peas, rosemary, thyme, dry mustard, and the remaining salt. Add ⅔ of the reserved cheese sauce, stirring until blended.

4. Spoon a heaping tablespoonful of the turkey mixture on each crêpe; roll up. Repeat until all crêpes are filled. Arrange crêpes in a shallow baking dish. Spoon remaining cheese sauce over crêpes.

5. Bake in a preheated moderate oven (375°) for 15 minutes, or until sauce is bubbly and lightly browned.

Crêpes: Combine 2 eggs, 5 tablespoons nonfat dry milk powder, 1 cup water, 1 cup flour, ¼ teaspoon salt, and 2 tablespoons melted margarine in the container of an electric blender; whirl until smooth. Or combine all ingredients in a medium-size bowl; beat with a whisk or beater until smooth. Refrigerate batter at least 1 hour. Heat a 7-inch skillet until hot; rub about ¼ teaspoon margarine on bottom of skillet to spread batter evenly over bottom. Cook crêpe until lightly browned on bottom; turn over and brown on other side. Stack cooked crêpes between layers of wax paper until ready to use. Makes 12 crêpes.

SERVING SUGGESTIONS: Garden Salad Mold■, broccoli vinaigrette, and Mousse de Bananes ■.

ENSENADA CRÊPES

Bake at 350° for 25 minutes.
Makes 12 servings.

Wrapper:
Basic Easy Crêpes
(recipe below)

Ensenada Filling*:*
1 **pound thinly sliced cooked ham (12 slices)**
1 **can (4½ ounces) whole green chilies, rinsed, halved, seeded, and cut into ¼-inch strips**

2 **tablespoons butter or margarine**
2 **tablespoons all-purpose flour**
1 **cup milk**
¼ **pound Cheddar cheese, shredded (1 cup)**
½ **teaspoon prepared mustard**
¼ **teaspoon pepper**
2 **tablespoons chopped parsley (optional)**

1. Prepare Basic Easy Crêpes; reserve.
2. Lightly butter a shallow baking dish. Halve ham slices lengthwise. Place a ham strip and a green chili strip in the center of each of 24 crêpes. Roll up crêpes; fasten with a wooden pick, if necessary. Arrange crêpes in a prepared baking dish.
3. Preheat oven to 350°
4. Melt butter in a medium-size saucepan; blend in flour. Cook, stirring constantly, for 1 minute. Stir in milk slowly. Cook, stirring constantly, until sauce thickens and bubbles. Stir in cheese, mustard, salt, and pepper; cook until cheese is melted and sauce is smooth. Spoon sauce over filled crêpes.
5. Bake in a preheated moderate oven (350°) for 25 minutes. Sprinkle with parsley if you wish.

---

*To use as a pastry filling: Chop ham, cheese, and chilies. Add just enough of the cheese sauce to moisten. Spoon into baked pastry shell; serve with remaining cheese sauce.

Basic Easy Crêpes (Makes 24 seven-inch crêpes.): Measure 1½ cups quick-mixing flour into a medium-size bowl. Add 1 cup cold water, 1 cup cold milk, 4 large eggs, ½ teaspoon salt, and ¼ cup (½ stick) melted butter. Beat with a wire whisk or rotary beater until blended. (Note: This batter does not need to rest.) Heat a 7-inch crêpe pan over medium heat. (If pan is well seasoned, there will be no need to butter it. If not, brush lightly with butter.) Pour in 3 tablespoons batter. Tilt pan to cover the bottom evenly. Cook over medium-high heat until the underside of crêpe is lightly browned. Turn and brown the other side. Stack cooked crepes between layers of wax paper until ready to fill.

SERVING SUGGESTIONS: Lima Bean Coleslaw ■, sliced tomatoes, and orange flan.

LITTLE EXTRAS THAT DON'T COST MUCH

- Serve fancy desserts on small doilies
- Form butter or margarine into curls or balls, or use a butter mold.
- Use candles.
- Fold napkins in unusual shapes, or tie them with pretty ribbons.
- Add color to punch bowls and tall drinks with a decorative ice ring (see page 285) and ice cubes. For making cubes, add lemon, lime or orange rind, mint leaves, or halved strawberries.
- Garnish food to give it a festive, finished look.
- If you can't afford flowers, use a healthy houseplant or a bowl of perfect fruit for a centerpiece.
- Chill beer glasses and salad plates; warm plates for hot foods.
- Serve rolls, bread, and muffins warm, for just-baked flavor.
- Add sliced lemon to ice water; serve in your best goblets.
- Use placecards for a touch of elegance.
- Decant less expensive wines into pitchers or decanters.

SENSATIONAL PIZZAS

It's practically impossible to miss with pizza. Just about everyone loves it—with good reason. Pizza is simply delicious and can be varied in countless ways. Here are 4 luscious versions, all based on the Homemade Pizza Dough (see page 271). We bet your guests will say "Sensational!"

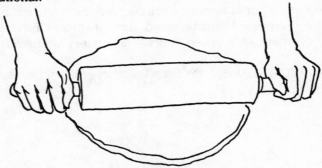

ROLLING DOUGH

Roll out dough, working from the center outward to a diameter 1 inch larger than the pan. Pick up dough often to stretch dough and to prevent sticking.

CUTTING PIZZA

To make pizza-cutting easy, slice with a strong, sharp pizza wheel or kitchen scissors.

HOMEMADE PIZZA DOUGH

Makes two 12-inch crusts or one 16-inch crust.

1 envelope active dry yeast	1 teaspoon salt
1 cup very warm water	3 tablespoons olive or
3¼ cups all-purpose flour	vegetable oil

1. Sprinkle yeast over very warm water. Stir to dissolve yeast.
2. Stir together flour and salt in a large bowl. Make a well in center; add yeast mixture and oil; stir until a rough dough forms. Turn out onto a lightly floured surface. Knead until smooth and elastic, 5 to 7 minutes. Shape into a ball. Place in a greased bowl; turn to coat. Cover; let rise in warm place, about 45 minutes or until doubled in volume.
3. Punch dough down; divide in half.* Proceed with following recipes.

---

*The dough may be frozen at this point. Shape into circles 1 inch thick. Wrap loosely in plastic wrap; freeze solid. Wrap securely in second layer of plastic wrap, then in aluminum foil. Freeze up to 2 months. To use, defrost. Punch dough down.

THICK PIZZA SAUCE

Makes about 4 cups (enough for four 12-inch pizzas).

2 cans (28 ounces each) peeled Italian plum tomatoes	¼ cup olive or vegetable oil
	1 teaspoon oregano, crumbled
2 large onions, chopped (2 cups)	1 teaspoon basil, crumbled
	½ teaspoon salt
4 large cloves garlic, minced	¼ teaspoon pepper

1. Pour tomatoes with their liquid, 1 can at a time, into the container of an electric blender; cover. Whirl until pureed.
2. Sauté onions and garlic in oil in a large skillet, stirring often, until onions are tender, 10 minutes. Add pureed tomatoes, oregano, basil, salt, and pepper; bring to a boil. Lower heat; simmer uncovered, stirring occasionally, until thickened, about 1 hour. (No liquid should be bubbling around edges.) Cool slightly before using. (Sauce can be stored in the refrigerator up to 5 days or in the freezer up to 4 months.)

HAM AND MUENSTER PIZZA

A delicious thin pizza not unlike; an open-faced sandwich.

Bake crust at 450° for 10 minutes; bake pizza at 450° for 20 minutes. Makes 6 servings (one 12-inch pizza).

	Cornmeal	**1**	**tablespoon red wine vinegar**
½	**recipe Homemade Pizza**	**2**	**teaspoons prepared mustard**
	Dough (see recipe page 271)	**½**	**pound thinly sliced**
	Or: packaged pizza dough		**Virginia ham**
	prepared for 12-inch pizza	**½**	**pound thinly sliced**
1	**tablespoon vegetable oil**		**Muenster cheese**

1. Preheat oven to 450°. Grease a 12-inch pizza pan; sprinkle with cornmeal.

2. Roll out dough on a floured surface to make a 13-inch circle. Fit into a prepared pan; roll edges under to make thick rim. Cover; let rise in a warm place for 15 minutes.

3. Bake in a preheated very hot oven (450°) for 10 minutes. Remove crust; leave oven on.

4. Mix oil, vinegar, and mustard in a bowl until blended. Brush ⅔ of mixture over crust, leaving ½-inch border. Arrange ham and cheese slices over top. Brush with remaining oil mixture.

5. Bake in a very hot oven (450°) for 15 to 20 minutes or until cheese is melted and lightly browned.

SERVING SUGGESTIONS: All-American Coleslaw ■ in lettuce cups and beer.

SPINACH PIZZA

Bake crust at 450° for 10 minutes; bake pizza at 450° for 15 minutes.
Makes 6 servings (one 12-inch pizza).

Cornmeal
½ inch recipe Homemade Pizza Dough (recipe page 271) Or: package pizza dough prepared for 12-inch pizza
2 packages (10 ounces each) frozen chopped spinach, thawed
2 medium-size onions, thinly sliced
3 tablespoons butter or margarine
¼ teaspoon ground nutmeg
⅛ teaspoon ground cloves
⅛ teaspoon cayenne pepper
½ cup dairy sour cream
1 egg
8 ounces shredded Swiss cheese (2 cups)
¼ cup grated Romano cheese
¼ cup chopped pimiento

1. Preheat oven to 450°. Grease 12-inch pizza pan; sprinkle with cornmeal.

2. Roll out dough on a floured surface to a 13-inch circle. Fit into prepared pan; roll edges under to make thick rim. Cover; let rise in a warm place for 15 minutes.

3. Bake in a preheated very hot oven (450°) for 10 minutes. Remove crust; leave oven on.

4. Meanwhile, place spinach in colander; squeeze out as much liquid as possible.

5. Sauté onions in butter in a large skillet until wilted. Remove about ¼ cup; reserve. Stir spinach, nutmeg, cloves, and cayenne into a skillet; cook, stirring often, until almost all liquid evaporates. Cool slightly.

6. Beat sour cream and egg in large bowl until well blended. Stir in spinach mixture, 1½ cups of the Swiss cheese and the Romano cheese. Spread evenly over crust, leaving ½-inch border. Sprinkle with remaining ½ cup Swiss cheese.

7. Bake in a preheated very hot oven (450°) for 15 minutes or until cheese is bubbly. Garnish with chopped pimiento and reserved ¼ cup sautéed sliced onion. Cool for 5 minutes.

SERVING SUGGESTIONS: Tomatoes vinaigrette, crisp carrot sticks, and orange sherbet.

PIZZA WITH "THE WORKS"

A real knife-and-fork pizza, topped with everybody's favorites. Since many of the toppings are salty, you may wish to use low-salt cheese.

Bake crust at 450° for 10 minutes; bake pizza at 450° for 15 minutes. Makes 12 servings (one 16-inch pizza).

	Cornmeal	6	ounces pepperoni, thinly sliced
1	recipe Homemade Pizza Dough (see recipe page 271) Or: packaged pizza dough prepared for 16-inch pizza	1	large green pepper, cored, seeded, and cut in thin rings
2	cups Thick Pizza Sauce (see recipe page 271)	1	can (2 ounces) flat anchovy fillets, drained
1	pound mozzarella cheese, shredded (4 cups)	1	jar (4½ ounces) sliced mushrooms, drained
		12	pitted black olives

1. Preheat oven to 450°. Grease a 16-inch pizza pan; sprinkle with cornmeal.

2. Roll out dough on a floured surface to a 17-inch circle. Fit into prepared pan; roll edges under to make thick rim. Cover; let rise in a warm place for 15 minutes.

3. Bake in a prepared very hot oven (450°) for 10 minutes. Remove crust; leave oven on.

4. Spread sauce over crust, leaving ½-inch border. Sprinkle with 3 cups mozzarella. Overlap pepperoni slices in a circle, 1 inch from edge. Overlap pepper rings in center; arrange anchovies. Sprinkle mushrooms over all. Sprinkle with remaining mozzarella.

5. Bake in a very hot oven (450°) for 15 minutes or until cheese is bubbly. Garnish with olives. Cool 5 minutes before slicing.

SERVING SUGGESTIONS: Tossed green salad and fresh fruit compote.

SAUSAGE AND ZUCCHINI PIZZA

Bake crust at 450° for 10 minutes; bake pizza at 450° for 15 minutes.
Makes 12 servings (one 16-inch pizza).

Cornmeal
1 recipe Homemade Pizza Dough (see page 271) Or: package pizza dough prepared for 16-inch pizza
1 large onion, thinly sliced
2 tablespoons vegetable oil
1 pound zucchini, sliced
1 pound sweet Italian sausage
2 cups Thick Pizza Sauce (see recipe page 271)
1 pound mozzarella cheese, shredded (4 cups)
½ cup grated Parmesan cheese

1. Preheat oven to 450°. Lightly grease a 16-inch pizza pan; sprinkle with cornmeal.

2. Roll out dough on a floured surface to 17-inch circle. Fit into prepared pan; roll edges under to make thick rim. Cover; let rise in a warm place for 15 minutes.

3. Bake in a preheated very hot oven (450°) for 10 minutes. Remove crust from oven; leave oven on.

4. Sauté onion in 1 tablespoon of the oil in a skillet until soft but not brown; remove to a bowl. Sauté zucchini slices in remaining 1 tablespoon oil in same skillet, stirring often, about 3 minutes. Remove to a second bowl. Cook sausage in same skillet in boiling water to cover for 10 minutes. Remove from skillet; cool. Cut into thin slices.

5. Spread Thick Pizza Sauce evenly over crust, leaving ½-inch border. Sprinkle with 3 cups mozzarella and the Parmesan. Arrange zucchini, sausage, and onion over cheese; sprinkle with remaining 1 cup of mozzarella.

6. Bake in a preheated very hot oven (450°) for 15 minutes or until lightly browned on top. Cool 5 minutes before slicing.

SERVING SUGGESTION: Celery and tomato salad and watermelon (or other seasonal fresh fruit).

BROCCOLI AND HAM SOUFFLÉ

Bake at 350° for 35 minutes.
Makes 4 servings.

2	tablespoons chopped onion	1	package (10 ounces) frozen
3	tablespoons margarine		chopped broccoli, thawed
3	tablesoons all-purpose flour	1	cup finely chopped cooked
½	teaspooon salt		ham (about 4 ounces)
⅛	teaspoon pepper	3	tablespoons grated Parmesan
1	cup milk		cheese
4	eggs, separated	1	teaspoon cream of tartar

1. Sauté onion in margarine in a medium-size saucepan, stirring occasionally, until tender but not brown, about 2 minutes. Stir in flour, salt, and pepper; cook for 1 minute. Stir in milk until mixture is smooth. Cook, stirring constantly, until mixture thickens.

2. Lightly grease a 1½-quart soufflé or other straight-sided dish. Preheat oven to 350°.

3. Beat egg yolks slightly in a small bowl; stir in a little of the hot mixture; return blended mixture to saucepan. Cook over low heat, stirring constantly, 2 minutes.

4. Drain broccoli in a colander, pressing with a spoon to remove excess moisture. Stir into sauce along with ham and cheese. Remove from heat.

5. Beat egg whites with cream of tartar in a large bowl until soft peaks form. Gently fold broccoli mixture into whites until no streaks of white remain. Spoon into prepared dish.

6. Bake in a preheated moderate oven (350°) for 35 minutes or until browned and puffed. Serve at once.

SERVING SUGGESTIONS: Crusty whole wheat rolls, Grated Zucchini and Green Pepper Salad ■, and baked custard, topped with fruit.

SIBERIAN MEAT STRUDEL

Bake at 375° for 40 minutes.
Makes 6 servings.

Siberian Meat Filling:
½ pound ground round
¼ pound ground lean pork
1 tablespoon water
1 medium-size onion, finely chopped (½ cup)
1 teaspoon dillweed
¼ teaspoon salt
⅛ teaspoon pepper

Wrapper:
1 package (8 ounces) phyllo or strudel dough
¼ cup (½ stick) butter or margarine, melted
¼ cup packaged bread crumbs
2 tablespoons butter or margarine, melted

1. Combine ground round, ground pork, water, onion, dill, salt, and pepper in a medium-size bowl; mix well. (Makes about 2 cups filling.)
2. Remove 6 leaves of phyllo or strudel dough from package; cover with a damp towel. Reseal remaining leaves in package; refrigerate or freeze.
3. Place 1 phyllo or strudel leaf on a damp towel; brush with some of the ¼ cup melted butter; sprinkle with some bread crumbs. Repeat with remaining 5 leaves, butter and crumbs.
4. Grease a shallow baking dish. Preheat oven to 375°.
5. Shape filling into a cylinder, about 3 inches shorter than one of the short ends of the phyllo; roll up phyllo leaves and filling, starting with of the long sides, using towel as an aid in rolling. Place on prepared baking dish, seam side down. Brush top with the remaining 2 tablespoons butter.
6. Bake in preheated moderate oven (375°) for 40 minutes or until golden brown. Cool slightly on a wire rack before cutting into thick slices with a serrated knife.

SERVING SUGGESTIONS: Tomato soup, tossed green salad, lemon-glazed carrots, and Spiced Peach Cake ■.

POTATO PIE

Bake at 400° for 20 minutes.
Makes 6 servings.

Crust:
1¾ cups *sifted* all-purpose flour
¾ teaspoons salt
9 tablespoons (1 stick plus 1 tablespoon) unsalted butter or margarine
1 egg yolk
  Ice water

Filling:
5 thick slices bacon (5 ounces), cut crosswise into ¼-inch-wide strips

1¼ pounds medium-size potatoes
¼ cup finely chopped parsley
½ teaspoon salt
⅛ teaspoon pepper
5 hard-cooked eggs, shelled and thinly sliced
¾ cup heavy cream

Egg Glaze:
1 egg yolk
1 teaspoon water

1. For crust: Sift flour and salt into a large bowl. Cut in butter with a fork or pasty blender until mixture is crumbly. Make a well in the center.

2. Beat egg yolk lightly in a 1-cup measure; add just enough ice water to make ¼ cup; pour into the well. Lightly mix flour into liquid just until the flour is moistened. Gather pastry together with hands into a ball.

3. Roll out dough on a lightly floured surface to a 12 x 8-inch rectangle; fold lengthwise into thirds. Wrap in plastic wrap; refrigerate overnight. Allow pastry to stand 1 hour at room temperature before using.

4. For filling: Cook bacon in a large skillet just until edges begin to turn brown; remove with a slotted spoon to paper toweling to drain.

5. Pare and thinly slice potatoes. Set in colander; rinse under cold running water; drain; pat dry with a kitchen towel; reserve.

6. Combine parsley, salt, and pepper in a small bowl; reserve.

7. Divide softened pastry in half. Roll out half on a lightly floured surface into a 12-inch round (you may have to shape pastry into a circle with your hands as you roll). Fit into a 9-inch pie plate. Trim overhand to ½ inch.

8. Arrange half the potato slices, overlapping slightly, in the bottom of the pastry-lined plate; sprinkle with half the parsley mixture. Sprinkle the bacon evenly over all; layer the egg slices over the bacon.

Arrange remaining potato slices, overlapping slightly, over top; sprinkle with remaining parsley mixture. Slowly pour cream over all.
9. Preheat oven to 400°. Roll out second half of pastry on lightly floured surface into a circle to fit over top of pie. Beat the egg yolk with the water in a small cup. Brush edges of pastry in pie dish with glaze. Fit pastry top over filling; trim overhang to ½ inch. Pinch edges to seal; turn edge up and in to seal. Pinch again to make a stand-up edge; flute. Cut slits in center of pie for steam vent. Refrigerate pie for 10 minutes.
10. Brush top crust lightly with remaining glaze.
11. Bake in a preheated hot oven (400°) for 20 minutes. Lower oven temperature to moderate (350°). Bake 1 hour longer.
12. Remove pie to a wire rack; cool 10 minutes before cutting.

SERVING SUGGESTIONS: Shredded carrot salad, buttered steamed spinach, and Apricot-Yogurt Whip ■

PORK AND CARROT EGG FOO YUNG

These Chinese omelet-like patties are a snap to make if you use a skillet with a nonstick surface. Even when reheated, the vegetables in these patties retain their crispness.

Makes 4 servings.

2	thin center-cut pork chops (½ pound)	1	cup chopped celery
6	tablespoons vegetable oil, or as needed	8	ounces bean sprouts, rinsed and drained (about 2 cups)
6	eggs	⅓	cup thinly sliced green onions
2	tablespoons soy sauce		Chinese Brown Gravy (recipe below)
1	tablespoon cornstarch		
1½	cups packed shredded carrot (2 large carrots)		

1. Cut away bone and excess fat from pork chops; cut meat into small cubes. Heat 1 tablespoon of the oil in a medium-size skillet over medium heat. Add pork; stir-fry until cooked through (meat should be completely white thoughout.) Remove meat; set aside.
2. Beat together eggs, soy sauce, and cornstarch in a large bowl. Stir in carrot, celery, bean sprouts, green onion, and pork.

3. Heat 2 tablespoons of the oil in a large skillet over medium heat until almost smoking. Pour ⅓ cup of the pork mixture into the skillet; spread into a 4-inch circle with a spatula, pushing back any egg that has run outward from the vegetables. Cook 2 or 3 patties at a time, without crowding the skillet. Cook until bottoms are golden brown, 2 minutes. Turn over; brown other side. Remove to a warmed platter; cover loosely with aluminum foil. Repeat with remaining batter, stirring each time to mix ingredients; add oil as necessary to prevent sticking.* (Patties can be kept warm in a preheated 200° oven for up to 30 minutes.)

4. Prepare Chinese Brown Gravy.

5. To serve: Arrange patties on a platter with cooked rice and green peas; spoon some gravy over patties; pass remaining gravy.

Chinese Brown Gravy: Stir together 1 cup beef broth, 1 tablespoon cornstarch, 1 tablespoon soy sauce, and 1 teaspoon sugar in small saucepan until smooth. Cook over medium heat, stirring constantly, until mixture thickens and bubbles. Makes about 1 cup.

SERVING SUGGESTIONS: Hot cooked rice, green peas, and gingered melon balls.

---

*To reheat leftovers, place patties in lightly oiled skillet over low heat; cook until heated through, about 3 minutes on each side.

GENOA SALAMI AND
BLACK OLIVE CROSTATA

Salami and vigorous Italian cheeses bake in a mellow custard for this sunny, open-face pie.

Bake at 425° for 5 minutes, then at 375° for 30 minutes.
Makes 6 servings.

½ package piecrust mix	½ cup grated Parmesan cheese
1 package (6 ounces) sliced salami, julienned	½ teaspoon salt
	¼ teaspoon pepper
12 pitted black olives, sliced	2 whole eggs
1 large ripe tomato, peeled, seeded, finely chopped, and juice drained	2 whole egg yolks
	1½ cups light cream
	1 tablespoon all-purpose flour
½ cup grated Italian Fontina cheese	

1. Preheat oven to 425°. Prepare piecrust mix. Roll out on a floured surface to a 14-inch round; fit into a 9-inch pie plate. Trim edges; flute.
2. Bake in a preheated oven (425°) for 5 minutes. Remove to a wire rack. Lower oven temperature to moderate (375°).
3. Combine salami, olives, tomato, Fontina cheese, half of the Parmesan, salt, and pepper in a large bowl; toss. Spoon into the partially baked pie shell.
4. Lightly beat whole eggs and yolks in a medium-size bowl. Stir in cream and flour. Pour over salami mixture. Sprinkle remaining Parmesan cheese over pie.
5. Bake, uncovered, in a preheated moderate oven (375°) for 30 minutes or until golden and puffed. A knife blade inserted 1 inch from edge should come out clean.

SERVING SUGGESTIONS: Spinach, Chick-pea, and Mushroom Salad ■, crusty whole wheat rolls, and lemon sherbet.

FRESH FRUIT SALAD WITH SOUR CREAM DRESSING

Prepare the fruit salad and dressing ahead and keep refrigerated until ready to serve.

Makes 12 servings.

1 large cantaloupe	1 cup dairy sour cream
Or: 1 large honeydew melon	⅓ cup mayonnaise
4 navel oranges	⅓ cup banana liqueur or
4 bananas, sliced	pineapple juice
1 package (8 ounces) pitted dates	

1. Cut melon in half; remove seeds. Scoop out balls with a melon baller or cut flesh into chunks. Peel oranges; section and remove with white membrane. Arrange melon, orange sections, banana slices, and dates in flat salad bowl. Chill.
2. Combine sour cream, mayonnaise, and liqueur in a small bowl until blended. To serve, spoon over chilled fruit.

PINEAPPLE-APRICOT YOGURT

Pineapple, apricots, and yogurt are laced with honey for a refreshing frozen dessert. Put squares of the frozen yogurt between honey graham crackers for you own frozen yogurt "sandwiches."

Makes 12 servings.

1   **can (15¼ ounces) crushed pineapple in pineapple juice**
1   **envelope unflavored gelatin**
¼   **cup honey**
1   **can (17 ounces) apricot halves**

1   **container (16 ounces) plain yogurt**
1   **teaspoon vanilla**

1. Drain juice from crushed pineapple into a medium-size saucepan; sprinkle gelatin over pineapple juice. Let stand 5 minutes to soften. Place saucepan over very low heat, stirring constantly, until gelatin dissolves. Remove from heat; stir in honey until smooth. Pour into a large bowl; cool.
2. Drain apricot halves; turn apricot halves into the container of an electric blender; cover; whirl until smooth.
3. Drain apricot puree, crushed pineapple, yogurt, and vanilla into honey mixture; stir until thoroughly combined. Pour into a 13x9x2-inch pan. Freeze, stirring occasionally so mixture freezes evenly, until partially frozen, 2 to 3 hours.
4. Spoon partially frozen mixture into a chilled large bowl. Beat with an electric mixer until very smooth.
5. Wash and dry pan. Tear off an 18-inch length of aluminum foil; line pan with aluminum foil allowing foil to extend up sides of pan. Pour yogurt mixture into pan. Freeze until softly frozen, about 2 hours, or freeze solid. Remove from freezer 15 to 30 minutes before scooping out into dessert bowls.

Variations: Substitute 1 can (16 ounces) Elberta peach halves, drained and pureed, for the apricot halves.

Sandwiches: Lift frozen yogurt with aluminum foil to kitchen counter. Cut yogurt into squares to fit honey graham halves (24). Sandwich together. Place on a cookie sheet and freeze. Wrap individually in aluminum foil and place in a plastic bag. Allow sandwiches to soften slightly before eating.

FROZEN GRAND MARNIER MOUSSE

A spectacular centerpiece for the buffet desserts. Prepare the frozen mousse up to a week ahead, and decorate just before serving.

Makes 12 servings.

⅓ cup sugar
1 envelope unflavored gelatin
2 teaspoons cornstarch
6 egg yolks
1 cup milk
⅓ cup Grand Marnier or orange juice

4 egg whites
¼ cup sugar
2 cups heavy cream
1 pint strawberries, washed, hulled, and halved
2 kiwis, pared and sliced

1. Combine ⅓ cup sugar, gelatin, and cornstarch in a medium-size saucepan; add egg yolks; beat until well blended. Gradually stir in milk. Cook, stirring constantly, over medium heat, just until mixture is slightly thickened. Remove from heat; stir in liquer.
2. Set pan in a larger pan filled with ice and water. Chill, stirring often, until mixture mounds when spooned.
3. While mixture is chilling, beat egg whites in a medium-size bowl with an electric mixer until foamy. Beat in ¼ cup sugar gradually until meringue forms soft peaks.
4. Beat 1½ cups of the heavy cream in a small bowl until stiff. Fold whipped cream, then meringue into gelatin mixture until no streaks of white remain. Turn into an 8-cup decorative ring mold; smooth top. Wrap mold with aluminum foil or plastic wrap. Freeze overnight or until firm. (The mousse can be frozen for up to 1 week.)
5. To serve, remove mousse from freezer. Loosen around edges with a small spatula. Unmold onto a serving platter. Beat remaining ½ cup cream in a small bowl until stiff. Pipe whipped cream around base and top of mousse. Garnish with strawberries and kiwis.

CREAMY PINEAPPLE-COCONUT PUNCH

This punch can be alcoholic or non-alcoholic, depending on which of the flavored decorative ice cubes you use.

Makes twenty-two 4-ounce servings.

1   can (46 ounces) unsweetened pineapple juice, chilled
1   bottle (28 ounces) club soda, chilled
1   can (15 ounces) cream of coconut

Orange-Rum Ice Cubes (recipe below)
"Shirley Temple" Ice Cubes (recipe below)

Combine pineapple juice, club soda, and cream of coconut in a punch bowl or pitcher; stir until well blended. Serve in punch cups with a flavored ice cube in each.

Orange-Rum Ice Cubes: Combine 1¾ cups orange juice and ¼ cup light rum in a measuring cup with a pour spout. Half fill an ice cube tray. Add strawberries, citrus slices, kiwi slices, or pineapple chunks to the ice cubes. Freeze to anchor the fruit. Fill with remaining juice; freeze until firm.

"Shirley Temple" Ice Cubes: Half fill an ice cube tray with a red-colored fruit drink. Add maraschino or candied cherries. Freeze to anchor the cherries. Fill with more juice; freeze until firm.

TANGERINE-APRICOT CHAMPAGNE PUNCH

*Tangy fruits and orange liqueur blend with champagne
for a refreshing drink.*
Makes twenty-six 4-ounce servings.

1 can (6 ounces) frozen
tangerine or orange juice
concentrate, thawed
1 can (12 ounces)
apricot nectar, chilled
½ can superfine granulated
sugar
½ orange-flavored liqueur
1 bottle (28 ounces) club soda,
chilled

1 bottle (750 ml.)
dry white wine, chilled
1 bottle (750 ml.)
champagne, chilled
Ice Ring or Ice Block
(recipe below)
Canned apricot halves
(optional)

1. Combine tangerine juice concentrate, apricot nectar, sugar, and orange liquer in a chilled large punch bowl; stir to dissolve sugar.
2. Stir in club soda, wine, and champagne. Float Ice Ring or Ice Block on top. Serve in punch cups or champagne glasses. Add apricot half to each, if you wish.

Make Ahead Tip: A few hours ahead, combine juices, sugar, and liqueur in a large pitcher; stir to dissolve sugar; chill. When ready to serve, follow recipe from step 2.

Decorative Ice Ring or Block: Fill a ring mold or metal pan ¼ full with water. Partially freeze. Add fruit of your choice: citrus slices, strawberries, pineapple chunks, maraschino cherries, etc. Arrange in decorative design. Freeze to anchor fruit; fill with ice water and freeze until firm.

14
Desserts

Al of the desserts here do more than just please the palate. In addition to being delicious, they are based on nutritious ingredients like fruit, nuts, cottage cheese, peanut butter, or carrots: Peanut Putter Brownies, Apricot-Glazed Peach Cake and Carrot-Nut Cake. Some are hearty and homey, like Raisin Bread Pudding, while others, Mousse de Bananes, are elegant enough for company.

Our chart on fruits will steer you to buy fruit when in season. You'll also learn how to get more juice from a lemon, what to do with leftover canned fruit syrup, and how to make a buttermilk substitute.

COTTAGE CHEESE POUND CAKE

Bake at 300° for 1 hour, 30 minutes.
Makes 16 servings.

3	cups *sifted* all-purpose flour	2	cups sugar
¼	teaspoon baking soda	6	eggs, separated
1	cup (2 sticks) butter or margarine, softened	1	teaspoon grated orange rind
		1	teaspoon vanilla
1	cup cottage cheese, sieved		10X (confectioners') sugar

1. Grease a 9-inch Bundt® pan (9 or 10 cup). Preheat oven to 300°.
2. Sift flour and baking soda onto wax paper.
3. Beat butter and cottage cheese in a medium-size bowl with an electric mixer until creamy and smooth. Slowly beat in sugar until fluffy. Beat in egg yolks, one at a time. Beat in orange rind, vanilla, and flour mixture until well blended.
4. Beat egg whites in a small bowl with an electric mixer until stiff but not dry. Fold into cake batter. Spoon into prepared pan, smoothing top evenly.
5. Bake in a preheated slow oven (300°) for 1½ hours or until top springs back when lightly pressed with fingertip.
6. Cool in pan on a wire rack for 10 minutes. Turn out on rack; cool completely. Sprinkle with 10X sugar. Store wrapped at room temperature.

APRICOT-GLAZED PEACH CAKE

Bake at 350° for 55 minutes.
Makes 8 servings.

2	cups *sifted* all-purpose flour	3	medium-size peaches
1	cup sugar	2	tablespoons sugar
3	teaspoons baking powder	½	teaspoon ground cinnamon
½	teaspoon salt	¼	teaspoon ground nutmeg
½	cup (1 stick) butter or margarine, softened	2	tablespoons butter or margarine, melted
1	egg	1	tablespoon slivered almonds
½	cup milk	¼	cup apricot preserves

1. Lightly grease a 6-cup baking dish. Preheat oven to 350°. Sift flour, the 1 cup sugar, baking powder, and salt into a large bowl; cut in the ½ cup butter until crumbly.

2. Beat egg in a small bowl until frothy; stir in milk. Pour milk mixture into flour mixture, stirring until well mixed. Spread batter in prepared baking dish.

3. Drop peaches into boiling water for 15 seconds; lift out with a slotted spoon; peel and slice. Arrange peach slices on top of batter. Combine the 2 tablespoons sugar, cinnamon, and nutmeg; sprinkle over peaches; drizzle melted butter over all.

4. Bake in a preheated moderate oven (350°) for 55 minutes or center springs back when lightly pressed with fingertip. Sprinkle almonds over top of cake. Heat apricot preserves until melted; brush over top of cake. Cool on a wire rack.

SPICED PEACH CAKE

Bake at 375° for 1 hour.
Makes 16 servings.

½ cup firmly packed light brown sugar	3½ cups *sifted* all-purpose flour
2 tablespoons all-purpose flour	4 teaspoons baking powder
	½ teaspoon salt
2 teaspoons ground cinnamon	½ cup vegetable shortening
¼ teaspoon ground nutmeg	1½ cups sugar
2 tablespoons butter or margarine, softened	2 eggs
	1 cup milk
1 cup coarsely chopped walnuts	Grated rind of 1 large lemon
	1 can (1 pound, 13 ounces) sliced cling peaches, drained

1. Grease and flour a 13 x 9 x 2-inch baking pan. Preheat oven to 375°. Combine brown sugar, the 2 tablespoons flour, cinnamon, nutmeg, and softened butter in a small bowl; blend. Stir in nuts. Set aside.

2. Sift the 3½ cups flour, baking powder, and salt onto wax paper.

3. Beat shortening, sugar, and eggs in a large bowl with an electric mixer, about 3 minutes or until creamy. Beat in milk. Add sifted flour mixture and lemon rind; beat until smooth and thick.

4. Turn cake batter into prepared pan; spread evenly. Arrange drained peach slices in rows on top of batter. Sprinkle with brown sugar topping over peaches.

5. Bake in a preheated moderate oven (375°) for 1 hour or until a wooden pick inserted in center comes out clean. Cool in pan on a wire rack. Cut into 16 pieces.

GINGERCAKE WITH HOT LEMON DRIZZLE

Bake at 325° for 35 minutes.

2 eggs
⅓ cup vegetable oil
½ cup molasses
½ cup water
2 tablespoons unsweetened cocoa powder
1½ teaspoons ground cinnamon

1½ teaspoons ground ginger
1 cup *sifted* all-purpose flour
1 cup whole wheat flour
2 teaspoons baking powder
Hot Lemon Drizzle (recipe below)

1. Grease and flour a 9 x 9 x 2-inch baking pan. Preheat oven to 325°.
2. Beat eggs in a large bowl until foamy; beat in oil and molasses; stir in water.
3. Combine cocoa, cinnamon, ginger, all-purpose and whole wheat flours, and baking powder in a medium-size bowl; mix well. Stir dry ingredients into egg mixture until batter is smooth. Pour into prepared pan.
4. Bake in a preheated slow oven (325°) for 35 minutes or until wooden pick inserted in center of cake comes out clean. Serve with Hot Lemon Drizzle.

Hot Lemon Drizzle: Combine 5 tablespoons sugar and 1 tablespoon cornstarch in a small saucepan; stir in 1 cup water. Cook over medium heat, stirring, until smooth and thickened, about 5 minutes. Add 1 tablespoon margarine, 2 tablespoons lemon juice, and ½ teaspoon dried lemon rind (or 1 teaspoon fresh); stir until margarine is melted. (Those on a diabetic diet can substitute fructose for the sugar. Unsalted margarine should be used by people watching their sodium intake.)

MORE JUICE FROM A LEMON

You'll get more juice from a lemon if you first soften it by pressing and rolling on a firm surface. Then squeeze the entire lemon. But, if you need only a few drops, make a small hole in the lemon and squeeze out only what you need. Wrap the lemon and refrigerate it.

CARROT-NUT CAKE

Bake at 350° for 1 hour.
Makes 8 servings.

1	cup *sifted* all-purpose flour	½	cup finely chopped walnuts
2	teaspoons baking powder	2	tablespoons rum, brandy,
⅛	teaspoon salt		or orange juice
½	cup vegetable shortening	1	teaspoon lemon juice
1	cup sugar		Apricot Glaze
3	eggs, separated		(recipe below)
1	cup shredded carrots		Walnut halves

1. Grease a 2-quart fancy tube pan (or you can use a 9-inch angel cake tube pan but cake will not be as high). Dust lightly with flour; tap out excess. Preheat oven to 350°.

2. Sift flour, baking powder, and salt onto wax paper.

3. Beat shortening, sugar, and egg yolks in a large bowl with an electric mixer on high speed for 3 minutes, scraping down side of bowl and beaters occasionally. (Finish mixing cake by hand.)

4. Stir in carrots, walnuts, rum, and lemon juice. Stir in flour mixture a little at a time until batter is smooth.

5. Beat egg whites in a small bowl with electric mixer until soft peaks form; fold into cake batter. Spoon into prepared pan, spreading top evenly.

6. Bake in a preheated moderate oven (350°) for 1 hour or until top springs back when lightly pressed with fingertip. Cool in pan on a wire rack for 10 minutes; loosen cake around edge with a metal spatula; turn out onto wire rack; cool completely. Brush with Apricot Glaze; garnish with walnut halves.

Apricot Glaze: Heat ⅓ cup apricot preserves in a small skillet; press through a sieve into a small bowl. Brush glaze over and side of cake.

SAVE THE SYRUP

If you've been discarding the syrup drained from canned fruits, don't any more. It can be used to poach fresh fruit or added to milk shakes, fruit whips, gelatin molds, and puddings.

Don't throw out orange rinds because they are always useful. The rinds can be grated and stored in the freezer to add zesty flavor to desserts and other dishes. You can also "candy" the rind by simmering it in a sugar syrup until tender and translucent; it's great for fruitcakes, cookies, and puddings. For a refreshing, low-calorie drink, drop a large piece of orange rind into a glass of chilled club soda.

ORANGE CHIFFON CAKE

Bake at 325° for 55 minutes, then at 350° for 10 minutes.
Makes 16 servings.

2¼ cups *sifted* cake flour	7 egg whites
1½ cups sugar	½ teaspoon cream of tartar
3 teaspoons baking powder	Orange Buttercream Frosting
1 teaspoon salt	(recipe below)
½ cup vegetable oil	Orange Date Filling
5 egg yolks	(recipe below)
¾ cup cold water	Orange slices (optional)
3 tablespoons grated orange rind	Grated orange rind (optional)

1. Preheat oven to 325°.

2. Sift cake flour, sugar, baking powder, and salt into a large bowl. Make a well in the center; add oil, egg yolks, cold water, and orange rind. Stir until smooth and well blended.

3. Beat egg whites and cream of tartar in a large bowl with an electric mixer until soft peaks form. Fold egg yolk mixture into beaten whites until well blended and no streaks of white remain.

4. Pour batter into an ungreased 10-inch tube pan with a removable bottom.

5. Bake in a preheated slow oven (325°) for 55 minutes; increase oven temperature to moderate (350°). Bake 10 minutes longer or until top springs back when lightly pressed with fingertip. Invert onto a funnel or tall bottle. Let hang until cool. Remove from pan.

6. Prepare Orange Buttercream Frosting and Orange Date Filling while cake cools.

7. Cut cooled cake into 3 equal crosswise layers, using a serrated knife. Add ½ cup of frosting to date filling, blending well. Spread on cake layers. Assemble cake. Frost with remaining Orange Buttercream Frosting. Decorate with fresh orange slices and grated orange rind, if you wish.

Orange Buttercream Frosting: Beat ⅓ cup softened butter and 1 tablespoon grated orange rind in a small bowl with an electric mixer until fluffy. Beat in 1 package (1 pound) *sifted* 10X (confectioners') sugar alternately with 4 tablespoons orange juice until frosting is smooth and spreadable.

Orange Date Filling: Chop 1 package (10 ounces) pitted dates. Combine with 1 cup orange juice and 2 tablespoons sugar in medium-size saucepan. Bring to a boil; lower heat; simmer 10 minutes, stirring often, until thickened. Cool.

APPLESAUCE CAKE

Bake at 350° for 65 minutes.
Makes 1 loaf cake.

2	cups *sifted* all-purpose flour	½	cup vegetable shortening
2	teaspoons baking soda	1	cup sugar
1	teaspoon ground cinnamon	2	eggs
½	teaspoon salt	1½	cups applesauce
½	teaspoon ground cloves		

1. Grease and flour a 9 x 5 x 3-inch loaf pan. Preheat oven to 350°.
2. Sift flour, baking soda, cinnamon, salt, and cloves onto wax paper.
3. Beat shortening, sugar, and eggs in a large bowl with an electric mixer until light and fluffy.
4. Add flour mixture alternately with applesauce, beginning and ending with the flour mixture; beat well after each addition. Turn into prepared pan.
5. Bake in a preheated moderate oven (350°) for 65 minutes or until a wooden pick inserted in center comes out clean. Cool in pan on a wire rack for 10 minutes. Turn out of pan onto wire rack; cool to room temperature.

BUY FRUITS IN SEASON AND SAVE $

FRUITS	JAN-FEB	MAR-APR
Apple	✹	✹
Avocado	✹	✹
Blueberry		
Cherry		
Grape		
Grapefruit	✹	✹
Lemon/Lime		
Melon		
Orange	✹	✹
Peach		
Pear		
Pineapple		✹
Plum		
Strawberry		✹

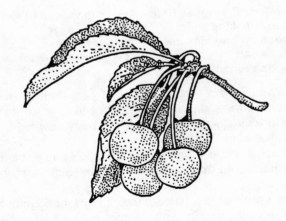

MAY-JUNE	JULY-AUG	SEPT-OCT	NOV-DEC
		●	●
●		●	●
●	●		
●	●		
	●	●	●
●			●
●	●		
●	●	●	
●			
●	●	●	
	●	●	
	●		●
●	●		
●	●	●	
●			

MUDPIE CHOCOLATE CAKE

Bake at 350° for 35 minutes.
Makes one 8-inch cake.

1½ cups all-purpose flour	1 tablespoon vinegar
1 cup sugar	1 teaspoon vanilla
¼ cup unsweetened cocoa powder	1 egg
1 teaspoon baking soda	1 cup water
6 tablespoons vegetable oil	⅓ cup walnuts, chopped

1. Preheat oven to 350°. Sift flour, sugar, cocoa, and baking soda into an ungreased 8 x 8 x 2-inch baking pan. Make 3 holes in mixture. Pour oil into first hole, vinegar into second hole, and vanilla into third hole.
2. Beat egg with water in a small bowl; pour over dry ingredients; add nuts. Stir with a fork until evenly blended.
3. Bake in a moderate oven (350°) for 35 minutes or until center springs back when lightly pressed with fingertip. Cool in pan on wire rack.

PEANUT BUTTER BROWNIES

Bake at 350° for 35 minutes.
Makes 24 brownies.

1 cup peanut butter	3 eggs
½ cup (1 stick) butter or margarine, softened	1 teaspoon vanilla
2 cups firmly packed light brown sugar	1 cup *sifted* all-purpose flour
	½ teaspoon salt

1. Grease a 13 x 9 x 2-inch baking pan. Preheat oven to 350°.
2. Beat peanut butter and butter in a large bowl with an electric mixer until well blended. Add sugar, eggs, and vanilla; beat until fluffy and light. Stir in flour and salt until well blended. Spread batter in prepared baking pan.
3. Bake in a preheated moderate oven (350°) for 30 to 35 minutes or until golden brown. Cool in pan on a wire rack. Cut into 24 brownies.

THE KNACK OF SNACKING

Kids are incorrigible snackers—so don't fight it! Just make sure they snack properly.

The Basic 10 Snacking Guidelines

• Consider snacks as part of your child's overall nutrition for the day. For example, if he has a snack of raw vegetables and dip, don't worry if he doesn't eat his peas at dinner.

• Remember *you're* the adult; *you're* the role model. Don't expect your child to snack on carrot sticks if he sees you constantly munching on potato chips and candy.

• Don't allow your children to snack 1 hour before a main meal.

• If your child is going through a fussy eating phase, avoid making mealtimes into emotional battles. Instead, use snacks as mini-meals.

• Overweight child? Low-calorie snacking is a necessity. Encourage this by controlling junk food, involving the child in snack preparation, making low-calorie snacks truly appetizing.

• Get all your children—not only those with a weight problem—involved in shopping for and/or making their own snacks. This way they learn firsthand about what goes into good eating.

• Yes! Kids do have a sweet tooth. Studies show that we're born with a preference for sweet-tasting things. Help satisfy that craving by keeping *lots* of fruit on hand—it's got its own natural sugar. Kids *will* eat grapes, watermelon, and the like, instead of a piece of candy.

• Kids tend to grab what's handy, so keep what *you* want them to eat up front in the refrigerator.

• Serve ice cream and chips and other packaged treats once in a while. Doctors agree that if you treat them as "forbidden fruit" they'll assume exaggerated importance for your children.

• And last, but not by any means least, children should brush their teeth after snacks as well as following regular meals.

DELICIOUS AND NUTRITIOUS

Peanut butter is one of America's favorite sandwich spreads. It deserves its popularity because of its delicious flavor, inexpensive price, and good nutrition (protein, niacin, and thiamine). If you've never ventured beyond peanut butter sandwiches, try enriching desserts and snacks with peanut butter. With a glass of milk, kids and adults alike, will have a delicious and nutritious treat.

CINNAMON-NUT COOKIES

Bake at 350° for 8 minutes.
Makes 4 dozen cookies.

¼ cup (½ stick) margarine,
  softened
1 cup firmly packed brown
  sugar
1 egg

½ cup milk
1 teaspoon vanilla
1½ cups *sifted* all-purpose flour
1 teaspoon baking soda
¾ cup walnuts, chopped

1. Grease 2 large cookie sheets. Preheat oven to 350°. Beat margarine, sugar, and egg in a medium-size bowl until light and fluffy. Stir in milk and vanilla.
2. Sift flour, cinnamon, and baking soda over; mix well. Stir in walnuts. Drop by rounded teaspoonful onto prepared cookie sheets, leaving 2 inches between cookies.
3. Bake in a preheated moderate oven (350°) for 8 minutes or until lightly browned around edges.

Chocolate Cookies: Omit walnuts and cinnamon; sift ¼ cup unsweetened cocoa powder with flour and baking soda. Makes 3½ dozen cookies.

OATMEAL-RAISIN COOKIES

Store these cookies in a tightly covered container and
they'll keep all week.

Bake at 375° for 12 minutes.
Makes 4 dozen.

1 cup *sifted* all-purpose flour
2 teaspoons baking powder
¼ teaspoon salt
½ cup (1 stick) margarine,
  softened
½ cup granulated sugar

½ cup firmly packed brown
  sugar
1 egg
½ teaspoon vanilla
2 cups quick-cooking oats
½ cup raisins

1. Combine flour, baking powder, and salt on wax paper.
2. Beat margarine, sugars, egg, and vanilla in a large bowl with an electric mixer until light and fluffy. Stir in flour mixture by hand until well blended. Stir in oats and raisins.

3. Drop by rounded teaspoonsful onto ungreased cookie sheets, spacing about 2 inches between cookies.

4. Bake in a preheated moderate oven (375°) for 12 minutes or just until set. Cool a few minutes before removing from cookie sheet to wire racks.

POWERHOUSE PUDDING

Serve hot with milk or cold as pudding.

Makes 8 generous servings.

7½ cups water	¼ cup sugar
1 teaspoon salt	2 teaspoons vanilla
2⅔ cups nonfat dry milk powder	½ teaspoon almond extract
1⅓ cups quick enriched farina	½ to 1 cup raisins
4 eggs	

1. Bring 6½ cups of the water and the salt to a boil in a large saucepan.

2. Mix the remaining 1 cup water and dry milk until blended. Pour into the boiling water, stirring constantly; bring to a boil again.

3. Slowly pour in farina; lower heat; cook, stirring constantly, for 2 to 3 minutes or until thickened. Remove from heat.

4. Beat eggs lightly in a medium-size bowl. Stir a little of the hot cereal into the eggs; pour back into saucepan; cook and stir 1 minute longer. Remove from heat. Stir in the sugar, vanilla, almond extract, and raisins. Serve hot or cold.

NONFAT DRY MILK

One of the biggest nutrition bargains is nonfat dry milk. It has all the nutrients of whole milk—at about half the calories and cost. Two 8-ounce glasses of milk provide as much protein as a small serving of steak. Use nonfat milk for cooking and drinking. For best flavor, reconstitute the milk at least 6 hours before you drink it and serve it well chilled. If a slightly richer flavor is desired, you can mix some whole milk with the reconstituted nonfat milk and still cut costs.

RAISIN-BREAD PUDDING

Make the bread crumbs from dried-out bread in an electric blender;
then use the blender to mix the rest of the pudding.
Serve with a little jelly for dessert, or try it with milk for breakfast.

Bake at 325° for 1 hour.
Makes 10 servings.

4	cups homemade bread crumbs (about 8 slices bread)	3	eggs
		¾	cup sugar
		½	teaspoon salt
2	cups nonfat dry milk powder	1	teaspoon vanilla
6	tablespoons margarine	½	cup raisins
6	cups hot water		

1. Lightly grease two 6-cup baking dishes. Preheat oven to 325°.
2. Sprinkle the bread crumbs into prepared baking dishes.
3. Combine the dry milk, margarine, and 2 cups of the water in the container of an electric blender; whirl until margarine is melted. Add eggs, sugar, salt, and vanilla; whirl until mixed.
4. Pour mixture into baking dishes, dividing evenly. Add remaining 4 cups of water to dishes, dividing evenly; mix well; add the raisins. Let stand 10 minutes.
5. Bake in a preheated slow oven (325°) for 1 hour or until top is lightly browned. Cool on a wire rack. Serve warm or cold.

HEARTY BREAD PUDDING

Cottage cheese, eggs, and milk give this delicately-flavored bread
pudding the protein value of a main dish. Leave leftovers in the
refrigerator labeled "for snacking" and it will disappear pronto.

Bake at 350° for 45 minutes.
Makes 6 servings.

1	container (12 ounces) cream-style cottage cheese (1½ cups)	¼	teaspoon salt
		2	tablespoons butter or margarine, melted
¾	cup milk	1	teaspoon vanilla
2	eggs	4	slices white bread, cut into ¼-inch cubes (2¼ cups)
½	cup sugar	½	cup snipped dates
½	teaspoon ground cinnamon		

1. Lightly butter a 1½-quart casserole. Preheat oven to 350°. Place cottage cheese, milk, eggs, sugar, cinnamon, salt, butter, and vanilla in the container of an electric blender; cover; whirl until smooth.

2. Pour into a prepared casserole; add bread cubes and dates; stir to moisten. Let stand 15 minutes; stir again.

3. Set pan in a larger pan on oven shelf; pour boiling water in larger pan to a depth of 1 inch.

4. Bake in a preheated moderate oven (350°) for 45 minutes or until knife inserted ½ inch from edge of pudding comes out clean. Remove the pudding from water. Serve warm or cold with light cream, if you wish.

RICE PUDDING (Risgrynskaka)

Bake at 350° for 1 hour.
Makes 6 servings.

½ cup converted rice	½ cup sugar
2½ cups water	1 teaspoon vanilla
1 teaspoon salt	3 eggs, slighty beaten
3 cups milk	

1. Combine rice, water, and salt in a small saucepan; bring to a boil, stirring often; lower heat; cover. Simmer over low heat for 25 minutes or until water is absorbed. Grease a 1½-quart casserole. Preheat oven to 350°.

2. Add milk, sugar, vanilla, and eggs; mix well. Pour into prepared casserole. Set casserole in a larger baking pan. Pour hot water into pan to a depth of 7 inches.

3. Bake in a preheated moderate oven (350°) for 1 hour or until knife inserted 1 inch from edge comes out clean.

4. Remove from hot water to a wire rack; let cool.

SUBSTITUTE & SAVE $

You can often make do by using the ingredients on hand. For instance, there's no sense in buying a whole quart of buttermilk if the recipe calls for only 1 cup—especially if you hate drinking buttermilk. You can easily make a substitute for buttermilk by putting 1 tablespoon of vinegar in a 1-cup measure and then adding enough milk to make 1 cup.

VANILLA PUDDING

Makes 4 servings.

1¾ cups milk
⅓ cup sugar
3 tablespoons cornstarch

½ cup cold milk
1 teaspoon vanilla

1. Heat the 1¾ cups milk in the top of a double boiler over boiling water until bubbles appear around edge of milk. Combine sugar and cornstarch in a small bowl; stir in the ½ cup cold milk until smooth. Gradually stir mixture into the heated milk.
2. Cook over boiling water, stirring constantly, until mixture thickens. Cover; cook over simmering water for 20 minutes, stirring occasionally.
3. Remove from heat; stir in vanilla. Pour into a serving dish; place a piece of plastic wrap directly on surface of pudding to prevent skin from forming. Cool to room temperature; refrigerate until cold.

Chocolate Pudding: Increase sugar to ½ cup; add ⅓ cup unsweetened cocoa powder and ⅛ teaspoon ground cinnamon to the cornstarch.

APRICOT-YOGURT WHIP

Makes 6 servings.

1 envelope unflavored gelatin
½ cup orange juice
1 can (17 ounces) apricot halves, drained
2 tablespoons honey
1 teaspoon grated lemon rind

1 teaspoon lemon juice
½ teaspoon almond extract
1 container (8 ounces) plain yogurt
Yogurt (optional)
Sliced almonds (optional)

1. Sprinkle gelatin over orange juice in a 1-cup measure; let stand 5 minutes to soften. Place cup in hot, not boiling, water. Heat until gelatin is clear; let cool.
2. Place apricots in the container of an electric blender; cover; whirl until smooth. Turn into a large bowl. Stir in honey, lemon rind, lemon juice, almond extract, and the cooled gelatin mixture.

3. Place bowl in a pan partly filled with ice and water to speed setting; chill, stirring frequently, until mixture is thickened.

4. Beat with an electric mixter on high speed, 3 minutes, or until mixture triples in volume; add yogurt; beat 1 minute longer. Spoon into 6 dessert glasses. Chill until set. Garnish with additional yogurt and sliced almonds, if you wish.

MOUSSE DE BANANES (Banana Mousse)

Makes 6 servings.

3	small firm-ripe bananas (each about 6 inches long), unpeeled	1	tablespoon lemon juice
		¼	cup sugar
		1	cup heavy cream

1. Cut bananas, through skin, in half lengthwise. Carefully remove the fruit without tearing the skins. Set the banana shells aside.

2. Place bananas in a large bowl with lemon juice; mash with a fork until smooth. Or place banana and lemon juice in the container of an electric blender. Cover; whirl *just* until smooth. Scoop into a large bowl; stir sugar into banana mixture.

3. Beat cream in a small bowl with an electric mixer until stiff; fold into bananas.

4. Spoon banana mousse into pastry bag fitted with a ½-inch star tip tube. Pipe mousse, using a circular motion, into banana shells.* Serve immediately.

---

*If you wish, spoon banana mousse into parfait glasses.

FRUIT BARGAINS

Check over the supermarket "bargain" tables in the produce section and you'll probably find several good buys. Bruised apples can be used in pies and applesauce and pears can be poached in a spiced syrup. Overripe bananas are great in milk shakes, bread, or cakes. When frozen, bananas can be eaten like popsicles. Overripe peaches can be cooked and puréed to make a wonderful sauce for cake or pudding. Chopped fruits can be added to pancake, muffin, or waffle batter.

INDEX

Beef *(cont'd)*
  Burgundy, 49
  and cabbage pasties, 254-255
  chili con carne, 159
  Hungarian noodles and, 219
  Javanese curried noodles and, 109
  liver 'n' peppers, 160
  meat loaf with shredded vegetables,
    158
  -rice loaf, chili, 238-239
  Stroganoff, quick, 157
  sweet and sour cabbage and, 69
  zesty picadillo, 233
  see also Hamburgers
Beets, 51, 179
  with orange sauce, 182
Biscuits, mini, 256-257
Bourbon-mustard marinade, 138
Bratwurst and onions in beer, 164
Bread crumbs, 27
  seasoned, 34
Bread dough
  doubled, 29
  frozen, 30, 32
  kneading of, 23
  know-how, 23
  punching down of, 29
  rising of, 23
Breads, 11-36
  alfalfa wheat, 20
  autumn barley loaf, 16-17
  in casserole toppings, 36
  cooling and slicing of, 25
  cracked wheat, corn, and sesame loaf,
    14-15
  freezing of, 11, 15, 225-226
  garlic, 25, 214
  giant whole wheat twists, 28-29
  herb-onion rolls, 31
  honey and cream cheese whole
    wheat, 13-14
  nut and raisin, 22
  pans for, 21
  post-dated, 26
  pudding, hearty, 300-301
  -raisin pudding, 300
  savory, 17
  shaping of, 19
  stale, 27
  testing for doneness of, 20
  using up, 32
  -vegetable soup, Italian, 39
  wheat germ, 18
  white honey, 12
  see also Bread dough
Breads, quick, 24-27, 30-26
  apple griddle cakes, 36
  freezing of, 226
  mini biscuits, 256-257
  orange-flavored doughnuts, 35
  parathas, 27
  sweet breakfast squares, 34

  whole wheat-raisin, 21
  see also Cornbread; Muffins
Breadstick bundles, 30
Broccoli
  basic fried rice with bacon and, 111
  creamy shells with ham and, 218
  and ham soufflé, 276
  stir-fried, 183
Broiler meals, 10
Brownies, peanut butter, 296
Budget savvy, 4-5
Bulgur-chick-pea salad, 96
Bulk purchases, 7
Burritos, cheese and bean, 206-207
Butter, 139
  baste, lemon-herb, 150
  and oil sauce, garlicky, 100
  seasoned, 29
  stretching of, 26

Cabbage, 59
  and beef pasties, 254-255
  red, and apple salad, 58
  sweet and sour beef and, 69
  unstuffed, 70
  see also Coleslaw
Cakes, 288-293
  applesauce, 293
  apricot-glazed peach, 288-289
  blender banana, 222
  carrot-nut, 291
  carrot-pineapple upside-down,
    247
  cottage cheese pound, 288
  freezing of, 226
  ginger, with hot lemon drizzle, 290
  mudpie chocolate, 296
  orange chiffon, 292
  spiced peach, 289
Canned food, 8
  grades of, 7-8
  leaking or bulging, 9
Carrots
  cornbread, 24
  herbed, 191
  -nut cake, 291
  -pineapple upside-down cakes,
    247
  and pork egg foo yung, 279-280
  salad in lemon and mustard
    dressing, 53
  and spinach salad, 259
  and turkey loaf, 153
  versatility of, 191
Casseroles, 67
  California, 79
  chili pie, 236
  crunchy chicken, 217
  lima bean, 71
  range-top cooking of, 50
  surfside, 174

toppings for, 36, 75
tuna-rice, 73
Celery, complete use of, 193
Cereals
  hot cooked, 96
  raisin granola, 221
Cheese, 117-123
  all-American pasta and, 242-243
  and bean burritos, 206-207
  chicken Parmesan, 142
  -chicken sandwich, 205
  chilies rellenos and chili sauce,
    132-133
  eggplant Parmesan, 181
  fettuccine with green onions, dill,
    and, 120-121
  gentle cooking of, 124
  ham, turkey trio, 202
  ham and muenster pizza, 272
  'n' ham puff, 121
  -lasagne rollups, 119
  layered brown rice, spinach, and, 114
  -lentil loaf, 92
  and macaroni pies, 241
  rice, and spinach bake, 123
  -rice balls, Italian, 122
  sauce, Cheddar, 115-116
  sauce, turkey crêpes with, 267-268
  and sausage pizza, 134-135
  shells stuffed with four-, 118
  soufflé, 135-136
  -spinach strata, 237
  spreads, 33
  squares, easy spicy, 120
  storing of, 123
  -stuffed potatoes, 186
  super macaroni and, 240
Chicken, 141-152
  basic fried rice with curried, 111
  breast, boning of, 143
  casserole, crunchy, 217
  -cheese sandwich, 205
  cutting a whole, 148-149
  'n' egg, 205
  flautas with salsa, Texas, 209
  frankfurters, 159, 166
  giblets, 141
  glazed wings, 146
  hash, 74-75
  with hot pepper, 145-146
  Normandy style, 142-143
  Parmesan, 142
  and parsleyed-dumpling stew, 47
  in the pot, 46
  pot pie, 83-84
  primavera, 147
  Provencal, 141
  ragout of, with garlic, 74
  and rice skillet meal, 220
  and rotelle salad with pesto
    dressing, 62
  salad, company, 263

salad, Oriental, 230
stir-fry, 144-145
stuffed twin, 150
tacos, Cuban, 264
tarragon, 144
and vegetables in puff ring,
  curried, 76
Chicken livers, 141
  polenta with, 78
  and rice, savory, 152
  risotto with, 77
  and sausages en brochette, 165
Chick-peas, 90
  -bulgar salad, 96
  spinach, and mushroom salad, 59
Chili
  beef-rice loaf, 238-239
  con carne, 159
  pie casserole, 236
  sauce, 133, 140, 167
Chocolate
  chewy squares, no-fuss, 223
  mudpie cake, 296
  pudding, 302
Chutney
  baste, 140
  -stuffed eggs, 126
Cinnamon
  muffins, 32
  -nut cookies, 298
Clam sauce
  linguine and, 172
  spaghetti with, 172-173
Coconut-pineapple punch, creamy, 284
Coleslaw
  confetti, 58
  lima bean, 260
  tomato, 259
Containers, airtight, 8
Cookies
  cinnamon-nut, 298
  freezing of, 226
  no-fuss chocolate chewy squares,
    223
  nutmeg leaves, 246
  oatmeal-raisin, 298-299
Cooking
  of cheese, 124
  clever, 8-10
  fast, 215
  of legumes, 90
  microwave, 211-213
  of pasta, 98
  pressure, 221
  range-top casserole, 50
  rotisserie, 151, 166
Cookware, energy-efficient, 10
Corn
  cracked wheat, and sesame loaf,
    14-15
  frittata, 131
  fritters, fresh, 190-191

Yeast
  activating dry, 12
  proofing of, 22
Yogurt
  -apricot whip, 302-303
  gingered marinade, 138
  pineapple-apricot, 282

Zucchini
  and green pepper salad, grated, 53
  oven "fried," 194
  and potato omelet, party, 129
  -rice loaf with Cheddar cheese sauce,
    nutted, 115-116
  and sausage cornbread, 24-25
  and sausage pizza, 275